INCLUSIVE LEGAL POSITIVISM

Inclusive Legal Positivism

W. J. Waluchow

CLARENDON PRESS · OXFORD
1994

Oxford University Press, Walton Street, Oxford OX2 6DP
Oxford New York Toronto
Delhi Bombay Calcutta Madras Karachi
Kuala Lumpur Singapore Hong Kong Tokyo
Nairobi Dar es Salaam Cape Town
Melbourne Auckland Madrid
and associated companies in
Berlin Ibadan

Oxford is a trade mark of Oxford University Press

Published in the United States
by Oxford University Press Inc., New York

British Library Cataloguing in Publication Data
Data available

Library of Congress Cataloging in Publication Data
Waluchow, Wilfrid J.
Inclusive legal positivism / W. J. Waluchow.
p.   cm.
Includes bibliographical references.
1. Legal positivism.   I. Title.
K331.W35   1993
340'.1—dc20   93–24903
ISBN 0–19–825812–7

1 3 5 7 9 10 8 6 4 2

Typeset by Create Publishing Services Ltd., Bath, Avon
Printed in Great Britain
on acid-free paper by
Bookcraft Ltd., Midsomer Norton

For Donna,

who made it all seem worthwhile again

ACKNOWLEDGEMENTS

Some of the ideas developed and defended in this book originated in my doctoral thesis, 'Adjudication and Discretion', submitted at Oxford University. I am delighted once again to acknowledge my overwhelming debt to Herbert Hart who supervised the thesis and provided me with the kind of guidance and encouragement of which doctoral students' dreams are made. Professor Hart has continued to offer his insightful comments on my written work, and for his ongoing assistance and generosity I am extremely grateful.

During the past decade I have incurred several other debts of gratitude. Many friends and colleagues commented on drafts of essays in which my ideas were being developed. These include Dick Bronaugh, who first introduced me to legal philosophy; Steven Dehaven; Ronald Dworkin, who despite his almost complete disagreement with my ideas has on several occasions offered an encouraging word; Chris Gray; Les Green, with whom I have had many fruitful conversations on the issues addressed in this book and who commented on drafts of several sections of the book; R. M. Hare; Michael Hartney; Barry Hoffmaster; John King-Farlow; Ken Lloyd, my first graduate student in legal philosophy, from whom I learned at least as much as he learned from me; Neil MacCormick, who along with John Mackie served as examiner of my doctoral thesis and offered many helpful suggestions; Joe Murray; Spiro Panagiotou, who helped me through some difficult times; Joseph Raz, who encouraged me to submit my manuscript to Clarendon Press and who provided many insightful comments on papers in which my ideas were being tested; and Roger Shiner, with whom I have had many discussions in legal philosophy and who taught me how to write a publishable paper. I also wish to thank my brother, Ted, whose encouragement and assistance were extremely beneficial. Finally, I wish to express my sincerest gratitude to Donna Farkas, whose support helped sustain me during the long process leading up to the completion of the manuscript. Without her warmth and inspiration this book would not have been completed.

I greatly benefited from the opportunity provided by the Social Sciences and Humanities Research Council of Canada to spend a year on the book free from the demands of teaching. For this tremendous opportunity I offer my sincerest gratitude. I am also grateful to McMaster University for a further year free of teaching.

Parts of this book contain material previously published in a series of articles. Chapter 3 contains material which first appeared in 'The "Forces" of Law', *The Canadian Journal of Law and Jurisprudence*, 1990. Chapter 4 is a greatly expanded and revised form of 'The Weak Social Thesis' which appeared in 9 *Oxford Journal of Legal Studies*, 1989. Chapter 5 is a slightly revised version of 'Charter Challenges: A Test Case For Theories of Law', published in 29 *Osgoode Hall Law Journal*, 1990. Chapters 6 and 7 contain substantially revised and expanded material from 'Herculean Positivism', 5 *Oxford Journal of Legal Studies*, 1985, and 'Strong Discretion', 33 *The Philosophical Quarterly*, 1983. Finally, Chapter 8 contains ideas first entertained in 'Hart, Legal Rules and Palm Tree Justice', 4 *Law and Philosophy*, 1985. I am grateful to the publishers of these articles for permission to redeploy some of my ideas and arguments.

CONTENTS

1. INTRODUCTION   1
   1. Indeterminate Boundaries   1
   2. The Structure of Our Inquiry   4

2. THEORIES AND CONCEPTIONS   9
   1. The Grounds of Law   9
   2. The Force of Law   12
   3. Dworkinian Conceptions of Law   13
   4. Conceptions and Evaluation   15
   5. Values and Legal Theory   19
   6. Conclusion   29

3. THE FORCES OF LAW   31
   1. Introduction   31
   2. Law, Compliance, and Adjudication   33
   3. The Institutional Forces of Law   42
   4. Rights Against Hercules   46
   5. The Theory of Compliance   58
   6. Separate But Connected   64
   7. An Alternative   73
   8. Conclusion   78

4. INCLUSIVE V. EXCLUSIVE POSITIVISM   80
   1. The Forms and Limits of Positivism   80
   2. Hart's Arguments   84
   3. Bentham's Causal/Moral Argument   86
   4. The Invalidity of Causal/Moral Arguments   88
   5. A Dubious Causal Connection   95
   6. The Argument From Intellectual Clarity   98
   7. Three Popular Arguments   103
   8. The Argument From Explanatory Power   113
   9. The Argument From Function   117
   10. The Authority Argument: An Outline   123
   11. The Authority Argument: A Critique   129
   12. Taking Stock   140

5. CHARTER CHALLENGES   142
   1. Introduction   142
   2. Moral Arguments?   143
   3. Does It Figure in the Right Way?   155
   4. An Alternative Exclusive Account?   163
   5. Conclusion   164

6. HERCULES   166
   1. Introduction   166
   2. The Validity Argument   168
   3. The Pedigree Argument   174
   4. The Argument From Function   182

7. DISCRETION AND LEGAL THEORY   191
   1. The Discretion Argument   191
   2. Strong and Weak Discretion   192
   3. Two Interpretations   195
   4. Two Objections   204
   5. Having and Exercising Strong Discretion   207
   6. A Significant Distinction?   213
   7. A Return to the Discretion Argument   219
   8. Raz's Challenge   226
   9. Conclusion   229

8. MORALS AND THE MEANING OF LAWS   232
   1. Introduction   232
   2. Hart's Early Theory   234
   3. The Necessity Argument   236
   4. The Desirability Argument   250
   5. The Intention Argument   254
   6. The Rule of Law Argument 1   259
   7. The Rule of Law Argument 2   263
   8. Later Hart   269

References   273

Table of Cases   281

Index   283

1

INTRODUCTION

1. INDETERMINATE BOUNDARIES

Legal theory is in a perplexing state. Traditional boundaries between rival views have been blurred to the point where one wonders just what the issues are and whether the protagonists are more often than not arguing at cross purposes. On the one hand we have apparently dyed-in-the-wool legal positivists like Joseph Raz and Neil MacCormick claiming that it is perfectly consistent with legal positivism to suggest that law, as an important social institution, necessarily has some moral merit. According to MacCormick, 'legal systems have as such a certain moral value in virtue of the formal (and of itself amoral) character which positivist theories ascribe to them; but this is only an inconclusive and readily over-rideable element of moral value.'[1] How does one reconcile this position with John Austin's famous battle-cry of legal positivism that the existence of law is one thing, its merit or demerit quite another? Is there not a contradiction here?

On the other hand, one finds John Finnis, whose contemporary theory of natural law seems about as close as one can get to the traditional natural law theories of Aquinas and Augustine, suggesting that it was never a major concern of classical natural lawyers to deny legal validity to unjust state enactments. One wonders just what it is, then, that characterizes the natural-law tradition and how one is to interpret Augustine's famous claim, thought to be definitive of that approach, that 'an unjust law seems to be no law at all'. Isn't there a contradiction here too? Someone approaching legal philosophy for the first time couldn't help but be terribly confused by all this. Those more familiar with the path taken by general jurisprudence over the past several years would be forced to admit to at least a tiny bit of perplexity and concern. If positivism isn't the view that law does not necessarily have moral merit, that wicked legal

[1] MacCormick, 'A Moralistic Case for A-Moralistic Law?', 27.

systems of absolutely no redeeming moral value whatsoever are conceptually possible, then just what is legal positivism? If natural-law theory isn't the view that there is a 'higher law' defining an objective, fundamental standard of justice which human enactments violate only at the expense of being denied the status of valid law, then just what is it that the natural lawyers have been trying to tell us?

One of the aims of this book is to help dispel at least some of the chaos into which general jurisprudence seems to have fallen in recent times. Our main focus will be legal positivism, once dubbed 'the ruling theory of law' by its chief contemporary critic Ronald Dworkin. Though perhaps still the ruling theory, at least in the sense that most legal scholars and commentators claim (uncritical?) allegiance to some form of the theory, the survival of positivism is now in question, and it has even been suggested that the theory has 'self-destructed'.[2] It is my intention to show that positivism is alive and well, and quite able to fend off its chief challengers, most notably Ronald Dworkin whose 'natural-law' theory poses no more of a threat to positivism than its predecessors did, e.g. Lon Fuller's procedural natural-law theory. Other challengers besides Dworkin will be considered as circumstances dictate, but the principal focus will be Dworkin, whose powerful critique of positivism, particularly the elegant statement of that view one finds in H. L. A. Hart's *The Concept of Law*, reveals several ways in which Hart's 'model of rules' must be modified, or at least expanded and clarified. The trick will be to effect the required alterations without abandoning the essential thrust of Hart's theory. That is what I hope to do.

The version of positivism developed and defended in this book will be called 'inclusive legal positivism'. A distinguishing feature of inclusive positivism is its claim that standards of political morality, that is, the morality we use to evaluate, justify, and criticize social institutions and their activities and products, e.g. laws, can and do in various ways figure in attempts to determine the existence, content, and meaning of valid laws.[3] Political morality,

---

[2] See J. D. Goldsworthy, 'The Self-Destruction of Legal Positivism'.

[3] I do not wish to become embroiled in any conflicts there might be as to the nature and objectivity of moral standards, nor in any controversies concerning whether there is an important and viable distinction between political and personal morality, where the latter constitutes the standards of morality appropriate for judging private, individual behaviour. We will merely assume that people do appeal to standards like the principles of equality, liberty, fairness, and justice in assessing social institu-

on this theory, is included within the possible grounds for establishing the existence and content of valid, positive laws, that is, laws enacted or developed by human beings in legislatures, courts of law, or customary practice. In proposing such a central role for political morality in determinations of law,[4] inclusive positivism runs the risk of collapsing into a version of natural-law theory—and only adding to the chaos into which jurisprudence seems to have fallen. Another of my hopes is to show how this collapse can be avoided without surrendering the main insights of positivists like Bentham, Austin, and Hart, all of whom, I shall argue, adhere to inclusive positivism.

Yet another of my aims is to demonstrate that one need not follow the lead of Joseph Raz, who vehemently opposes the distinguishing feature of inclusive positivism (that morality can figure in determinations of law) in order to provide a viable alternative to natural-law theory which remains faithful to the insights of Austin and Bentham. Raz's 'exclusive legal positivism', which excludes morality from the logically or conceptually possible grounds for determining the existence or content of valid law, is neither the only nor the most viable version of positivism. A good deal of effort will therefore be directed towards fending off Raz's critique of inclusive positivism. In short, then, this book is designed to show that there is a positivistic theory to be found somewhere between Raz's exclusive positivism and Dworkin's (natural) law as integrity (henceforth referred to as the integrity theory). Finding a secure middle ground will not be easy, but the task is undertaken with a hope once expressed by John Stuart Mill in *On Liberty*. As Mill observed, 'conflicting doctrines, instead of one being true and the other false, share the truth between them, and the nonconforming opinion is needed to supply the remainder of the truth of which the received doctrine embodies only a part.'[5] It is my belief that somewhere between the conflicting views of Raz and Dworkin lies inclusive legal positivism, a viable and illuminating theory of law.

tions and their products; that these activities are not totally nonsensical as some radical moral nihilists might argue, but are open to at least some degree of rational argument and assessment; and that it is these kinds of standards that we have in mind when we ask about the possible role of political morality in determining the existence and content of valid laws.

[4] Henceforth we will mean by 'determinations of law' attempts to determine the existence, content, or meaning of valid, positive laws.

[5] C. Shields, edn. (1956), 56.

As should now be clear, the version of positivism to be explored in this book is in no way revolutionary, or even very novel. It represents what I hope is merely a refinement or clarification of H. L. A. Hart's position(s), one which attempts to accommodate the doctrines and insights of Raz and Dworkin while remaining faithful to the positivist tradition adopted and developed by Hart. As a consequence, I shall be making liberal use of theories and concepts introduced by Hart and addressing criticisms which have been, sometimes justifiably, directed at them only when necessary for the purposes of this book. For instance, I shall assume that Hart's theory that a rule of recognition lies at the foundation of all legal systems is more or less correct, and that Dworkin's critique of the rule of recognition as a conventional, social rule, indeed his critique of Hart's entire theory of social rules, can be satisfactorily answered, as I think it can.[6]

I make no apologies for my lack of novelty in this book, nor for the fairly narrow scope of my principal concern: to defend a Hartian version of inclusive positivism against two of its principal opponents, Raz and Dworkin. Comprehensiveness and novelty are all too often purchased in philosophy at the cost of clarity, precision, and ultimately understanding. Given the current state of general jurisprudence, this is a cost we must strenuously seek to avoid. I shall be content if this book succeeds only in helping to clarify at least some of the issues disputed in current debates about the nature of law. I shall be absolutely delighted if I am able to establish inclusive positivism as a viable, positivistic theory of law.

2. THE STRUCTURE OF OUR INQUIRY

Much of the current confusion within general jurisprudence results from differences of opinion concerning (a) what it is exactly that one is supposed to be doing in offering a theory of law, and (b) what it is that one's opponents are doing in articulating their theories of law. Here is an example. Despite his claim in *The Concept of Law* to be offering an essay in 'descriptive sociology', Hart is characterized by Dworkin as providing a semantic theory concerning the meaning of

---

[6] For a thoroughly persuasive answer to Dworkin's critique of Hart's theory of social rules, see P. H. Nowell-Smith, 'Dworkin v. Hart Appealed: a Meta-ethical Inquiry'.

words like 'law' and 'legal system', or propositions such as 'Canadians have a legal right to equality'. Dworkin himself eschews both descriptive sociology and semantic theories in favour of what he calls 'conceptions of law'. These are inherently controversial, normative accounts of the 'meaning' of (our) legal practices, accounts which are neither linguistic in nature nor purely descriptive.[7] They are normative through and through, attempts to place the legal practice of the author's community in its best moral light, to make of it 'the best that it can be'.

So here we seem to have two of the most important legal philosophers of our time radically at odds concerning what it is they are up to in offering a legal theory. We also have one of those two disputants (Dworkin) apparently mistaken about, or ignoring, what it is that the other is up to. Is it any wonder, then, that a certain degree of perplexity is encountered when one attempts to come to grips with the 'Hart–Dworkin debate'?

But matters are even worse than this. In his general jurisprudential writings, Hart's main concern has always been to provide a philosophically illuminating account of an important social institution, law, which recurs in different societies and periods 'exhibiting many common features of form, structure and content'.[8] In so doing, Hart tells us, he is concerned to occupy, not the perspective of a judge deciding a case, but 'that of an external observer'. In particular he is not out to justify the legal practice of adjudication and the coercive enforcement of its results, let alone any specific instance of that practice as found in some particular legal system. On the contrary, his aim is to describe the common form, structure, and content of all (or at least most) forms of legal systems, and to discover how these forms of social regulation relate to such things as morality, brute force, and forms of social organization which some wish to call 'law' but others not, for example international law. Hart's perspective, then, is that of an external observer out to describe and analyse a particular kind of social system, and the concepts in terms of which we conceive of it, in a philosophically illuminating way. Dworkin's perspective, by contrast, is that of a judge out to justify what he does in holding people liable for violating legal rights and

---

[7] By 'our law' Dworkin apparently means the legal systems of Western constitutional democracies, though this is not entirely certain. If this is not what Dworkin means, then it is not clear what he does mean. Henceforth we will assume that the above represents Dworkin's intentions.

[8] Hart, in *Issues in Contemporary Legal Philosophy*, 36.

duties. As he so provocatively puts it, jurisprudence is only 'the general part of adjudication' and 'no firm line divides it from adjudication or any other aspect of legal practice'.[9] Hart, then, seems to want to offer a morally and politically detached, descriptive theory about the nature of all or at least most legal systems; Dworkin a fully committed, normative, or as he prefers to call it 'interpretive', theory of adjudication, or the adjudicative practices of 'our' legal systems. One might begin to wonder at this stage whether there really are any useful points of comparison between Hart and Dworkin, and whether they really have been arguing at cross-purposes.

The aim of the preceding paragraphs has not been to show the futility of attempts to assess the disputes between Hart and Dworkin. Rather the aim has been to show that we must be extremely careful to distinguish different kinds of legal theories and to realize that apparent differences of opinion in jurisprudence can often be traced to differences in starting points and aims, and resulting differences in methodology. In Chapters 2 and 3 I shall try to demonstrate the utility of distinguishing carefully between what I call theories of law, theories of adjudication, and theories of compliance. It will be argued that Dworkin in effect collapses these three into one, and that this leads him to highly counter-intuitive consequences. I shall also follow Hart's lead in arguing that descriptive-explanatory accounts of law and legal systems are both possible and valuable, contrary to Dworkin's opposing suggestions. We shall explore how value enters into descriptive accounts in ways which do not transform them into Dworkinian interpretive conceptions.

Having set the groundwork in place, we will turn in Chapters 4–7 to a defence of inclusive positivism as a general theory of law and legal systems. The theory will be carefully distinguished from its main competitors and its intuitive appeal will be highlighted. A good deal of effort will be made attempting to demonstrate the respects in which inclusive positivism seems to account better than Raz's exclusive version for certain salient features of legal practice. Of particular interest will be the respects in which inclusive positivism offers a better account of the interpretation and application of constitutional documents like the Canadian *Charter of Rights and Freedoms* or the American *Bill of Rights*. In allowing political morality to figure in determining what such documents mean and

[9] *Law's Empire*, 90.

the impact of their various provisions on the validity of subordinate laws, say statutes, inclusive positivism provides a much better account of these common legal practices. In this respect, it will be argued, inclusive positivism is decidedly superior to exclusive positivism whose account of these practices is often forced and counter-intuitive.

If, according to inclusive positivism, political morality can indeed figure in determining the existence and content of valid law, then the question naturally arises: How does it differ from Dworkin's integrity theory, or from the natural-law theories of Aquinas and Augustine? Just how far can one go in admitting a determining role for morality and maintain one's claim to be offering a version of legal positivism? One way to explore these issues is to examine the extent to which inclusive positivism is compatible with Dworkin's insights into the nature of our legal systems, at least to the extent that these are sound. To that end, we shall explore the extent to which the identification of law via the kind of 'Herculean' legal reasoning Dworkin sketches in *Taking Rights Seriously* and *Law's Empire* is consistent with inclusive positivism. As we shall discover, there is much in Dworkin's account of adjudication which is perfectly compatible with this particular version of positivism, and to that extent Dworkin provides no convincing grounds for rejecting it as a general theory of law.

If the arguments of Chapters 4–7 are sound, then what we will have is a positivistic theory according to which it is possible for political morality to play a role in determining the existence and content of valid laws. A separate though no less important question which naturally arises is whether morality should serve this role. *chap 8* Should legal practice pursue the role which inclusive positivism *p232-270* warrants as possible? Or should our practices be such that, as a matter of contingent social fact, the existence of law really is one thing; its merit or demerit another thing altogether? Should legal validity, as determined by our rules of recognition, depend on conformity with certain standards of political morality? Alternatively, should the content, i.e. the very meaning, of valid laws ever be thought to depend, in part at least, on factors of political morality? It is this latter question which will concern us in Chapter 8 where it will be argued that standards of morality and rationality should be allowed to function as partly determinative of the very meaning of valid laws. I shall argue that 'liberal', 'purposive' approaches to legal interpretation are generally to be preferred to approaches which restrict judges to discovering, so far as possible, 'neutral', 'plain' meanings. It will be further argued that Hart's doctrine of the core and penumbra is sensitive to the possibility and desirability of such purposive approaches to legal interpretation.

2
THEORIES AND CONCEPTIONS

1. THE GROUNDS OF LAW

In *Law's Empire* Dworkin introduces an important distinction between what he calls the 'grounds' and the 'force' of law. The former primarily interest Dworkin in *Law's Empire* and concern the 'circumstances in which particular propositions of law should be taken to be sound or true'.[1] Propositions of law, we are told, are 'all the various statements and claims people make about what the law allows or prohibits or entitles them to have'.[2] That Canadians owing income tax to the federal government must file their returns before 30 April or face a late penalty is presumably an example of a proposition of law. That no person may profit from his own legal wrongdoing is another proposition of (common-law) jurisdictions. That Ontario residents may file for divorce following one year's separation is another still. All these propositions of law report the current state of the law in the relevant jurisdiction. They describe, or in some other way make reference to, existing legal rights, duties, powers, liabilities and so on. On Dworkin's account, the legal duties cited in, or entailed by, propositions of law should normally be respected by citizens, and their violation normally licenses state coercion. It justifies a judge in holding the offender liable.

As Dworkin sees it, competing jurisprudential theories of law differ in what they posit as the appropriate grounds for propositions of law. They also differ in their views on how one must go about discovering those grounds. Legal positivism suggests that the grounds of law are exhausted by a finite set of rules validated by the will of the sovereign (Austin and Bentham), a chain of validity culminating in a presupposed 'Grundnorm' (Kelsen) or a socially constituted, master rule of recognition (Hart). The grounds of law, according to Dworkin's rendering of positivism, can always be

---

[1] *Law's Empire*, 110.   [2] Ibid. 4.

[handwritten margin notes: "Disconception of posim!"; "D:"; "are these always empirically discovered?"; "D says 'yes'."]

empirically discovered. Their existence is always a matter of social fact and their content can be discovered without resort to moral, or any other sort of evaluative, argument or judgment. Law is, according to Dworkin's rendition of positivism, simply an 'amoral datum'.[3]

Dworkin's early attack on positivism in effect argued that positivists mistake part of the grounds of law for the whole. The grounds of propositions of law like 'No person may profit from his own legal wrongdoing' are not to be found in 'pedigreed' rules emanating from the sovereign's will or the rule of recognition, something whose existence and content can be empirically discovered. Rather they are to be found in true but inherently contestable principles of political morality which lack the kind of social pedigree that positivists claim to be essential to the grounds of law.

[handwritten margin note: "Law as Integrity ≠ grounds of law →"]

Dworkin's alternative conception, 'law as integrity', is offered as a theory which properly captures the full range of the grounds of law figuring in (at least) common-law systems. What is most distinctive about these grounds, so far as they relate to Dworkin's dispute with positivism, is that their existence and impact upon cases cannot be determined empirically. Discovering the grounds of law is not a matter for empirical discovery but requires complex, inherently controversial arguments of political morality. One must ask which principles of political morality best justify morally 'the settled law' of the jurisdiction in question. In other words, the real grounds of law are the principles of political morality underlying, and justifying the coercive enforcement of, what the positivist (mis)identifies as the grounds of law.

[handwritten margin note: "D:"]

Another distinctive feature of Dworkinian grounds of law is that they are not members of a finite set, inclusion within which is determined by the standard's historical relation to a foundational rule or social fact, i.e. its pedigree. Principles of law are those which figure in the soundest interpretive theory of the legal system, the one which accords the legal system the maximum degree of coherence and moral virtue, i.e. integrity. Discovering the grounds of law is not a matter of tracing a linear chain of validity back to a foundational norm or social fact. The process is 'holistic' and justificatory. The fundamentally moral grounds of law hang together, not as links in

[handwritten margin notes: "not historical tracing back to foundational norm or social fact."; "but 'holistic' justificatory criteria for 'grounds' law"]

---

[3] This is Fuller's phrase. See 'Positivism and Fidelity to Law–A Reply to Professor Hart', 94.

a chain anchored to empirically discoverable, foundational social *web*
facts, but as strands in a complex, fully normative web tentatively *metaphora*
attached at various points to social, political, and moral 'facts' and
conjectures.

To sum up, on Dworkin's conception of positivism the grounds of *Summary*
law are finite in number and can be empirically discovered in, *Contrast*
ultimately, foundational social norms or facts. According to Dwor- *bt Posm*
kin's integrity theory, there are no foundational, social grounds of *+ LI.*
law. The grounds of law lie in an interpretive, fundamentally
normative theory of the settled law. Discovering this theory requires
holistic, non-linear reasoning. It requires that a lawyer delve very
deep into arguments of political morality.[4] The grounds of law are *NB*
reported in true propositions of law, the citing of which normally
settles moral questions concerning the conduct of citizens and
judges. Propositions of law cite requirements which should
normally be respected but which might justifiably be disobeyed or
disregarded in exceptional cases.

According to Dworkin's integrity theory, then, a true proposition
of law does not necessarily imply a conclusive answer to questions
like: What should I (a citizen) do? What should I (a judge) do in
deciding this case in which a citizen has not complied with requirements described in a true proposition of law? Should I (a judge)
bring the coercive power of the state to bear upon this citizen?
Merely citing the grounds of law does not, in Dworkin's view, *evidence*
provide conclusive answers to these difficult questions in all cases. *in D ?*
There are exceptional cases in which we must resort to a different
notion. Though a positivist is likely to applaud Dworkin's claim
that true propositions of law do not always settle questions of
obedience to and application of law, he is likely to complain that
Dworkin has failed to take his insight far enough. As we shall see, it
is distinctive of legal positivism to claim that the grounds of law fail
to provide conclusive answers to practical questions in all cases, not
just those which are for some reason exceptional. It is to this issue
that we now turn.

---

[4] Legal positivists can accept that there are true propositions of law. Even if one
conceives of laws as general commands or rules which are, as such, incapable of truth
value, there is nothing to prevent a positivist from speaking of propositions whose
truth value is derivable from these non-propositional items. A Hartian positivist can
accept that a proposition of law is true if (but not necessarily only if) there is at least
one rule validated by a rule of recognition which prescribes or entails what the
proposition reports.

2. THE FORCE OF LAW

D: grounds of law normally settle ~~moral~~ practical questions (how should I act?)

In explaining his claim that the grounds of law normally settle practical questions, Dworkin introduces us to a notion which plays a key part in his theory. The 'force' of law, he tells us, is 'the relative power of any true proposition of law to justify coercion in different sorts of exceptional circumstances'.[5] In hard cases where the grounds of law seem at odds with the requirements of moral principle, we must ask difficult questions concerning the law's power to justify coercion. Owing to the fact that the grounds of law lie in the best interpretive theory of the settled law, and the fact that settled law is sometimes morally deficient, it is possible, even in a flourishing legal system, for the grounds of law to depart from the requirements of justice, fairness, and due process. The principles which provide the best 'justification' of morally deficient settled law may yet be morally bankrupt. In such cases the answer to the hard question posed by a law's existence might be that a judge or citizen should act contrary to its requirements. The grounds of law do not, in such a hard case, impose justified requirements on the citizen, and most certainly do not license the use of force by the state or its agents.

Traditional questions such as whether civilly disobedient persons should be punished for their transgressions, or whether judges must ever enforce immoral law in corrupt regimes, presumably concern, in Dworkin's view, the force as opposed to the grounds of law. It may be a true proposition of law that a Black South African who enters a Whites-only beach is guilty of a legal offence; there may be no consistent and coherent way of reading the relevant apartheid laws in such a way as to avoid this conclusion. However one cuts it, the only principles which 'justify' such laws are principles of racial supremacy. Nevertheless, the force of the law in such a case is very weak, perhaps even non-existent. Whether, on Dworkin's theory, the force of law is ever totally non-existent is a question to which we will return later. For now, it is enough to note that, in Dworkin's view, the force of a true proposition of law may be so weak as to warrant a refusal to apply state coercion against the legal offender. The grounds of law may furnish a reason for coercion, but the reasons competing against it may be much stronger. A judge would

---

[5] *Law's Empire*, 110.

therefore not be justified, morally or legally, in acting upon the grounds of law in such a case.

Surprisingly enough, then, Dworkin's distinction between the grounds and the force of law seems to suggest, along with the positivists, that it is one thing to say what the law is on some matter, quite another to say whether it has any moral merit and therefore any call upon our respect and our obedience. In this respect he is in total agreement with Bentham who in effect claimed that the force of law may, in some rare instances, be so weak as to license a refusal to comply; this despite Bentham's famous prescription that normally, in the face of morally deficient law, we should obey punctually and censure freely.[6] Despite their agreement on this issue, however, there are crucial differences between Bentham and Dworkin on how one is to understand the force of law in relation to its very existence. Unlike Bentham, Dworkin in no way seeks a conceptual separation between the law and its force, between the grounds of law and its moral force in justifying coercion. But this is not the time to explore these important differences. Which of the two theorists has the better position on these questions is an issue to which we shall return later.

3. DWORKINIAN CONCEPTIONS OF LAW

According to Dworkin, legal philosophers rightly concentrate on the grounds of law, while political philosophers are typically concerned with questions of its force. It is nevertheless Dworkin's view that a plausible legal theory regarding the grounds of law (a legal-grounds theory) will inevitably entail a fairly general answer to questions about what we might call the 'non-exceptional' or 'normal' force of law. A legal-grounds theory does not commit its adherents to concrete claims about what we should do, but it does nevertheless commit us to general moral conclusions about how citizens should behave and how judges should decide cases. Unless a legal-grounds theory is a deeply sceptical one, which accords absolutely no justification for obedience or state coercion, 'it must be understood as saying what judges [and citizens] should do in principle, unless circumstances are special'.[7]

Dworkin's suggestion is that whatever a non-sceptical legal-grounds theory identifies as the grounds of law will almost always

[6] Bentham, 'A Fragment On Government', 399.   [7] Law's Empire, 112.

be conceived, within that same theory, as at least prima facie binding on citizen and legal official alike.

A conception of law must explain how what it takes to be law provides a general justification for the exercise of coercive power by the state, a justification that holds except in special cases, when some competing argument is specially powerful.[8]

In a flourishing legal system the fact of law provides a case for coercion that must stand unless some exceptional counterargument is available.[9]

In more familiar terminology, legal-grounds theories typically posit, explain, and articulate the scope of, a prima-facie moral obligation to abide by the law, an obligation the violation of which actually serves, morally, to justify state coercion of recalcitrants in all but exceptional cases.

It is crucial to realize that a Dworkinian legal-grounds theory normally posits such an obligation because of the kind of theory it is. It is a conception of law, a fully normative, morally committed justification or 'interpretation' of legal practice, not a morally-neutral, detached description as some legal positivists seek to provide. It is not, as for example Hart thought his theory to be, an essay in 'descriptive sociology'.[10] A conception of law is an interpretive theory, which sets out (in part at least) to justify the legal practices of the author's community. It purports to articulate and defend grounds which normally do justify the use of the coercive power of the author's own legal system. In offering a conception of law one is trying to characterize law in such a way that one can see both that, and how, it justifies coercion. This goal governs how one chooses to characterize the object of study.

A conception of law is a general, abstract interpretation of legal practice as a whole. It offers to show that practice in its best light, to deploy some argument why law on that conception provides an adequate justification for coercion.[11]

Dworkin does acknowledge exceptions to his general description of conceptions of law; but they do not lie in the descriptive theories of Hartian jurisprudence. Rather they lie in those interpretive conceptions whose authors find nothing in existing legal practice which actually warrants state coercion. For example, certain so-called

---

[8] Ibid. 190.   [9] Ibid. 110.   [10] The Concept of Law, p.v.
[11] Law's Empire, 139.

Margin note: Yes. Certainly a legal theory should have this role, acc. to D.

Marxist theories, according to which the rule of law is a pernicious sham masking the dark forces of class oppression, find no redeeming moral value in legal practice. A competent proponent of Marxist legal theory will, along with Dworkin, attempt to make legal practice the best it can be. The difference is that he will fail. He will become what Dworkin calls a 'global internal sceptic',[12] one who can find no moral justification within existing legal practice, or within legal practice as it might develop in light of sustained and effective moral censure, for state coercion. A Dworkinian conception of law, then, does not necessarily end up providing a justification for state coercion. It must, however, at least make a serious attempt to do so. Otherwise it is not a competent interpretation of legal practice.

4. CONCEPTIONS AND EVALUATION

Dworkinian conceptions of law are thoroughly normative in nature. They are morally charged theories which do not try to describe or characterize what a theorist sees if she takes a morally neutral, detached look at legal systems. They are attempts to justify morally what is observed within the author's own community. They are what Gerald Postema calls 'participant' as opposed to 'observer' theories of law.[13] There is a descriptive element in Dworkinian conceptions, if only because any justification of a social practice like law must in some way characterize, or at the very least presuppose a characterization of, what the theorist seeks to justify. The 'object' to be interpreted must in some way be identified and this requires an element of description. Dworkin expresses the descriptive component of interpretation by saying that any adequate interpretation of a social practice like law must, to some significant though indeterminate degree, 'fit' the practice as it exists. One could not offer a plausible interpretation of the American legal system without accounting for the undeniable fact that it contains a written constitution or that judges cite precedents in justifying their decisions. These are true descriptions of the American legal system; any remotely adequate interpretation of American law must fit the data described by these propositions.

But it is important to stress that descriptive fit is only one feature

[12] Ibid. 79 ff.   [13] See Postema, 'The Normativity of Law', 85.

relative importance of descriptions
justif. in D.
yes

of a plausible Dworkinian interpretive conception and, perhaps more importantly, that the process of description is fundamentally governed, not merely motivated, by the goal of justification. The aim is always to make what is 'described' the best it can be, and a good description is one which succeeds in doing this. According to Dworkin's account, what one 'sees' in legal practice is in part a function of whether what is seen morally licenses state coercion. If it does not, then one has likely not seen the practice correctly, not seen it for what it really is. The parallel with Fuller's attack on 'pos-

parallel with Fuller

itivistic' jurisprudential method is striking. In response to Hart's call for morally neutral description, divorced from a direct concern for questions of fidelity to law, Fuller wrote: '[D]efinitions of "what law really is" are not mere images of some datum of experience, but direction posts for the application of human energies.'[14] A similar view is advocated by Philip Soper who insists that we accept as a datum to be accounted for by a legal theory, the widespread belief in, and likely truth of, the proposition that law imposes justifiable demands upon us. Having done so, Soper suggests, we can then set out to ask the fundamental jurisprudential question: What is law that I should (normally?) obey it? According to Dworkin, Soper,

NB
law's normativity
[cf. Shiner]

and Fuller, that the fact of law normally does provide (not merely is widely believed to provide) a case for coercion is part of the very data to be explained by a jurisprudential theory about the nature of law. As a consequence, a legal theory cannot be a morally de-tached, neutral essay in descriptive sociology. In attempting to in-terpret law in such a way as to explain why normally it really does justify state coercion one simply must exercise moral judgment. So the positivist's insistence that we separate law and morality con-ceptually leads, in the view of these three authors, not only to a false theory but to a deficient jurisprudential methodology.

It is important to be clear that Dworkin's meta-theory about conceptions of law goes well beyond suggesting what philosophers of science have been saying for some time now. It is a commonplace within philosophy that the manner in which one views the data dealt with by a theoretical account will be causally influenced by a vari-ety of forces. According to contemporary feminist critiques of science, gender bias has not only determined what it is that scientists study, it has often shaped the very formation of the scientific theories offered. Apparently it never occurred to Kohlberg to include young

[14] Fuller, 'Fidelity to Law: A Reply to Professor Hart', 83.

women and girls in the sample upon which he based his scientific theories about moral development.[15] Similarly, legal realists and advocates of 'critical legal studies' are fond of pointing out that what a judge or legal scholar 'finds' in the law will be as much a function of his moral biases and personal predilections as what is 'really' there in the books. All this is commonplace and beyond dispute, even for a legal positivist like Kelsen who sought, in developing his 'pure theory of law' to minimize such influences as much as possible. There is no doubt that all theorists are subject to causal influences regarding what it is they select for study, how they conceptualize the problems they study, and ultimately what they say about those problems. But it is one thing to utter these cautionary notes about the causal forces to which all theorists are subject; it is quite another to suggest that we should deliberately permit our moral values and beliefs about the justification of state coercion to shape how we understand a social practice like law. And it is precisely this that Dworkin would have us do. But there are problems in this approach.

For one thing, in following Dworkin's lead we run the serious risk of wishful thinking, of disguising reality behind a sweet coating of moral rationalization. There is little doubt that in trying to understand the products of human activities like law, literature, or the customs of a foreign culture we should be charitable. In striving to understand the words of someone from a foreign culture, for example, the principle of charity requires that we do not, at least initially, attribute false or irrational beliefs to our interlocutors. Likewise, in interpreting a practice in which people are coerced in ways which are claimed (at least by the coercers) to be justified, the principle of charity requires that we do not too quickly describe the practice in such a way that its participants' claims are obviously false or irrational. We should, at least initially, strive to characterize their practice in such a way that it would at least make sense for someone to believe that the practice, so understood, really does

Yes!

---

[15] For Kohlberg's provocative theories see e.g. *Essays on Moral Development. Volume II. The Psychology of Moral Development*, 170–211. For an extensive critique of Kohlberg's theory see the various essays included within the above. See also C. Gilligan, *In a Different Voice: Psychological Theory and Women's Development*, passim. As noted by James Rest, 'Gilligan contends that the male bias in justice-oriented scoring systems came about (at least partly) because Kohlberg is a male, used only male subjects in his dissertation and longitudinal sample, and uses male protagonists in his hypothetical stories' (Rest, *Moral Development*, 111).

justify coercion. In other words, we should try to avoid making those whose activities we interpret look like idiots. It is important to add, however, that one can do this without attributing true beliefs to the participants and setting out to show why they are true. An interpretation of law which characterizes law in such a way that the belief in justification is understandable—i.e. it makes sense—but the question of its truth value is left open to be answered at another time by way of another type of theory is as live an option as one which sets out to show the belief to be true or false. A theory which ignores the belief in justification entirely, or which simply condemns it as ludicrous without attempting to give it sense, is perhaps not a good theory. But one can avoid this *faux pas* without tackling the question of justification directly, without offering either a positive or a sceptical moral theory about whether the practice really does license coercion.

True enough, it might be replied, but the alternative to Dworkinian interpretation tacitly suggested here—i.e., morally neutral, detached description—is simply not possible. Kelsen notwithstanding, a pure, scientific theory of law, devoid of all evaluative influences from ethics, politics, and social theory cannot be constructed. Such a theory is no more possible than a pure theory of mental illness or a pure description of moral development. Since pure theories are unavailable in jurisprudence, we are left with only one alternative: Dworkinian conceptions which not only acknowledge but highlight the role of moral value in the construction of legal theories. If (1) morally neutral description is not possible; (2) we are, like it or not, subject causally to moral and political beliefs, prejudices and biases when fashioning a theory of law; then (3) we are better off placing our normative commitments front and centre, recognizing that our so-called neutral descriptions are in fact rationalizations serving our moral predilections. In offering Dworkinian conceptions we at least display the virtue of intellectual honesty. We recognize that our beliefs in justification shape how we see and understand a practice like law.

The problem with this reply lies in its failure to recognize alternatives lying between Kelsen's antiseptic science of law and Dworkinian conceptions. As I shall now argue, we can acknowledge the role of value, including moral value, in legal theory without going all the way with Dworkin. One can find a central role for value without proposing that we deliberately try to make the data under investigation morally 'the best it can be'. One can allow value to influence, and indeed in some instances govern, theoretical description without courting the threat of moral and intellectual deception lurking in Dworkinian conceptions.

5. VALUES AND LEGAL THEORY

In discussing the role of values in legal theory, Joseph Raz reminds us that 'evaluative' and 'moral' are not equivalent in meaning. A theory which describes and explains—i.e. a descriptive-explanatory theory—can be based upon and even guided by non-moral, evaluative considerations. We have already seen how the principle of charity operates in theory construction. Simplicity provides another evaluative criterion to which appeal is often made in constructing and appraising theories of all kinds. This is obviously true in the case of fully normative theories, say normative ethical theories. Despite its many weaknesses, one of the decided virtues of act utilitarianism, as opposed, say, to the pluralistic theory of Sir David Ross, is its simplicity. Compared with Ross's long list of irreducible, non-lexically ordered principles of morality which compete in various complex ways, the principle of act utilitarianism—Act always so as to maximize the balance of utility over disutility caused by one's actions—is a simple measure to understand.[16] Of two theories, more or less comparable in terms of the data for which they account (i.e. describe and explain in the case of a descriptive-explanatory theory; justify in the case of a normative theory), the simpler will be judged better, a more worthy theory. For those who wish to speak in these terms, it will be judged more likely to be true. Leibniz thought that this was the case with scientific theories because God's moral perfection requires laws of nature which are as simple as is compatible with the variety of phenomena that God, in his infinite goodness and power, chose to create. This world is the best of all possible worlds, and the best of all possible worlds is one which maximally combines simplicity of governing laws with richness of effect. Modern scientists seldom, if ever, ascribe validity to the simplicity criterion on such grounds, and it is

[16] David Ross, *The Right and the Good*. Of course, act utilitarianism is not as easy to understand and apply as many of its advocates think. Problems surrounding the possible incommensurability of preferences, pleasures, and so on, plague the theory.

not abundantly clear why, in the absence of some such explanation, the simpler of two theories should be thought more likely true, not merely more useful. But the fact remains that simplicity is a value in theoretical inquiries of all kinds. It represents what we will call a 'meta-theoretical-evaluative' criterion: a meta-theoretical criterion governing the assessment or evaluation of theories.

The value of simplicity is not restricted, of course, to situations where two or more competitors account for precisely the same data. It is also possible that, of two competing theories, the simpler theory is preferable even though it accommodates less of the relevant data than its more complicated competitor. In such a case, the recalcitrant data will be viewed as somehow mistaken (due, for example, to a faulty measuring device), or accountable in some way consistent with the simpler theory but not yet discovered. In effect, it will be usefully set aside, if only for the moment. In this way the value of simplicity might be said to control the data and how we see it, just as moral value does in Dworkin's account of conceptions of law. The difference, however, is that, with the possible exception of Leibniz, no one views the value of simplicity as moral in nature. It is not a moral belief which leads us to set aside data which conflicts with the simpler account: it is the intellectual concern to discover what things are really like, to understand how they in fact hang together. We are better able to reach this goal with a simpler theory.

We do, of course, also want to know sometimes how things should hang together. It may even be that, deep down, most of our intellectual energies are or should be motivated by moral concerns. We may, at least in part, want to know the laws of physics so that we can control our environment to reduce suffering and enhance flourishing. Analogously, we may want to know what law is like because it sometimes seems to present us with moral dilemmas, and it is crucial to know how morally we ought to behave in such situations. But there is no compelling reason to think that our efforts to solve moral dilemmas can best be accomplished by merging our descriptive explanations and our moral evaluations in the way Dworkin suggests. As Hart notes, 'the positivist's insistence that there is a task and need for a descriptive analytic jurisprudence is salutary even if it is regarded only as a preliminary to the articulation of a justificatory theory of a community's legal practices and not, as it in fact is, a contribution to the study of human society and culture.'[17]

So descriptive-explanatory theories are ultimately governed by meta-theoretical-evaluative considerations like simplicity, comprehensiveness, coherence, and the like. It may even be that our motivation for constructing such theories often lies in the moral concerns we have. In the case of jurisprudence, the relevant moral concerns are not hard to find. Coercion, for example, is something we morally suspect wherever we encounter it, and one of the law's most salient features is its characteristic use of coercion. So immediately we have moral reason to understand, not necessarily justify, what law is all about. But the role of these moral concerns may not end at the point where we are furnished with motivation to investigate the nature of law. Morality may also serve to guide us, and perhaps even justify us, in what we choose to centre on in our descriptive-explanatory accounts. As Raz suggests, 'any good theory of [law] is based on evaluative considerations in that its success is in highlighting important social structures and processes, and every judgment of importance is evaluative'.[18] Legal theory, even of the descriptive-explanatory sort, 'does engage in [moral]-evaluative judgment for such judgment is inescapable in trying to sort out what is central and significant in the common understanding of the concept of law'.[19] It is perhaps worth pausing to explore this suggestion a bit further so that we may be clear how it differs from Dworkin's account of how conceptions of law are developed.

It is obvious that how we see the world can differ depending on our interests and concerns. As Leslie Green observes, legal theory, like all types of theory, must be 'value-relevant'.[20]

Any [theory] of law can have no deeper ground than the complex set of interests and purposes to which legal and political theory responds. Should law be distinguished from custom? From morality? Does canon law count as a legal system? Does international law? Abstracted from political [and moral] concerns, there are no answers to these questions.[21]

With a characteristically coercive social practice like law, many of our interests are undoubtedly moral. As noted, law resorts to coercion, so, as theorists, we will centre to some extent on the coercive

---

[17] *Issues in Contemporary Legal Philosophy*, 37.
[18] 'Authority, Law and Morality', 320.
[19] Ibid. 322.
[20] 'The Political Content of Legal Theory', 15.
[21] Ibid.

elements in legal practice. We are likely, for example, to follow Hart's lead in noting that law and morality differ in the sorts of coercive sanctions to which they appeal.[22] Law typically employs organized sanctions which are often physical in nature; morality typically employs diffuse social pressure as its form of 'sanction'. That we choose to make these observations about morality and law is no doubt to be explained, in part, by our moral concerns about coercion.

Another example: law typically asserts the authority to pre-empt individual judgment concerning our social responsibilities. The law may leave us to judge for ourselves in some instances, as it does in our choice whether or not to have children. But it does not always do so, as in our choice whether to assault a neighbour because he supports the wrong hockey team. Even more to the point, the law seems to claim the authority to decide for itself when and where and to what extent it will pre-empt personal judgment about social responsibilities. Owing to the fact that we value moral autonomy and look with suspicion upon attempts to deny it, this feature of legal practice seems well worth highlighting in a theory of law. In fact, Raz ascribes so much importance to this feature that he is led to describe law as a set of standards purporting to provide 'exclusionary reasons for action'. In the case of law, these are reasons which not only argue directly in favour of actions prescribed by law; they also purport to exclude from practical deliberation reasons of any other sort which would otherwise be relevant. It is Raz's concern for autonomy which no doubt leads him to centre on this particular aspect of legal practice and to place it at the very heart of his descriptive-explanatory theory.[23]

So what, it might be asked, distinguishes the kind of moral value-relevance espoused by Raz and Green on the one hand, and the kind of value-relevance espoused by Dworkin (and Fuller and Soper) on the other? One crucial difference lies in the level of moral commitment that is involved in the two different enterprises: offering value-relevant, descriptive-explanatory theories versus value-determined interpretive conceptions. Discovering certain elements of legal practice worth highlighting because they are morally relevant in no way commits one to saying that these are elements in virtue of which the practice is actually justified (or unjustified) morally. One can see

---

[22] See *The Concept of Law*, 175–6.
[23] This feature of Raz's theory will be explored more fully in Chapter 4.

that the use of coercion is morally relevant without knowing whether and when coercion is ever justified morally. One can give an account which highlights this morally relevant feature of law without arguing or even suggesting that coercion is (or is not) morally justified. In short, one can see moral relevance without making a moral commitment.

Consider a parallel case in ethics. It is obviously morally relevant to the abortion debate that a living entity which, if allowed to develop naturally could become a fully-fledged human being, is killed when abortions are performed. One can know that this killing is a morally relevant feature of abortion without knowing whether abortions are ever justified. Indeed, the relevance issue is one upon which all sides of the abortion debate agree even though they disagree radically on the effect of this feature on the ultimate justification of killing foetuses. All participants in the debates would find totally inadequate any theory which neglects even to mention or account for the fact that killing does take place.

But seeing moral relevance without taking a moral stand is not at all what is involved in Dworkinian conceptions. According to Dworkin, a legal theorist attempts (and may fail if the ultimate conclusion is global scepticism) to impose morally worthy purposes on legal practice. He does this, Dworkin thinks, in much the same way as a literary theorist attempts to impose an aesthetically valuable purpose on the object of his interpretation, say a novel. Each theorist's choice of an interpretive conception 'must reflect his view of which interpretation proposes the most [moral or aesthetic] value for the [object]—which one shows it in the better light, all things considered'.[24]

It is important to keep stressing that the ascriptions of purpose contained within Dworkin's interpretive theories of law are fully committed moral justifications. The morally detached, neutral perspective of analytical jurisprudence sought to varying degrees by Kelsen, Hart, Raz, and Green is dismissed by Dworkin as a hold over from the misguided positivistic quest for semantic theories of law, or a value-free science of law. A viable legal theory is fully committed, offered from the *participant's* point of view. This is not the perspective of one who seeks merely to understand the practices of others and somehow to describe those practices in a morally neutral fashion. Rather, it is the perspective of one who, in offering

[24] *Law's Empire*, 52–3.

his theory, actually engages in the practice himself. In Dworkin's view, it is just not possible to understand a social practice like law without engaging in it directly. And by this I mean not merely that we cannot, according to Dworkin, understand the practice without first engaging in it, and then setting out to offer a description of what we have experienced. In other words, he is not saying that one should actually practice law before one comes to legal philosophy. Dworkin's point is a different one. In his view, there just is no theoretically important difference between interpreting and engaging in a practice. Legal theory is not meta-theory according to Dworkin. A legal theorist must, by the very logic of interpretation, 'use the methods his subjects use in forming their own opinions about what [the practice] really requires. He must, that is, join the practice he proposes to understand; his conclusions are then not neutral reports about what [the participants] think but claims about [the practice] competitive with theirs.'[25] '[N]o firm line divides jurisprudence from adjudication or any other aspect of legal practice.'[26]

So, for Dworkin, a legal theorist's job is not unlike that of a judge who sets out to interpret a statute or a line of precedents. Both must attempt to make their objects of study the best they can be, to find in them as much moral value, i.e. moral justification, as they can. Both the judge and the legal theorist are trying to find something that licenses state coercion. The judge wants to know what justifies coercion in this particular case before him; the legal theorist wants to know what, in general, licenses coercion in all (or most) cases coming before the courts of a particular legal system, or legal systems in general. So according to Dworkin legal theory is not essentially different from adjudication: it is just that the former is more general and encompasses more material than the latter.

Legal theory, according to Dworkin, is also not essentially different from interpretive theories in the arts, or even from theories in the hard sciences like physics and chemistry. Dworkin provocatively suggests that all interpretive theories attempt to impose purpose and value on their objects. Upon noting that the construction and appraisal of scientific explanations utilize standards like simplicity and elegance, Dworkin proposes that his account of constructive interpretation might apply to interpretations of all kinds, including scientific 'interpretations' of physical phenomena. Perhaps, he suggests, 'all interpretation strives to make an object the

[25] Ibid. 64.	[26] Ibid. 90.

best that it can be', and interpretation takes different forms in law, literature, and science only because each of these enterprises has its own unique standards of value. 'Artistic interpretation differs from scientific interpretation ... only because we judge success in works of art by standards different from those we use to judge explanations of physical phenomena.'[27]

What are we to make of these provocative suggestions? Surely something has gone wrong here, something which may reflect badly on Dworkin's general theory of interpretation and ultimately his account of the nature of legal theories. There is no doubt whatsoever that scientists are guided by evaluative judgments of a variety of kinds in developing, choosing, and assessing scientific theories. The same is true in jurisprudence. That value plays a crucial role is, as we have seen, something which no positivist, with the possible exception of Kelsen, would wish to deny. Appeals to simplicity and elegance, for example, clearly presuppose a range of meta-theoretical-evaluative judgments about the features of a good scientific or jurisprudential theory. And it is undeniable that at least sometimes what a legal theorist or scientist chooses to study and highlight is motivated by, perhaps even guided by, moral concerns. There is also no doubt that we naturally speak of scientists and legal theorists attempting to 'interpret' the data their theories purport to explain. Finally, it is clearly the case that all scientists and legal theorists are out to make their theories, their 'interpretations' of the data, the best that they can be. With this we can have no quarrel. It is one thing to say all this, however, quite another to suggest that physicists are attempting to make their data the best that it can be. It is obvious (perhaps to all but Leibnizians) that scientists do not set out to find value in what they seek to explain and describe. It's the theory not the data to which value is properly ascribed in the manner Dworkin proposes.[28]

Perhaps Dworkin would wish, at this point, to withdraw his

[27] Ibid. 53.
[28] This is not to deny, of course, that it is ever proper to ascribe value to data. New data which allows us to test competing theories is properly described as valuable. But its value clearly lies in its role in testing the theories and advancing our understanding of the phenomena in question. The theories are not attempts to find value in the data—to impose a valuable purpose on it. There is perhaps a second sense in which value can always be attributed to data, regardless of the particular field of inquiry. It is plausible to think that all interpretations strive to impose *intelligibility* upon the object of interpretation, and intelligibility may be as much a value as elegance and simplicity. (I owe this point to my colleague Sami Najm.) There is nothing here which

suggestion of a parallel between scientific, legal and aesthetic theories. It was after all just that, a suggestion. Nevertheless, a suspicion would linger that the misguided parallel has revealed something of significance about Dworkin's general account of interpretation and its implications for jurisprudence. Once we apply Dworkin's theory of interpretation to science, the importance of distinguishing between trying to make the object of interpretation— i.e. the data—the best it can be, and attempting to make a theory about that object the best that it can be, comes clearly into focus. Dworkin has simply conflated meta-theoretical values with values which are sometimes pursued by the participants of some practices (e.g. law and art) but not others (e.g. physics). The differences between these are ignored, however, only at the cost of considerable error and confusion, at least in the case of science. But if this is so, then one wonders if the same might not be true when we turn to art and legal theory. It seems plausible to suppose that here too we should distinguish between seeking value in an interpretation (i.e. trying to make our interpretation a good one) and seeking value (e.g. a justification for coercion) in the object of the interpretation. There is no doubt that in providing an interpretation of a painting, a novel, or the customs of a foreign culture one tries to make something the best it can be; hence the initial plausibility of Dworkin's theory. But once we draw our distinction, much of the plausibility vanishes. Why suppose that here, unlike in the sciences, the thing that we attempt to make the best of its kind is necessarily the object not its interpretation? Why should our aim not be, as it is in science, to illuminate the object, enhance our understanding of it and other things to which it is related? Perhaps too our immediate aim in offering a legal theory is not to find moral value in, to impose a morally worthy purpose on, legal practice, but rather to 'sort out what is central and significant in the common understanding of the concept of law',[29] or to provide an 'improved analysis of the distinctive structure of a municipal legal system and a better understanding of the resemblances and differences between law, coercion, and morality as types of social phenomena'.[30] To be sure, our efforts

undermines our critique of Dworkin's general theory of interpretation, so long as one is careful to add that it is intelligibility, not moral value, which a descriptive-explanatory theory attempts to impose on legal practice. So even if all theories attempt to find value in data, we are not forced to conclude that a theory of law must attempt to find moral value in legal practice.

[29] 'Authority, Law and Morality', 332.   [30] *The Concept of Law*, 17.

good! (margin annotation)

along these lines must be guided by meta-theoretical-evaluative judgments, (partly) moral judgments as to what is important to highlight as distinctive about law as a social phenomenon, and the desire to avoid making legal participants look stupid. But there is no reason to think that our efforts along these lines must be determined by the immediate aim of finding a true or adequate moral justification for the object we set out to examine. That is something we could do if we chose to do so, if we chose to engage in normative as opposed to analytic jurisprudence. But why must we make this choice? And why should we try to do two things at once? Indeed, there is every reason to think we should not.

Another related difficulty with Dworkin's meta-theory about legal theories concerns his claim that the proper theoretical role is that of an engaged participant, one who does not merely seek somehow to understand legal practice 'from the outside' but to engage the practice directly by offering a justification for coercion. The theorist's conclusions are not, Dworkin thinks, neutral reports about what the participants think and do but claims about the practice which are competitive with theirs.[31] Offhand, the identification of participant and theorist is suspect. Consider these parallels. One can offer a theory about what it is to be in love without actually being in love; and it is certainly true that philosophical theories about love are not themselves expressions of love. Call it what you will, but *Law's Empire* is not a love poem. One can also offer theories of sexuality without thereby engaging in sexual behaviour. Theorists do get excited about their theories; but they do not confuse this excitement with the attainment of sexual orgasm.

But let us look a bit more closely at Dworkin's attempt to merge observer and participant and consider the kernels of truth in his suggestion. There is no doubt that one who seeks to understand a social practice like law should be very familiar with how its participants view what it is they are up to. Participants' claims and understandings should be taken very seriously and carefully examined. If the account is to be at all illuminating, philosophically, it must somehow characterize the participant's point of view and provide a sensible account of it. It must, at the very least, make sense that people should behave as the observer's account says they do and believe the things the account says they do. Hart made a similar point long ago when he criticized Austin for ignoring what

[31] *Law's Empire*, 64.

Hart called the 'internal point of view', and centring instead on the 'external point of view', the view of those within society whose concern with the law is simply to avoid its coercive measures. Austin failed to represent the view of the vast majority within a flourishing legal system who willingly accept and use the law as a guide to conduct. Hart is no doubt correct that the normal participant's internal point of view must be acknowledged, explained, and represented as being intelligible. But it is one thing to say this; quite another to suggest, along with Dworkin, that the only way to characterize the participant's point of view is to take it on oneself and offer claims which are competitive with his. Why should we think this necessary? Why are we forced to take the internal point of view in attempting to understand and depict it? What might lead one to think that the internal point of view cannot be understood and represented from the external point of view?

One reason for thinking this way might lie in the likely fact that a theorist can make strides towards understanding the social practices of others only because he himself engages in practices of a similar kind. One doesn't have to be a participant in a social practice identical to the one under study, but perhaps there must be some degree of similarity. Could one understand law if one had never before encountered or been subject to practices of social regulation somewhat like law, morality, or custom? This seems doubtful. It may also be the case that the closer one's own social practices are to the objects of study (the limiting case being that where the object of study just is a practice to which one is subject) the easier it will be to gain understanding. For example, perhaps a theorist must have had experience of rule following if he is to interpret what he sees in others as rule-governed behaviour. This doesn't get us very far, of course, since everyone follows rules at some time or other. Perhaps, though, we can go a bit further and suggest that it is essential to have, or to have had, moral beliefs oneself if one is to understand the practices of others as being motivated by moral beliefs. We might even go so far as to agree that the closer the participants' behaviour is to ours the easier it will be to understand them as engaging in a moral practice of some kind. But this doesn't seem to be essential. It seems possible to understand very different moral belief systems as many sociologists, anthropologists, and some philosophers seem to have done.[32] It is

[32] For a discussion of the very different moral belief system of the Hopi Indians, see R. B. Brandt, *Hopi Ethics: A Theoretical Analysis*, *passim*, and *Ethical Theory*, 96–9.

perhaps even possible that we can sometimes understand these systems better than we can systems which are closer to our own. Often a bit of 'distance' allows one to see things for what they really are, as opposed to what one's ingrained beliefs, assumptions, and biases lead one to think that they are. In the everyday sense of the term, distance sometimes provides us with a bit more 'objectivity'.

Perhaps, though, the possibility of interpreting radically different moral (and legal) practices hinges on our knowledge of certain very basic facts about human beings, in particular the kinds of things people, as human beings, tend to value, things like survival in close proximity to their neighbours.[33] Perhaps it is because we all value survival that we are able to interpret the norms of other cultures as legal or moral rules against killing and violence. We are able to effect the interpretation because we are all participants in the 'practice' of human survival. But notice how watered down Dworkin's claims about the necessity of occupying the participant's point of view would be were he to take this route in explaining why the theorist's claims are competitive with those made by participants. If this is all that is meant in insisting that the theorist must take the participant's point of view, then we can easily accept the recommendation. But it hardly tells us much about the nature of legal theory, and surely does not lead to the conclusion that legal theories necessarily attempt to provide moral justification for coercion. At best it leads to the conclusion that Martians might have difficulty interpreting our social practices. Of course, even in this case the degree of difficulty would depend on how different Martians are from us, and the similarities might outweigh the differences.

[margin note: watered down D. view]

6. CONCLUSION

So what has this long excursion into the theory of conceptions of law revealed? It has shown that we should be careful to distinguish the variety of ways in which values of various kinds can enter into and shape legal theories without their becoming justifications for coercion. Once our distinctions are drawn, the possibility of viable descriptive-explanatory theories of law emerges. We are not driven

---

[33] See *The Concept of Law*, 188 ff.

to conclude from the fact that Kelsen's desire for pure theory of law is unattainable that morally committed, Dworkinian conceptions of law are the only alternative. We can and should distinguish between (*a*) meta-theoretical-evaluative and moral-evaluative considerations; (*b*) seeing (moral) value relevance and offering a moral justification; (*c*) attempting to make a theory the best it can be and making the object of the theory the best that it can be; and (*d*) wanting to justify morally what one sees and wanting to avoid making those who engage in the practice (the object one studies) look stupid. Once we draw such distinctions, the possibility of an 'impure' and enlightening descriptive-explanatory theory clearly emerges as a viable and desirable alternative to the morally committed rationalizations represented by Dworkinian conceptions of law. In what follows we shall treat inclusive and exclusive positivism, together with natural-law theory and Dworkin's integrity theory as descriptive-explanatory theories of law, and assess them in these terms. Our principal aim is to show that inclusive positivism is a better descriptive-explanatory theory than its rivals so understood.

needed distinctions well drawn't drawn by W.

3

THE FORCES OF LAW

1. INTRODUCTION

In the preceding chapter we introduced Ronald Dworkin's distinction between the grounds and the force of law. We noted his suggestion that whatever a legal-grounds theory identifies as law will almost always be conceived by its author as justifying the use of state coercion. This led us to examine Dworkin's theory of interpretive conceptions of law and to draw several distinctions ignored in Dworkin's account. We saw how value can enter legal theories in a wide variety of ways without their being turned thereby into attempts to justify coercion.

In this chapter I wish to give further consideration to Dworkin's distinction between the grounds and the force of law and argue that, while on the right track, it needs to be developed and fleshed out more precisely in ways apparently not contemplated by Dworkin. I shall expand upon the intuition that the question 'What is the present law on this matter?' is logically distinct from questions concerning how citizens and judges should, both morally and, in the case of judges, legally, respond with respect to that law. As will be seen, this is a distinction which applies not only in cases where the law is wicked and disobedience is called for; it also seems to apply in very ordinary cases in which judges depart from authoritative precedent.

In section 2 it will be argued that we should distinguish carefully between the law and what I shall call its 'institutional force'. This is a distinction to which Dworkin's and other theories of law are insufficiently sensitive but which ought to be accommodated within a plausible theory of law. In illustration of this point we shall examine some rather peculiar and troublesome difficulties to which Dworkin's theory is led, difficulties which seem traceable in part to its failure to respect the difference between law and its institutional forces. These may not be problems which are fatal to Dworkin's

enterprise, or which Dworkin could not avoid by altering his interpretation of law, in particular his theory of legal rights, but they do
serve to illustrate the importance of the distinction between the law
and its institutional force. They also highlight the importance of
distinguishing between what I shall call a theory of law and a theory
of adjudication. Hart, Raz, Kelsen, Austin, and Aquinas all offer
theories of law and have only a secondary interest in a theory of
adjudication, that is, a theory about how judges do or should decide
legal cases. At best, Dworkin has it the other way round, i.e. he is
primarily interested in a theory of adjudication from which he
attempts to derive a theory of law. More likely, however, he actually collapses the two into one. As Joseph Raz has noted, Dworkin's theories are offered from 'the lawyer's perspective', and from
that perspective it is natural, though not necessarily enlightening
philosophically, to identify the law with whatever considerations
judges take into account in justifying their decisions in legal cases. It
is also natural to provide an account of law which is in effect a
theory of adjudication.[1] Raz is right in thinking that much is lost in
terms of our understanding of the nature, structure, and characteristic functions of legal systems if we follow Dworkin's lead. One of
my aims in the present chapter is to lend further credence to that
insight. Once we see the importance of distinguishing the law from
its institutional force, we see the immense danger in Dworkin's
approach. Several paradoxes emerge which can be easily dissolved
by drawing the appropriate distinctions and beginning with a theory
of law which, though related to, is not derived from, nor identical
with, a theory of adjudication.

Once these major points are established, we will turn in section 4
to a theme to be explored more fully in later chapters: that law and
its institutional force are each different, conceptually, from what
will be termed the law's 'moral force'. We have already seen that
Dworkin identifies as law that which normally provides a moral
justification for state coercion. In so doing, Dworkin comes perilously close to collapsing the distinction between law and its moral
force. This too leads to troublesome difficulties, of the sort traditionally highlighted by legal positivists in their critiques of
classical natural-law theory, as the positivists have understood that
theory, i.e., as summarized in Augustine's slogan: An unjust law
seems to be no law at all. Finally, section 5 presents a sketch of an

[1] See Raz, 'The Problem About the Nature of Law'.

alternative theory of law, based on the insights of Hart and Raz concerning the nature of law as a social institution characterized by a set of binding standards validated by a socially constituted rule of recognition. It will be seen how easily this positivist alternative can accommodate the distinctions drawn in sections 2–4 and how it is therefore free of the many difficulties faced by Dworkin's theory. That such a positivist theory is superior in these ways counts heavily in its favour.

2. LAW, COMPLIANCE, AND ADJUDICATION

Dworkin's distinction between the force and the grounds of law contains an important insight, though it is obscured somewhat by the suggestion that legal-grounds theories are constructive interpretations of legal practice and that they must therefore be understood as saying what judges and citizens should normally do—what the normal force of law is for them. As legal positivists like Austin, Bentham, and Hart have always stressed, and if John Finnis is right, no natural lawyer ever denied,[2] it is one thing to say what (the) law is, it is quite another to say what the obligations and responsibilities of citizens are with respect to that law. It may also, I should like to add, be quite another thing to say what the legal-adjudicative obligations and powers of judges are with respect to that law. One need not consider anomalous, borderline cases of wicked law, in which the judge's moral duty seems dramatically to conflict with her institutionally defined judicial responsibilities, in order to see the importance of distinguishing between the law and its force. We have only to look to the familiar practice of overruling undesirable or mistaken precedents. This practice signals the need to distinguish carefully between what the law is and the institutional powers and responsibilities of judges with respect to that law, between the law and its 'institutional force'. Put simply, we need to recognize, and accommodate within our jurisprudential theories, that the law is not always legally binding on judges. Sometimes its force may, indeed must, legally, be overcome by judges. One immediate and crucial implication of this point is that it is very dangerous to identify a

---

[2] See Finnis, *Natural Law and Natural Rights*, ch. 2. Cf. Summers, *Lon L. Fuller*, 71–2, where Summers suggests the following: 'Thus he [Aquinas] like many others in the natural-law tradition, severed the issues of legal validity and obedience.'

theory about the nature (or grounds) of law with a theory of adjudication. If the law is sometimes not legally binding on judges, but we nevertheless attempt to identify the law with whatever is binding on judges in adjudication, we run a serious risk of missing our mark, or at least a good deal of it. As we shall see presently, Dworkin does just that.

It may sound odd, perhaps even shocking, to say that judges may not be legally bound to apply the law. It may sound even more peculiar to claim that they may be legally bound not to apply existing law. But the appearance of paradox can easily be dissolved with an example. Imagine a jurisdiction in which a middle-court judge has decided case C1 on the basis that paternity leave should extend to adoptive fathers only. On this basis he denies the plaintiff, a natural father, the right to such leave. We may suppose that the decision was a proper one, that is, that no other binding precedents, statutes or constitutional provisions were infringed by the decision in C1, and that a decision about paternity leave was well within the court's jurisdiction. One might think the decision misguided morally or socially, but there are no legal grounds for disputing its validity. Suppose further that lower-court judges within our imaginary jurisdiction are strictly bound by precedents set by their colleagues in the middle court. When a lower-court judge confronts a relevantly similar case, C2, in which yet another natural father seeks a ruling that he is legally entitled to paternity leave, the lower-court judge is under a legal-adjudicative obligation, that is, an obligation established by the ground rules of adjudication accepted by the judges within the legal system, to decide against the natural father. The law, established in the middle-court judge's decision in C1, denies the legal right sought, and the lower-court judge, in virtue of the ground rules of precedent practised within the legal system, lacks the Hohfeldian power to change that law so as to escape its effect upon his decision. In the absence of such a power, he is under a legal-adjudicative obligation to apply that law even if he thinks it wrong or stupid, or that the middle-court judge should really have decided C1 in a different way.

But the same might not be true of another judge. Imagine that the decision in C2 is eventually appealed to a higher court and that higher-court judges are not bound by precedents set by middle-court judges. They have, by way of the ground rules of precedent practised within their jurisdiction, or if one likes, the best Dworkinian interpretation of their system's practices of precedent, the legal power to overrule a precedent set by a middle-court judge. They may do so if they think the precedent was legally in error, say because it violated a constitutional right of greater institutional force than the offending precedent, or if they think the precedent, though legally valid, is, for some other reason recognized as appropriate by the legal system, worthy of overruling. Perhaps, to cite an old English case, allowing the precedent to control the instant case would be 'manifestly absurd or [morally] repugnant'.[3] The higher-court judge decides that it is manifestly absurd, i.e. blatantly irrational, to deny paternity leave to natural fathers when adoptive fathers are accorded that very same right. So, notwithstanding the decision of the middle-court judge in C1, our higher-court judge rules that paternity leave must extend to natural fathers too. He therefore overrules his middle-court colleague thereby changing the law established in that earlier decision. The law does now extend the legal right sought. The natural father in C2 is granted a legal right to paternity leave.

This simple example illustrates an obvious but important truth: some judges, sometimes, have the Hohfeldian legal power to change the law which is otherwise binding on them, while others do not. In one case the institutional duty of the judge, i.e. the duty established by the ground rules of adjudication accepted within the judge's legal system, may be to enforce the law that already exists. In another, the opportunity to change the law may exist. In making this simple observation I do not mean to deny that all judges necessarily have discretion in some cases where the law is indeterminate, and that in exercising this discretion they add to and thus modify the law. Indeed, in Chapter 7 I shall argue, *contra* Dworkin, that judges always do have, and are often forced to exercise, what Dworkin terms 'strong discretion'. My present concern is only to establish the simple truth that some judges sometimes have the legal power to change the law that presently exists while others, in exactly similar cases, do not. In a second case, involving exactly the same facts, exactly the same law, but a different judge, the situation may well be

---

[3] This phrase derives from B. Parke in *Becke* v. *Smith* (1836). In Chapter 8 I will defend an approach to the interpretation of legal rules according to which a rule does not apply to a set of facts if manifest absurdity or moral repugnance would be the result. Here we are supposing a different, though by no means incompatible, practice: manifest absurdity or moral repugnance are grounds for changing a legal rule, not determining what it meant all along.

different. Here the judge may not be strictly bound by existing law. He may enjoy the legal power to change (or correct) the law so as to avoid its effect upon his decision and upon the litigants before him.

This last point is not something which any legal theorist would wish to deny. Even Dworkin, who sometimes talks as if the law is never changed but simply clarified and then declared by judges, does not wish to deny that precedents are sometimes binding though mistaken. Consider his theory of the 'embedded mistake', one whose 'enactment force' on cases precisely like the precedent-setting case cannot be overcome (i.e. the same mistaken decision must be made) but whose 'gravitational force' lacks effect. An embedded mistake must be followed by at least some judges in cases indistinguishable from the precedent, but it need not be accounted for in a judge's best interpretive theory of the law, the theory to which he repairs in deciding hard cases.[4]

It is not my intention to provide a descriptive-explanatory account of when judges within common-law jurisdictions are empowered to escape the institutional force of existing law. Many others, far more qualified than me, have done so already. I will simply draw upon their analyses when appropriate. A prime example of such an analysis is Sir Rupert Cross's classic text *Precedent in English Law*, to which reference will be made shortly. It is also not my aim to argue for the existence of Hartian secondary rules of adjudication which define the varying institutional forces which laws have for different judges. At this stage, I want merely to stress the obvious: that judicial powers to overcome the institutional force(s) of precedent, of the existing law, vary from case to case and depend, crucially, upon the level of court in which the judge finds himself. This, as we have observed, is something Dworkin would not wish to deny.

These differences in the judges' powers to overcome the institutional force(s) of existing law are illustrated well by Cross who observes that the doctrines of precedent under which English judges labour have a 'strongly coercive nature'. 'English judges are sometimes obliged to follow a previous case although they have what would otherwise be good reasons for not doing so.'[5] Being strictly bound by earlier decisions is a fate which can apply even to the

---

[4] On embedded mistakes, see *Taking Rights Seriously*, 121. Dworkin's theory of mistakes will be investigated more fully in Chapter 6.

[5] *Precedent in English Law*, 4.

supreme court of the system. Prior to its famous Practice Statement of 1966 the English House of Lords had considered itself absolutely bound by its own earlier decisions.[6] In *Nash* v. *Tamplin and Sons Brewery Ltd.*, for example, Lord Reid said: 'It matters not how difficult it is to find the ratio decidendi of a previous case, that ratio must be found. And it matters not how difficult it is to reconcile that ratio when found with statutory provisions or general principles: that ratio must be applied to any later case which is not reasonably distinguishable.'[7]

As Cross goes on to note, when they are 'unable to detect a rational distinction between the instant case and a former unsatisfactory decision which binds them, the lot of the judges of the [English] Court of Appeal may be as unenviable as that of the members of the House of Lords'.[8] As an example, he cites *Olympic Oil and Cake Co. Ltd.* v. *Produce Brokers Ltd.*, where Buckley LJ remarked: 'I am unable to adduce any reason to show that the decision which I am about to pronounce is right ... But I am bound by authority which, of course, it is my duty to follow.' Philmore LJ added: 'With reluctance—I might almost say with sorrow—I concur in the view that this appeal must be dismissed. I trust that the case will proceed to the House of Lords.' The case did proceed to the House of Lords where the appeal was allowed, Lord Sumner observing that 'the members of the Court of Appeal had been right in indicating objections to the earlier decisions, although they were bound to follow them'.[9]

It appears, then, that the institutional powers of judges to alter or correct the law differ considerably, at least in the English legal system. And if these differences occur here, there is no reason to think they do not also occur elsewhere. Yet if these judicial powers can differ in these ways, then it is clear that something within the spirit of Dworkin's distinction between the grounds and force of law needs to be marked out in a general jurisprudential theory. Dworkin's distinction goes at least some way towards recognizing that there is a difference between a statement of what the law presently is, and a statement of what the responsibilities of a judge or citizen are with respect to that law.

Yet Dworkin's distinction does not take us nearly far enough.

---

[6] See ibid. 109–16.   [7] [1952] AC 231, at 250.
[8] *Precedent in English Law*, 37.
[9] [1916] AC at 334; cited in *Precedent in English Law*, 37.

moral force vs institutional force

Simply referring to the 'force' of law obscures the fact that law subjects citizens and judges to very different 'normative forces'.[10] As observed above, some judges, sometimes, have the legal power to change the law which they are otherwise legally bound to apply, thus escaping its force. Other judges do not. Whether and the extent to which a judge does enjoy this power seems to be governed by institutional rules or standards of adjudication which help define the extent to which existing laws of various kinds have force over judicial decisions. The difference between being 'strictly' and 'moderately' bound by precedent seems to reflect different degrees of this institutional force.

Private citizens, on the other hand, have no such comparable role and are governed by no such comparable institutional rules. They do, of course, have private powers to change private legal relationships, as in the case of contracts or wills; or relationships between themselves and governments, as when one successfully applies for welfare and thereby imposes a legal duty on the government to provide assistance. But these private powers aside, the question for the ordinary citizen is not whether and how institutional rules of adjudication empower him to change the law which applies to someone else whose case he must adjudicate, but whether to conform his own behaviour to the law which applies to him and which he cannot change. The force here seems clearly to be moral and has, in the case of citizens, to do with compliance. It is not a role-specific, institutional force concerning the duty either to apply the law or to escape its force by changing it. Private citizens, and judges with no legal power to alter the law in the case in question, may of course plead for changes in the law. This the English Appeal Court judges did in *Olympic Oil and Cake Co. Ltd.*[11] But until such time as the law is modified in an appropriate way by one with legal power to do so, both citizens and judges are expected, by the law, to apply its standards to their decisions and their behaviour. In the case of judges with no legal power to effect the desired change, there is a legal-adjudicative obligation, defined by the rules of adjudication practised by the judges, to apply the existing law in their decisions, as the lower-court judge did in our earlier example and as the judges

[10] I use the term 'normative' in a very wide sense. A normative power or right is one held under norms of some kind or other, including customary, moral and of course legal norms.

[11] *Olympic Oil and Cake Co. Ltd.* v. *Produce Brokers Ltd.* (1915), 112 LT, 744 at 750.

did in *Olympic Oil*. This is so even when the judge has every reason to expect that a further appeal to have the law changed will rightly succeed in a court whose judges do have the power to change the offending law.

The institutional force of law exists even when the moral force of the present law is weak or even non-existent, as it may be in certain wicked regimes. In the latter instance the judge may have no institutionally recognized power to change the law, but he may have the moral right, perhaps even the moral duty, as a morally responsible, autonomous person in a position of some influence and (non-normative) power, to try to escape its institutional force in any way he can. Perhaps he must quietly attempt to subvert the existing law, say by providing a pernicious statute with a legally unwarranted reading. It is by no means inconceivable, though, that he might be morally required, in the appropriate circumstances, to subvert the law publicly, despite his judicial commitment to uphold the law. He might, thereby, risk his credibility as a judge, but he will also affirm his position as a responsible moral agent whose role-defined, institutional responsibilities provide him with only a framework within which his moral duties must be ascertained and discharged. These questions concerning the moral force of law for judges cannot be pursued here, and most certainly cannot be answered briefly and in the abstract. The moral dilemmas in which judges sometimes find themselves are no less difficult and complex than those faced by private citizens contemplating civil disobedience. They are certainly no less complicated and context-sensitive than the moral dilemmas facing other individuals with role-defined duties, e.g., a nurse within the pro-life movement who is called upon, in her capacity as professional care-giver and employee, to assist with non-therapeutic abortions. Or a police officer, vehemently opposed to abortion, who is called upon to provide police protection outside a community abortion clinic.

There appear to be significant differences, then, between what we have been calling the moral as opposed to the institutional forces of existing law, both for citizens and judges. Institutional force, as we have here defined it, is a function of the person's legal power (if any) to alter existing law so as to nullify its effect upon a decision. Moral force, as we have defined it, concerns the extent to which, if at all, there is a moral obligation to abide by the law's requirements. In the case of citizens, the only real questions concern the moral force of law. They have no powers to change it, though of course they can argue for change in courts of law where there may be someone, the presiding judge, with the power to bring about the desired change. In the case of judges, however, both the moral and institutional forces of law can come into play. Dilemmas arise when the law's institutional and moral forces point in opposite directions, when, e.g., the judge is not free to change a morally undesirable law but his moral duty is to escape the law's institutional force, even after taking into account his institutional role and the rules of adjudication which partly define that role for him.

distinctions obscured by D's claims about 'force of law'.

All of these important points are obscured if we follow Dworkin's lead and speak simply of the force of law in exceptional circumstances. We would do well to introduce further distinctions which are sensitive to the differences noted above. In what follows we shall continue to distinguish between the moral and institutional forces of law for judges and citizens. We shall also observe related distinctions between: (a) theories of law, which seek to describe and explain the nature of law and its various relationships with morality, custom, the use of force, and so on; (b) theories of compliance, which concern the (normal or exceptional) moral force of existing law, both for judges and for private citizens; and (c) theories of adjudication, which deal (among other things) with the variety of institutional forces various kinds of laws have—or should have—for different judges in different judicial contexts.[12]

As these labels are to be understood here, a theory of law is not a Dworkinian interpretive conception which seeks to justify the law and its characteristic use of coercion. Rather it is a descriptive-explanatory theory about the nature of legal systems, a theory which finds a role for meta-theoretical and moral-evaluative elements and premises, in the manner outlined and defended in Chapter 2, but which does not set out to justify legal practice. It allows value-relevance to influence what is highlighted as important without allowing moral value the robust, controlling influence which Dworkin ascribes to it. The same is true of a descriptive-explanatory theory of adjudication. The analysis provided by Cross in *Precedent in English Law* is a paradigm example of a descriptive-

---

[12] In 'Legal Positivism and Natural Law Reconsidered', at 364–87, David Brink urges a similar distinction between a theory of legal validity and a theory of adjudication, arguing that much of Dworkin's attack on the positivist's theory of validity (i.e. his theory of law) is misplaced in so far as Dworkin is concerned with issues surrounding the theory of adjudication.

explanatory theory of adjudication. It purports to describe the English doctrine of precedent in an accurate and illuminating way by, among other things, noting the variety of institutional forces precedents have for English judges at various levels within their judicial hierarchy. Cross does not set out to justify what he believes one discovers if one looks to the adjudicative practices of English judges, though it is clear that he finds much to applaud in those practices as well as some aspects which need to be criticized. But his fundamental goal is neither justification nor moral or rational critique. His aim is a descriptive-explanatory theory which illuminates, provides understanding. As we saw in Chapter 2, there is no reason to think that illumination comes only when we seek to justify what we illuminate.

Justification does, however, play a decisive role in what we will call a normative theory of adjudication. A prime example of such a theory is Richard Wasserstrom's analysis in *The Judicial Decision*. Here Wasserstrom is concerned not only with describing a number of possible adjudicative practices, but with justifying the common-law practice of following precedents. Later, in Chapter 8 we shall turn to questions which one addresses by offering a normative theory of adjudication. Having outlined the ways in which moral standards can and do seem to figure in, among other things, the interpretation of statutes, I shall attempt to show the desirability of pursuing a liberal approach to the interpretation of statutes. This is an approach which provides a strong role for morality in determining the very content of laws. Here we will obviously be involved in normative, not descriptive theory.

Theories of compliance are clearly normative in nature. They are moral theories concerning the moral responsibilities we have in the face of law and the coercion it will bring to bear upon us should we disobey its sometimes dubious demands. Theories of civil disobedience are prime examples of normative theories of compliance, and, according to Dworkin, fall mainly within the province of political philosophy. Whether this is true is, for our purposes, immaterial. What is material is that we be aware that what is offered in this book is not a moral theory of compliance with law. We shall follow the lead of Austin and Hart and insist that questions of compliance are separate conceptually from questions concerning the nature of law. This is not to say that the former are any less important than the latter, just that they are different. The philosophical utility of distinguishing theories of compliance and theories of law is not something which can be established here. In effect, this entire book offers reasons for thinking that such a separation is both feasible and illuminating. The proof, so to speak, will be in the pudding. Should we succeed in refining, and rendering more plausible, a Hartian theory of law, then we will have shown that the positivists were on the right track. Should we be able to do so while accommodating some of Dworkin's important insights concerning the nature of legal practice, then we will have taken a rather large step along the path of illumination.

3. THE INSTITUTIONAL FORCES OF LAW

In this section it will be argued that Dworkin comes perilously close to collapsing his theories of law and adjudication into one, and that he is, as a consequence, led to serious difficulties.[13] Dworkin's difficulties clearly demonstrate the dangers of defining law in terms of the adjudicative responsibilities of judges, and lend considerable credence to the suggestion that theories of law should be distinguished from theories of adjudication, the latter being related to, but not identical with, the former. It is best to begin by examining in some detail how Dworkin conceives his theory about the grounds of law, about what makes propositions of law true or sound. It is here that the trouble begins.

Dworkin, as we have seen, vehemently denies the positivist's thesis that a legal system contains a finite set of special rules distinguishable, according to some master test, from all other rules which might be in some way applicable to human behaviour. As we saw in Chapter 2, law is not, according to Dworkin, a specially demarcated, finite set of pedigreed rules to be used in the disposition of legal cases. Rather law is, according to Dworkin's integrity theory, best conceived or interpreted as a (more or less) coherent, seamless web of moral rights and responsibilities which are the special products of institutional history and political morality. By 'institutional

---

[13] As noted earlier, it is not a novel observation that Dworkin identifies, or at least confuses, the theory of law with the theory of adjudication. See Joseph Raz, 'The Problem About the Nature of Law'. Of equal relevance are Brink (see note 11 in this chapter); and P. Soper, 'Dworkin's Domain' (review of *Law's Empire*). So far as I am aware, however, no one has discussed the particular difficulties to which I draw attention below.

history' Dworkin means the various rules, principles, procedures and decisions which constitute the (largely uncontroversial) fruits of the judicial and legislative practices of a particular legal system. Presumably a good deal of this 'institutional history' is to be identified by way of something rather like a Hartian rule of recognition. How else is it to be identified? Unfortunately, however, Dworkin says little about how the materials of institutional history are to be determined, and so one cannot be sure if he would be in agreement with this suggestion. In any case, by 'political morality' we are to understand the morality actually implicit in institutional history, a morality of rights which legal practice seeks to concretize in its settled rules, decisions, and procedures and which serves as its point and justification. It is, so to speak, the 'spirit of the law', what the law stands for. The enforcement of rights of political morality is what judicial decisions are really all about.

At one time, Dworkin referred to the political morality implicit in institutional history as 'the best theory of the settled law' and it appeared as though he wanted to say that this best theory is relevant only in those hard cases where the settled law proves in some way indeterminate, 'when the standard materials provide uncertain guidance'.[14] It appeared, in other words, that Dworkin was suggesting the following.

In easy cases judges invoke pedigreed rules to justify their decisions, much in the way that Hart suggests. But when a hard case is encountered, in which the pedigreed rules prove in some way indeterminate, the judge must repair to the political morality implicit in the pedigreed rules. This morality consists of a scheme of principles (and policies) which best explains and justifies the pedigreed rules. These principles are as much law as the rules they support, and establish existing legal rights which judges must enforce. Owing to the existence of legal principles, there is no need for judges ever to 'exercise strong discretion', to invent new law, as the positivist Hart wishes to say.

As noted, this appears to be the picture presented in Dworkin's early writings. Political morality, on this view, serves as a supplement to settled law, to be engaged only when 'the settled materials provide uncertain guidance'. But it is now clear that the best theory of the political morality embedded in settled law is to play a far greater role than was initially suggested. It figures importantly in all cases, hard and easy. The law is not to be found, initially, in the

14 *Taking Rights Seriously*, 326.

settled rules and practices of the system and then in political morality; political morality is always the determining factor. Law is not a system of rules and principles of political morality. Rather it is a scheme of moral rights. The rules and practices which the positivist wishes to identify as the law are merely attempts, sometimes failed attempts, to articulate the concrete implications or instantiations of that scheme of moral rights. As such, the status (and interpretation) of a rule as binding law depends crucially, in all cases, on whether it protects or extends the appropriate rights of political morality. Judging is not, therefore, a matter of following settled legal rules until their guidance is uncertain, at which point one repairs to political morality. It is always a matter of enforcing rights of political morality which a legal rule may not in fact express accurately. A good deal of what the positivist would identify as the law can fail, on Dworkin's account, to express what is really the law. In Dworkin's latest terminology, 'propositions of law are true if they figure in or follow from the principles of justice, fairness, and procedural due process that provide the best constructive interpretation of the community's legal practice'.[15] 'The law of a community on this account is the scheme of rights and responsibilities that meet that complex standard.'[16] In short, law just is an important part of political morality; it is not a set of special rules supplemented by political morality.

So as to forestall any possible confusion here, we should draw careful attention to Dworkin's distinction between political and background morality. The latter is what a theorist might wish the law to embody, the moral rights which, in principle, the theorist believes the law ought to protect and enhance. A Marxist judge, for example, might espouse a theory of background morality according to which private property should be abolished. If he had the power to construct a legal system anew, he would institute rules and procedures which gave expression to that moral view. Our Marxist judge would be hard pressed, however, to offer a theory according to which the political morality actually implicit in common-law legal systems recognizes no private proprietary rights. This is because political morality is the scheme of moral rights which the law actually does attempt to instantiate. One finds this morality by asking which scheme of moral rights and responsibilities best explains and justifies, offers the best constructive interpretation of, the settled

---

[15] *Law's Empire*, 225.   [16] Ibid. 93.

rules and practices of the legal system as a whole. And no remotely plausible constructive interpretation of common-law legal systems can deny that private proprietary rights are part of the political morality implicit in these systems. One just couldn't explain, let alone justify, real-estate law, without assuming some such rights, any more than one could interpret *War and Peace* without assuming that it is a novel.

In a decent legal system the two schemes of rights, political and background morality, are likely to be more or less congruent. At the very least, any points of divergence will be slight and a judge or citizen will consider the political morality implicit in his legal system sufficiently good as to warrant respect and compliance. It is perhaps not what the judge or citizen would choose were the slate clean and we could start again, but there are no serious violations of background rights. One can easily live with it. A judge confronted with this slightly deficient, though perfectly tolerable, political morality will, for reasons of fairness, consider herself morally bound to enforce it in her decisions. Fairness, according to Dworkin, requires the consistent enforcement of the rights of political morality implicit in the legal system as practised, so long as that morality does not vary too much from true background morality.

In some instances, however, political morality and background morality will diverge to such an extent that disobedience may be called for, by both citizens and judges. The best constructive interpretation of the political morality implicit in the legal system yields a scheme of rights which in fact justifies nothing. It is a 'political morality' which in no way justifies the imposition of state coercion. Nor can the demands of fairness be invoked in such a case. Fairness cannot even begin to justify the consistent enforcement of a wicked scheme of rights. What the judge must do in such a case is at least partly a question concerning the moral force of law. But it is also important to note that it is, for Dworkin, a question concerning the grounds of law as well, and this poses difficult questions for Dworkin. If the law is identified as the implicit scheme of moral rights which justify state coercion, and this implicit scheme can in fact justify nothing, then do we have law? If legal rights, by definition, normally serve morally to warrant state coercion, then can there be legal rights in wicked regimes? How could there be? Is it not true, on Dworkin's account, that a 'law' which is (sufficiently) unjust is in fact no law at all? These are questions which cannot be answered here but will be more fully investigated later in section 5. At this stage all we need note are the potential pitfalls of Dworkin's legal-grounds theory as he conceives it: as a constructive interpretation, i.e. justification, of judicial practice.

4. RIGHTS AGAINST HERCULES

In order to facilitate discussion of his theory about the grounds of law, Dworkin introduces us to Hercules, a judge of super-human philosophical and legal acumen, who is able to fashion a most impressive constructive interpretation of his legal system. Al-though, as we shall see shortly, Dworkin is not entirely clear about this, it appears that the law consists, in Dworkin's view, of the rights and responsibilities of political morality figuring in Hercules' con-structive interpretation, i.e. his best theory, of the legal system. There is, of course, no real Hercules and so we cannot consult him, as we might a sage on a hill top, to determine our legal rights and duties. Nevertheless, it is the adjudicative responsibility of real judges and lawyers to emulate Hercules as best they can, to offer constructive interpretations which are as close as humanly possible to those Hercules would offer. Hercules is like the ideal observer in ethical theory. We are to emulate Hercules when seeking to discover the law just as we are to emulate the ideal observer when seeking to discover our moral duties.

But notice now how Dworkin characterizes the rights figuring in the constructive interpretations fashioned by Hercules and his less able judicial colleagues. 'A judge who accepts integrity will think that the law it defines sets out genuine rights litigants have to a decision before him.'[17] A legal right is 'the right to win a law suit'.[18] Again, a person has a legal right 'if he has a right, flowing from past political decisions, to win a law suit'.[19] So legal rights are not merely rights of political morality, they are a particular species of that genus: moral rights to win law suits. A second species is legisla-tive rights: moral rights to have certain pieces of legislation intro-duced into law. Yet another is to be found in what Dworkin calls 'background rights'.

This view of legal rights as rights to a decision before a court is

---

[17] Ibid. 218, emphasis added.   [18] *Taking Rights Seriously*, 89.
[19] *Law's Empire*, 152.

not, it would seem, a purely accidental or easily jettisoned feature of Dworkin's theory of law. Having rejected the notion that the law can best be conceived as a special set of pedigreed standards to be applied in everyday conduct and in courts of law, Dworkin proposes instead that we conceive of the law as a special scheme of rights of political morality which those standards seek, and sometimes may fail, to embody. Cognizant of the obvious fact that legal rights are, at least in part, creatures of special institutional activities and practices undertaken by judges and legislators, Dworkin is led to distinguish legal rights from other kinds of 'institutional rights', and from background rights of political morality. None of these share with legal rights their special relationships to legal institutions. None of these is especially relevant to legal decisions.

Background rights provide justification for political decisions by 'society in the abstract',[20] but not for legal decisions in courts of law. When arguing before the House of Commons for a wholesale revamping of property law, one might properly appeal to background rights of political morality. But it would be inappropriate to argue in court that, by law, a murderer is not entitled to inherit the private property of his victim because all private property schemes are morally pernicious. Background rights may legitimately be urged as grounds for new legislation, or for radical reform of the law or the political system of which it is a part, but they are unenforceable, as such, in courts of law. Once again, a Marxist can meaningfully, if not persuasively, argue that there is a background right of political morality that material goods be distributed according to need. But even he would be forced to recognize that the political morality implicit in common-law legal systems provides for no such enforceable right, and that an argument against a murderer's inheriting the property of his victim based upon the pernicious qualities of all private proprietary rights would be out of place in a common-law courtroom.

Background rights are to be distinguished from institutional rights. The latter 'provide justification for a decision by some particular and specified political institution'.[21] Within the general category of institutional rights we find legislative and legal rights. Legislative rights are held against a legislature and are entitlements to the enactment of legislation on some particular matter. Dworkin does not tell us when we have such rights, but he does describe

[20] *Taking Rights Seriously*, 93.   [21] Ibid.

conditions under which we do not have them: when introducing the legislation in question would violate (a sufficiently just?) constitution. Americans, he suggests, do not have a legislative right to laws granting them the property of others if they need it more. Such legislation, even if warranted as a matter of background moral rights, would violate the American constitution.

Legal rights constitute the second kind of institutional right discussed by Dworkin. Having rejected the attempt to carve out the grounds of law in terms of a special set of pedigreed standards of which the law consists (positivism), wanting instead to view the law as a scheme of special institutional rights (and corresponding obligations, powers, and responsibilities), and finally having defined institutional rights as rights to decisions from specific institutions like legislatures and courts of law, Dworkin is inexorably led to conceive of law (the grounds of law) as a scheme of rights to decisions from judges. Legal rights are a species of institutional rights, where the latter are distinguished from background rights by the fact that they are rights to a decision from a specific institution and not 'society in the abstract'. Legal rights are distinguished from other kinds of institutional rights by the fact that the institutions from which decisions may be demanded as of right are legal institutions, i.e. courts of law. One may have a non-legal right to X, but unless one has a right to a decision from a judge providing one with X, one has no legal right to it. Hence Dworkin's claim that a legal right is 'a right to win a lawsuit', a 'right to a decision before a court'.

Dworkin's way of conceiving legal rights seems innocent enough and has a measure of surface plausibility. It seems sensible to think of legal rights, which are, after all, rights which we expect to have enforced when we go to court, as rights to win lawsuits. But careful examination of this theory reveals several paradoxes which are not easily dealt with within the terms Dworkin has set for himself. By contrast, these can easily be avoided by the positivist's alternative of conceiving of law as a special set of standards with varying institutional forces.

Consider the following questions. Against whom, in Dworkin's view, are legal rights held, and who is it that has the corresponding legal obligations? If a legal right is a right to a decision from a judge, then legal rights are always held against judges who have the corresponding obligations. Now there is no denying that some of our legal rights are held against judges. We have a legal right to impartiality, for example, when our case is being decided. We also have a legal right that any law whose institutional force cannot be overcome by the judge before us be respected and applied by her in a fair and impartial manner. These are obviously legal rights and it makes perfectly good sense to say that they are held against judges and concern the decisions they make about our legal entitlements, powers, liabilities, and so on.

But surely not all our legal rights fall into this category. Suggesting that all our legal rights are held against judges seems to render Dworkin's theory vulnerable to criticisms closely analogous to *yes!* those made by Hart against Kelsen's theory that all laws are commands addressed to judges and instructing them to apply sanctions. To define law as consisting of rights to legal decisions before judges is seriously to misconstrue, or at least obscure, the way law characteristically functions in people's lives. As Hart notes, the law's primary role is to guide individual conduct in day-to-day life, to define what we may expect from fellow citizens, governments, corporations, and the like. Surely we obscure this important feature of law as a means of social control and guidance if we conceive of law as a set of rights against judges.[22]

An even bigger problem for Dworkin's account is that it leads to serious muddles concerning how to conceive the law in relation to the legal-adjudicative powers and responsibilities of judges. Consider the following example. If Ron has validly contracted with Brian for the use of the latter's sail boat, then the legal right, if it exists, is against Brian and not Judge Sally who might be called upon to settle a dispute to which the contract gives rise. Of course if such a dispute does arise and is brought to court, Ron (or Brian) may also have a legal-adjudicative right against Sally to a decision in his favour. If the law is determinate, then Ron (or Brian) will indeed have a right to a decision in his favour. But it is crucial to notice that this is a different, ancillary right, and more importantly, it might not exist even though the right against Brian (or Ron) does exist. This possibility is evident if we recall our earlier distinction between the law and its institutional force.

The present law, established in a precedent binding on lower courts, may be that Ron is entitled to use of the sail boat in the circumstances in question. But suppose that the case goes, on appeal, to Justice Harry, who sits in a higher court whose ground rules

[22] See on this *The Concept of Law*, 39.

of adjudication impose upon him a legal-adjudicative obligation to overrule the precedent in such a way that, as a consequence, Ron will no longer be legally entitled. Perhaps it would be 'manifestly absurd or morally repugnant' to grant title to a person in Ron's circumstances, despite the precedent. If so, then Ron does not have a right to a decision in his favour. Indeed, if Harry, unlike Justice Sally from the lower court for whom the precedent has overwhelming institutional force, is obliged to overrule the precedent which establishes Ron's right, then Brian is the one who has a right to a decision in his favour. This will be so even though Brian presently has no legal right against Ron to use of the sail boat.

Dworkin is barred from conceiving our contract case in the manner just described. Given his theory that legal rights are rights to decisions from judges, he seems compelled to say that if Harry was required to overrule the precedent, then the law is, and was, for Brian. The law was for Brian because Brian had an institutional right to a decision in his favour from Harry. It's not that Ron had a legal right which Harry was obliged or at liberty to expunge by exercising his Hohfeldian power to overrule the precedent which established it. That requires acceptance of what Dworkin's theory seems to deny, namely, a distinction between our legal rights and any legal-adjudicative rights we may have to a decision in our favour.

That it would force us to claim that the law was already for Brian because of Harry's adjudicative obligation to overrule the precedent gives us some reason to question Dworkin's theory of legal rights as institutional rights to decisions before courts. The problem is seriously compounded, however, when we recall that the institutional forces of law can vary from one court to the next. Consider again our earlier example involving paternity leave.

The lower-court judge, it will be recalled, was under a legal-adjudicative obligation to find against the natural father (call him Nathan), whereas the higher-court judge enjoyed the power to overrule the precedent set by the middle-court judge, thus establishing new law in Nathan's favour. How, on Dworkin's view of legal rights, are we to conceive of this legal situation? What are Nathan's legal rights before he initiates litigation?

One would, of course, like to say: (a) that the law presently denies Nathan a legal right to paternity leave; (b) that the lower-court judge is bound to respect this legal right in his decision in so far as he lacks the legal-adjudicative power to escape the precedent's institutional force—for him it is an embedded mistake; (*c*) that Nathan therefore has no legal-adjudicative right to a decision in his favour from the lower-court judge; (*d*) that Nathan does, however, have a legal-adjudicative right to a decision from the higher-court judge (at least that he has a right that the latter consider exercising his power to overrule the precedent, thereby granting Nathan a new legal right); and finally (*e*) that once the higher-court judge's decision is made, the law will have changed in such a way that Nathan and other natural fathers now do have a legal right, against their employers or the government, to paid paternity leave, as well as a legal-adjudicative right against lower- and middle-court judges to decisions in their favour.

But none of this seems possible if we follow Dworkin's lead and identify legal rights with rights to a decision from a court. So what can we say if we accept that theory? There would appear to be only two possible alternatives: (*a*) that Nathan's legal rights differ depending on which court we are talking about; or (*b*) that his legal rights are really those which would be enforced in some particular court within the judicial hierarchy, perhaps the highest court. Dworkin himself seems to acknowledge these two possibilities when he writes:

> In some circumstances any accurate judgment about what the law is must in some way be indexed to refer to the level of court in which the issue is assumed to arise. Suppose a lawyer thinks that the highest court of some jurisdiction has a duty ... to overrule a precedent and so find for the plaintiff, but that a lower court, bound by a strict doctrine of precedent, has a duty to enforce that precedent and so decide for the plaintiff. He might say (this is one way to put the point) that the law for the higher court is different from the law for the lower. Or he might say (this is another) that since the highest court has the last word, the law is 'really' for the plaintiff, though she must appeal to have that law recognized and enforced.[23]

There are two alternatives suggested in this passage, each with its own difficulties. Consider the first, the indexing option, as it would apply to Nathan's case. As we have noted, the legal-adjudicative powers and duties of judges differ from one court to the next. To this extent it makes perfectly good sense to say that 'the law for the

---

[23] *Law's Empire*, 452–3, n. 1.

higher court is different from the law for the lower'. The lower- and higher-court judges in Nathan's case have different legal powers and duties, and so, in that sense, the law for each is different from the law for the other. But this is not as far as Dworkin would have us go. Not only do the adjudicative duties and powers of the judges differ from one court to the next, so too do Nathan's legal rights regarding paternity leave. There simply can be no such thing as Nathan's legal rights, *simpliciter*, because his legal rights are rights to decisions within particular courts and, as we have seen, the adjudicative powers of courts differ crucially. Nathan's legal rights within the lower court will be different from his legal rights in the higher court. It follows that there is nothing which we can identify at any given time as the law bearing on Nathan's case: there is rather lower-court law, middle-court law, and higher-court law. There are no legal rights within Nathan's jurisdiction, only lower-court legal rights, middle-court legal rights, and higher-court legal rights. Rights must always be relativized to a particular court within the judicial hierarchy of a legal system. But this is not, I suggest, how we understand legal rights.

We can and must, of course, accept the indexing of law to the extent that law should always be conceived as the law of some particular jurisdiction. Even Aquinas accepts this point: Eternal and Divine Law are relative to God's jurisdiction, human law to the various communities into which groups of human beings naturally form themselves. The relativization of law to a particular jurisdiction seems to distinguish law from the fundamental principles of morality which are thought to be universally applicable and binding. That is, they are not thought to be jurisdiction-relative, except perhaps in theistic natural-law conceptions of morality like Aquinas' where the 'jurisdiction' in question is God's domain. But these special cases aside, moral principles are not conceived to be relative.[24] We don't speak of English versus Scots morality in the way we speak of English versus Scots law, or Federal versus Provincial law in Canada. Another example of proper indexing lies in the difference between Equity and Common Law. In the days when the two were clearly distinguishable as different bodies of law, it made perfectly good sense to say that our legal rights in Equity were

[24] This point is well made by Neil MacCormick in his 'Comment' on Gerald Postema's 'The Normativity of Law'. See *Issues in Contemporary Legal Philosophy*, 105–13.

different from our legal rights under Common Law. Again, there is
no mystery or puzzle here. Paradoxes emerge, however, when we are
asked to believe that there might be a different scheme of enforceable legal rights for two different courts within the same judicial
hierarchy sharing exactly the same institutional history, e.g., the
same constitution, conventions, statutes, and precedents. As
Stephen Perry notes, it is a requirement of institutional consistency,
grounded presumably in justice or fairness, that 'the state cannot
justifiably permit the parties in one of its courtrooms to be treated in
a manner that is at variance with how they (or any other set of
litigants) would be treated in a courtroom next door'.[25] This is true
even when one of these two courts has greater adjudicative powers
than the other to escape the institutional force of the laws they share
in common, laws which each must, in its own way, take into account
in arriving at its decisions. A theory which would have us accept that
our courts enforce different schemes of legal rights, even when they
appear to be dealing with the same laws, is one we should strive to
avoid if there is an alternative.

There are difficulties in the indexing option which apply specifically to Dworkin's integrity theory and its vision of law as a seamless web of moral entitlements. If law must be indexed to courts, it is
not easy to see how it can be conceived as a unified scheme of rights
(and responsibilities) recognized in Hercules' constructive interpretation of the legal system, a scheme which is to be applied consistently and equally, in the spirit of integrity and fraternity to all
citizens in all contexts. This is because Hercules is only one judge in
one court. The law will be different for other judges in other courts
and litigants will have different legal rights to different decisions
from them. Perhaps Dworkin must introduce a whole group of Herculean judges, one for each level of court. The law for that level of
court will be whatever rights the Herculean judge at that particular
level would see himself as bound to enforce. There is perhaps
nothing incoherent in this account, but it comes at a price. The
appealing picture painted in *Law's Empire* of a fraternal community
personified, speaking with one consistent voice through its judicial
and legislative officers begins to fade. How can the community
speak with one voice if the law to be recognized in one court is
different from the law to be recognized in another? The unity and

---

[25] Perry, 'Judicial Obligation, Precedent and the Common Law', 244.

integrity of law comes perilously close to vanishing on this account of legal rights.

That it leads to such serious difficulties is perhaps sufficient reason to avoid the indexing option. Of course Dworkin does consider a second alternative in the long passage quoted above. Perhaps it has more promise. On this option, the law is not the right to win a lawsuit in any court whatsoever. Rather, it is a right to win in the highest court. One's legal rights are held against the judges who preside over the highest court in the judicial hierarchy. The law on some question is whatever right(s) they are obligated to enforce. In short, the law consists of the set of rights and responsibilities that Chief Justice Hercules would see fit to enforce.

This alternative encounters its own difficulties. If the law is whatever rights would be enforced in the court of the mythical Chief Justice Hercules, then it would seem to follow that the law is largely unknown—indeed, a good deal of it, as it exists at any given time, will never be known. On this account, judgments of law would in all instances be based on counter-factual speculation about how Chief Justice Hercules, who will presumably be free of many of the institutional forces under which his less powerful colleagues in lower courts must labour, would decide were the case in question to come before him. They would not be based on the often much more easily answered question concerning what the settled law is that this judge in this particular lower court is bound to uphold. And of course it is this question which is normally asked in a court of law.

It also seems to follow that a great deal of what is really the law of some jurisdiction will never in fact be recognized as such. And even if it is, lower- and middle-court judges will often find themselves unable, legally, to enforce it—to enforce what is really the law on some matter before them.[26] Consider a case in which Chief Justice Hercules both could and would overturn a precedent were the case brought before him, but where the lower-court judge hearing the case (even if he is a lower-court Hercules) is barred, by the applicable rules and standards of adjudication, from taking any such step. The precedent is for him an embedded mistake; he has no

[26] It should be stressed again that Dworkin is well aware that undesirable or mistaken law is sometimes binding on lower- and middle-court judges. See e.g. *Taking Rights Seriously*, 118–23, for Dworkin's account of 'corrigible' and 'embedded' mistakes. My claim is not that Dworkin ignores what I have been calling the institutional forces of law, only that his conception of law is insufficiently sensitive to its importance.

power to overcome its institutional force. We will not be able to say in such a case that the lower-court judge is strictly bound to uphold the present law because he lacks Chief Justice Hercules' adjudicative power to change it. On the contrary, we must say that the lower-court judge is legally barred from enforcing the law, barred from recognizing the litigant's genuine legal rights, and may only hope that the case reaches the highest court where the law can actually be enforced! In short, we must say that the lower-court judge is duty-bound not to apply the law. It is important to be clear exactly what this means in this context. It is not that the judge should not apply the law because his legal duty is to change it in such a way that the law no longer requires him to make the undesirable decision but rather its opposite. It is not that he should decline to apply existing law because he has the power and the duty to make better law and apply it to the instant case. The point is that he cannot enforce what is now, already, better law: a law which exists at present and which he would like to apply, but which he must ignore because it is unenforceable at all but the highest level. This implication alone should give us sufficient cause to worry about Dworkin's second option. A theory according to which the law is largely unknown, and is for that reason not being enforced in the courts is bad enough. One according to which judges are routinely barred from enforcing what they know to be genuine legal rights seems beyond the limits of plausibility. But things get even worse.

A judge's hope that a case over which she presides will reach the highest court of appeal where the law can be enforced will often go unfulfilled. For one reason or another, few cases ever succeed in reaching the highest courts. Leave to appeal is only rarely granted, and sometimes an appeal which is denied would nevertheless have succeeded had leave to launch it been granted. Lawyers can be very persuasive when they actually get to argue their cases in person. And then there are all those cases where leave was not sought but which are such that Chief Justice Hercules, or one of his human colleagues, would have reversed a perfectly proper (proper because the lower-court judge lacked the power to escape the force of an earlier decision, as in Nathan's case) decision had anyone had the foresight to see this possibility, or could have financed a costly appeal. In all such cases, the judges in the lower courts will be failing to enforce existing legal rights, failing to enforce what is now really the law. This will be true despite the fact that they will properly be following established precedents, having been barred themselves from trying to escape their institutional forces.

Finally, we might consider the point that real judges, even those in highest courts, are not of Hercules' calibre. They will often err, denying rights which the mythical Hercules would have recognized. 'The law', then, will inevitably be quite different from what judges in the highest court consistently over time say it is. If they are not enforcing the rights which Hercules' constructive interpretation of legal history would ascribe to litigants, then they are not enforcing the law. One begins to wonder, at this point, whether the law can be so far removed from the actual concrete decisions of judges (and legislators?), or whether it becomes, on this second option, what Holmes called a 'brooding omnipresence in the sky'?

Putting all these points together, we seem led to the following conclusion: on Dworkin's alternative to the indexing option, the law is something far more ideal, speculative, unenforceable, and dependent on counter-factual speculation than it would appear to be. It becomes far too detached from what real judges in real courts seem, often quite properly, to be relying upon to justify their decisions. The law may not always be what the judges decide; but it should not be thought to be too far removed from what they routinely decide. We are no better off with this second alternative than we were with the indexing option, which led us to deny that there is anything we can call English or Canadian law.

These problems in Dworkin's theory of legal rights, arise, I suggest, because he fails to distinguish adequately between a theory of law and a theory of adjudication, where the former is designed, at least in part, to explain the nature of a legal system, while the latter explains or justifies, among other things, our legal-adjudicative rights against judges and the rules about how judges should apply or change the law in deciding legal cases. Collapsing a theory of law into a theory of adjudication, in this instance identifying law with adjudicative rights against judges, seems inevitably to lead to difficulties of the sort discussed above.

Perhaps, though, I have been uncharitable in characterizing Dworkin's view. Perhaps he might wish to withdraw his suggestion that legal rights are rights to win lawsuits, or to dissociate himself from the literal interpretation I have given his thesis. Maybe what Dworkin would really want to say (or had meant all along to say) is that a legal right is a right which is indeed normally held against other citizens, corporations, and the like, but which is also a right that necessarily underlies a separate adjudicative right to win a lawsuit. The right to win a lawsuit would be, on this alternative reading, a secondary, derivative right which results from the violation, by the defendant, of a primary legal right held against the plaintiff.[27] In other words, having one's primary legal right violated, e.g. by breach of contract, is the necessary antecedent of a secondary, legal-adjudicative right against a judge to a remedy.

There is nothing incoherent in this alternative account, so long as one is careful to develop it in a way which is sensitive to the discoveries made above. For instance, it is clear that we cannot simply identify a primary legal right as whatever right one has a secondary, adjudicative right to have enforced in a court. Once again, one may have a primary legal right which one is not entitled, legally, to have enforced in a court.

Consider in this regard *Olympic Oil and Cake Co. Ltd.*, where the party who had a secondary right to win in the Court of Appeal enjoyed no such right before the House of Lords. Instead the latter exercised its power to overrule the precedent establishing the primary legal right which the Court of Appeal was legally bound to uphold. Consider also our sail boat example. As the law stood at the time of their agreement, Ron seemed to have a primary legal right to use of Brian's sail boat. But if Justice Harry had a legal-adjudicative obligation to change the law by overruling the precedent which had been binding on lower-court judge Sally, in such a way that Ron no longer enjoyed his primary legal right, then Ron did not have a secondary legal right against Harry to a decision in his favour. This despite the fact that he did enjoy such a right against Sally. The violation of a primary legal right, then, is clearly not a sufficient antecedent of a secondary right to win a lawsuit in any and all courts within the system. But neither is it necessary. If Harry was obliged to overrule the precedent establishing Ron's primary legal right, then Brian had a secondary legal right against Harry to a decision in his favour, even though he lacked an antecedently existing primary right to what he sought from Ron.

So if we are to distinguish primary and secondary legal rights, we will either have to index both or find some particular court to which each can be relativized. Indexing brings with it all the problems discussed above, only now we have two sets of legal rights, second-

[27] I am indebted to Dick Bronaugh for bringing this possibility to my attention.

ary and primary, which must always be indexed to a particular court within the system. Again, there may be nothing incoherent in this account, but a theory which multiplies legal rights beyond necessity is one we would do well to avoid. Of course this meta-theoretical judgment (based on the value of simplicity) assumes that there is a viable alternative, which as we will see in a moment, there clearly is. But this viable alternative does not lie in Dworkin's second strategy of defining legal rights in relation to the highest court within the judicial hierarchy. There must be a way of conceiving of law which renders it less dependent on counter-factual speculation about what some ideal Chief Justice Hercules would be obliged to decide were the case to arise before him. It would be desirable if we could avoid defining our primary legal rights as whatever rights we have a secondary legal right to have enforced within an ideal highest court.

Whether, in the end, a coherent, plausible account of legal rights as institutional rights to decisions from judges can be developed may still be open to question. We have by no means refuted Dworkin on this issue, merely shown some of the serious pitfalls of his approach. Yet enough has been said to warrant our drawing the following important conclusions:

(a) One must distinguish between the law and its institutional force(s).

(b) A jurisprudential theory which identifies law with whatever rights judges must legally enforce in courts of law is in danger of ignoring (a) and falling into (i) incoherence, (ii) an unnecessary proliferation of (indexed) legal rights, or (iii) an over-idealizing of law as whatever a mythical high-court judge would decide were the case before him.

(c) A jurisprudential theory which carefully distinguishes a (legal-grounds) theory of law and a theory of adjudication is far less likely to fall into these traps.

5. THE THEORY OF COMPLIANCE

Let us now turn briefly to the distinction between law and its moral force, and to the related distinction between a theory of law and a theory of compliance. Once again, there is reason to think that Dworkin comes perilously close to collapsing the two. Recall how Dworkin would have us conceive a legal-grounds theory. If we

follow Dworkin in thinking that a non-sceptical theory of what the
law is entails a view about the (normal) moral force of law, about
'what judges [and citizens] should [morally] do in principle', then
one will inevitably have difficulty with what Dworkin calls 'a
wicked legal system'.[28] In other words, if (a) one thinks that a legal-
grounds theory is a constructive interpretation of legal practice, i.e.
an interpretation which attempts to put that practice in its best
moral light in order to show that it almost always justifies coercion
against disobedient citizens; (b) one thinks that the scheme of moral
rights such an interpretation identifies is what the law really is, not
what it ought to be or what it aspires to be; then (c) one will inevitably become entangled in difficulties with which classical
natural-law theory has long been associated, perhaps unjustifiably.
Is wicked law really no law at all, as Augustine claimed? If, as
Dworkin insists, 'the fact of law' normally provides a case for coercion, then one will presumably be led to deny that the 'laws' of a
thoroughly wicked legal system can really be law because they
cannot even begin to justify coercion. There is no moral force whatsoever in wicked law, no grounds for justifying coercive measures. In
making much the same point, H. L. A. Hart considers the possibility
that the fairness inherent in the consistent application of a law,
regardless of the law's inherent moral worth, might provide the
necessary moral force, weak though it may be and clearly override-
able by more stringent moral considerations. As Hart notes, this
last ditch effort seems hopeless. How can there be a moral right in
point of fairness to the continued application of immoral laws or the
principles they embody? And how could fairness be invoked to
explain legal rights in cases of first instance where, for example, an
iniquitous statute is applied for the first time? In such a case, 'there
could be no legal right with a moral component; for since it is the
first case the alleged moral component, based on the fairness of
consistency, treating like cases alike, would be absent'.[29]

So if the law is identified as a scheme of moral rights justifying
coercion in most cases, one seems led to deny that wicked legal
systems have law. Yet as Dworkin is well aware, this conclusion
seems absurd: as he puts it, there does seem to be the fact of law. This
is so even in the case of highly immoral law which no one is in any
way morally obliged to obey and the violation of which can in no
way furnish a justification for coercive measures. Yet if Dworkin is

[28] *Taking Rights Seriously*, 342.   [29] *Essays on Bentham*, 152.

happy in according the status of law to rights under wicked regimes whose measures in no way justify coercion, the question arises: What distinguishes Dworkin from positivists like Bentham and Hart? As Hart himself observes, 'all that survives of the theory ... is the truism that in a good system of law the laws and the rights and duties that arise from them would have a moral justification and in an evil system they will not. This seems indistinguishable from legal positivism.'[30]

Dworkin is understandably unhappy simply to surrender to the positivists on this crucial point. It is not clear, however, that his means of dealing with Hart's dilemma succeeds. Dworkin's strategy is to appeal once again to the 'flexibility' and 'richness' of our language, the same flexibility which enabled him to employ the indexing and relativizing options criticized earlier in this chapter. In Dworkin's view, we have the same flexibility when we turn to our understanding of 'law' within the context of wicked regimes. '[O]ur language and idiom are rich enough to allow a great deal of discrimination and choice in the words we pick to say what we want to say, and our choice will therefore depend on the questions we are trying to answer, our audience, and the context in which we speak.'[31]

According to Dworkin we have two senses of 'law' within our language, and therefore more than one way to put the points we wish to make when talking about immoral regimes. One of these ways is captured by the positivists, the other by natural lawyers like Aquinas and Augustine. If by 'law' we mean the elements of institutional history which serve as the 'pre-interpretive' data of constructive interpretations of legal practice, then wicked law is indeed law.[32] In other words, if one means by 'law' pretty much what legal positivists like Bentham, Raz, and Hart mean by that word, then wicked law is indeed law. In this sense of the term, law is a system of pedigreed rules, decisions, and practices, and one will therefore wish carefully to distinguish between law and its moral force. One will, if it is this sense of the term that one has in mind, wish to endorse some version or other of the separation of law and morality and embrace Austin's slogan: the existence of law is one thing; its merit or demerit another.

If, on the other hand, one means by the word 'law' that which a

---

[30] Ibid. 151.   [31] *Law's Empire*, 103.

[32] On the pre-interpretive, interpretive and post-interpretive stages of legal argument, see ibid. 65–8.

non-sceptical, constructive interpretation of institutional history identifies as morally licensing coercive force, then wicked 'law' does not qualify for that honorific title. In this sense of the term, the identification of law necessarily ascribes moral force to that which is identified, a force which is lacking in dark times. If this is what we mean by 'law', and it seems to be Dworkin's view that this normally is what we mean, then we will not wish to distinguish between law and its moral force.[33] Law necessarily has moral force, as Augustine, Aquinas, and Fuller seemed to recognize. Nor will we wish to distinguish between theories of law and theories of compliance. Law will necessarily be something with which we normally should comply; we will not be able to answer the question 'What is law?' without asking Philip Soper's question 'What is law that I should obey it?'

In Dworkin's view, then, the answer one gives to the question whether Nazi law was really law depends on one's point of view and the context in which the question arises. Whether Dworkin's attempt to deal with these serious questions of law and compliance displays sensitivity to the richness and diversity of language, or whether it is really just an *ad hoc* attempt to have it both ways, is a question which naturally arises here. Flexibility in theories is sometimes a good thing and sometimes it is even unavoidable. The particle and wave theories of light have long competed as models with which to understand the properties and behaviour of light. In response to the question 'What is light really like, a wave or a particle?' the only available answer does seem to be 'It depends on one's point of view and the context in which the question arises.' In some contexts, and

---

[33] Philip Soper shares this view on which the very concept of law connotes an obligation to obey. See e.g. *A Theory of Law*, where he writes: 'We have seen that others, Hart for example, also take as a starting point the claim that an adequate concept of law must at least connote obligation. I simply go one step further: what better way, after all, to show that law connotes obligation than to show that it obligates in fact? In that sense, by insisting that actual obligation is one of the phenomena of legal systems for which theory must account, one is no less arbitrary in the selection of data than are those [e.g. Hart, Raz, and Austin] who focus only on that other entity, the legal directive.' (14). One might take issue with Soper's claim that there is no better way to establish that the concept of law connotes, i.e., has part of its very meaning, obligation than to show that it obligates in fact. It is a fact that no human being is over 20 feet in height. This in no way supports the proposition that the concept of a human being connotes being under 20 feet in height. Of course if law does connote obligation, then we may infer that it in fact obligates, just as we may infer from someone's being a bachelor that he is in fact unmarried. But the implication clearly does not go the other way round.

Crit of 'perspectival' approach!

for some purposes, light behaves more like a stream of particles than a wave; in other contexts, and for other purposes, it is best thought of as a wave. Sometimes, then, the perspectival approach advocated by Dworkin is perfectly appropriate, but usually as a stop-gap measure till such time as a more unified theory is devised, one which accommodates within a single model all the properties of the phenomenon in question. A perspectival theory like Dworkin's often sheds very little light, and ends up providing no answers at all. 'It all depends on what one means by X' and 'It all depends on one's point of view or which aspect of the phenomenon one wishes to consider' are sometimes legitimate replies to difficult questions. But often they simply sidestep the real questions which are 'What does X really mean?' and 'Which point of view is the most fruitful and enlightening one to take on these issues?' As Dworkin himself notes, positivists provide answers to these questions, at least when it comes to their theories of law, as opposed to their theories of compliance, if they have them.[34] Traditional natural lawyers do so too. That he tries to have it both ways may not, in the end, serve Dworkin's cause at all.

But there is even more reason to be unhappy with Dworkin's 'flexible' approach. A good deal of the appeal of Dworkin's theory of law has been in his attempt to articulate an alternative to legal positivism, what he likes to call 'the model of rules'. According to *Dis view of posm's error:* Dworkin, positivism misconceives what law is really like by missing the inherently normative nature of the question 'What is law?' and by thinking of law as a system of pedigreed rules whose content can be ascertained independently of all normative considerations. We are offered, in place of this supposedly barren and defective theory, a conception according to which law is a system of entitlements under political morality, entitlements which we all understand to be morally binding (normally). This is what law necessarily is, not some system of pedigreed rules which we can only hope imposes morally acceptable duties and responsibilities. It is the inherently moral nature of law which allows us to explain, among other things, why we refer to legal requirements using the normative terminology of rights and duties, and why the fact of law provides a case for coercion in all but special cases. It allows us to answer Soper's question: 'What is law that I should obey it?'

It is disappointing, to say the least, to be told now that by 'law' we

[34] *Law's Empire*, 104.

do not necessarily mean all this. This disappointment is perhaps no reason in itself to reject Dworkin's theory. But one is left wondering where the once robust alternative to positivism has gone. Will positivists not reply that Dworkin has only succeeded in verifying what they have insisted all along, namely, that laws and the use of coercion to enforce them are often justified morally—but only if their content is right? Sometimes, positivists will add, the content is not right, and so it is a mistake to conceive law in such a way as to necessitate justification. As Hart and others have insisted, we are much better off, philosophically, if we build this important fact about law right into our theories about it, by insisting upon an understanding of law which does not necessarily accord it moral honour. Dworkin is driven to accommodate this insight by creating two senses of 'law', one of which renders legal rights a species of moral rights and explains their nature in those terms, the other of which is left completely unexplained. Instead of recognizing that law sometimes has no moral worth and building this into his explication of its nature, Dworkin simply creates a new category, a second concept of law. This carving off of what is better thought of as part of the domain to be explained is bad enough. One might also ask whether Dworkin has the resources within his theory to deal with it. If law, in this special sense, is not a scheme of moral rights, what exactly is it? Presumably it cannot be a system of pedigreed rules validated by a rule of recognition, if only because Dworkin would still wish to insist that institutional history, even in wicked regimes, contains much more than valid legal rules. It will at the very least contain legal principles and policies. But how is this additional part to be identified? What distinguishes it as legal? Indeed, what does 'law' and 'legal right' mean from this particular point of view? To these important questions we find answers in legal positivism. Dworkin may still not like those answers, but if legal rights are not to be understood as rights of political morality, he seems to have no better alternative.

It is far from clear, then, that Dworkin's attempt to be flexible in the face of wicked law does justice to his cause. What he calls 'law', in that sense of the term according to which it does not designate a species of moral rights justifying coercion, seems better thought of as data which Dworkin's conception of law cannot easily accommodate but the positivist's can. Instead of conjuring up two different meanings of 'law', on one of which law necessarily justifies coercion while on the other it does not, we seem better off following the positivist by accepting a univocal understanding of 'law' according to which positive law sometimes, but only sometimes, justifies coercive measures. At least with positivism we are able to understand why law only sometimes justifies coercion (e.g. proper pedigree does not guarantee moral worth) and what it is that does justify coercion when the latter is warranted.

6. SEPARATE BUT CONNECTED

If the preceding arguments are on the right track, there is considerable conceptual advantage in separating theories of law, adjudication, and compliance. This is not to say, of course, that the three are not related to one another, only that they are not identical and do not answer the same sets of questions. There are obvious connections between the three. If, for example, one's theory of law says that laws are pedigreed rules which do not necessarily accord with minimal moral demands, then one's theory of compliance will likely, though not necessarily, demand that one always subject laws to moral scrutiny and comply only if they measure up. I say only likely because it is conceivable that one should offer a theory of compliance according to which disobedience is never, or almost never, warranted. Bentham, for example, who strongly recommended healthy moral scepticism concerning the law's demands, none the less urged prompt obedience. Recall his prescription: 'Obey punctually, censure freely.'[35] An even better example lies in Thomas Hobbes. Like Austin, Hobbes conceived of law as the command of a sovereign and recognized that the sovereign could very easily issue morally pernicious laws. Fearing a return to the state of nature, however, Hobbes was adamant in demanding strict compliance with law regardless of its moral merit. For him pure pedigree determines law, and disobedience is (almost) never warranted. On the other extreme lies Joseph Raz, whose account of the authoritative nature of law leads him to suggest that there is very seldom a moral obligation to obey the law as such. Raz is not just saying that there is seldom a conclusive obligation to obey the law. His point is that there is seldom even a prima-facie obligation to do so, seldom any sound reason at all to follow the law as such. This

[35] 'A Fragment On Government', in 1 *Works of Jeremy Bentham*, 221, 230.

despite the fact that Raz shares a positivistic stance with Bentham and Hobbes. According to Raz's exclusive legal positivism, the existence and content of laws can always be determined independently of all moral considerations and arguments. These three examples only reinforce our earlier point that a theory of law is not a theory of compliance and that we court disaster if we fail to distinguish between the two.

A theory of law is also likely to have important connections with a theory of adjudication. Take H. L. A. Hart's theory as an obvious example. If Hart is right that the law consists of a finite set of standards validated in various ways by rules of recognition, and that these standards are necessarily indeterminate or open-textured to some degree, then it follows that adjudication cannot always amount to the incontestable application of valid laws. Discretion of some sort will inevitably be necessary in some instances. Here we have an implication flowing from a theory of law (coupled with a semantic theory) to a theory of adjudication. Of course it does not follow from Hart's thesis that whenever an undeniably valid law applies incontestably to a case, the judge's adjudicative obligation is clear and points in the direction of application. We must again insist that law and its institutional forces be distinguished: a judge must sometimes decline to apply valid law. As we saw above, this is especially apparent in the case of legal precedent.

It is a common mistake to think that Hart's theory of law does imply that valid laws must be applied in all cases in which their core of settled meaning would seem to make them clearly applicable. But this is far from true.[36] Nowhere does Hart suggest this theory of adjudication, nor is there anything in his theory of law which commits him to that position. This is clear if one examines Hart's writings carefully with an eye towards the distinction between a theory of law and a theory of adjudication, and between law and its institutional forces. Whether a valid rule must be followed in a core case will crucially depend, in part, on the institutional rules of adjudication accepted within the legal system. These, together with rules of recognition, help define the varying institutional forces valid laws have for judges. There is nothing in Hart's theory of law or his thoughts on adjudication which denies the possibility that, in a core

[handwritten marginalia: correction of a common mistake in interpreting Hart.]

[handwritten marginalia: NB]

[36] Robert Moles makes this mistake in his *Definition and Rule in Legal Theory: A Reassessment of H. L. A. Hart and the Positivist Tradition*. For criticism of Moles on just this point see my review of his book in 8 *Canadian Philosophical Reviews*, 181–3.

case where an existing rule clearly implies an answer to the question before the court, the court may, or indeed must, exercise its legal-adjudicative power to change the law so as to avoid its institutional force.[37] The court may also enjoy the legal power to unsettle the settled core of a rule which it does not invalidate but only 'interprets' in such a way as to avoid having to apply it. All these possibilities[38] are open to Hart, and so it is simply inappropriate to saddle him with a naïve theory of adjudication according to which whatever is identified as valid law via a rule of recognition must always be applied by judges. Hart's theory of law does have implications for adjudication, but this is not one of them.

There is, of course, reason to think that a legal system could not exist in which all judges were totally free at all times to change or depart from valid rules in any way they saw fit. But this is not my suggestion: the institutional forces of existing laws are often powerful and cannot be overcome. A system of absolute discretion in which no law had any institutional force at all could not be a system of law because there would be no general standards by which, on the whole, both private actions and judicial decisions could be guided. There would be no rule of law only, as Cardozo put it, 'isolated dooms'.[39] But it remains consistent with the healthy existence of a legal system that change and departure be permissible, indeed mandatory, under certain defined conditions and in certain limited ways.

Further connections between the theory of law and the theory (and practice) of adjudication are apparent in controversies concerning the proper approach to judicial review and the interpretation of constitutional documents like the Canadian *Charter of Rights and Freedoms* and the American *Bill of Rights*. These disputes have raged for decades in the United States, at least since *Marbury* v. *Madison*[40] when the American Supreme Court definitively ruled that it did indeed have the prerogative to strike down legislation which offen-

[37] I am not sure that it's fair to say that Hart has a theory of adjudication, as opposed to remarks concerning adjudication which are intended to defeat rule scepticism, i.e. legal realism, as a theory of law.

[38] These and others will be taken up in Chapter 8 where we consider various approaches to dealing with what our theory of law identifies as valid law.

[39] In relation to a realist interpretation of the practice of precedent, Cardozo had this to say: 'In that view, even past decisions are not law. The courts may overrule them. ... Law never *is*, but is always about to be. It is realized only when embodied in a judgment, and in being realized, expires. There are no such things as rules or principles: there are only isolated dooms.' (*The Nature of the Judicial Process*, 126.)

[40] 5 US (1 Cranch) 137 (1803).

ded the *Bill of Rights*. Section 52 (1) of the Canadian *Charter* appears
to grant a similar right to judges. The only real question in the
United States and Canada is how this prerogative is to be exercised.
What exactly is it that judges are empowered to do when utilizing a
constitutional instrument to invalidate other less authoritative
legal measures? In short, what approach must judges take in interpreting a charter or bill of rights?

The answers which have been given to this question are numerous
and varied, but they all seem to fall roughly within one of three
categories: (a) those who think that judges should be faithful to the
text of the constitution; (b) those who believe that the proper object
of deference is the intent of the original framers; and (c) those who
claim that judges should view the constitution as a 'living tree' and
interpret it in ways which express an ever-changing and developing
political morality.[41] Position (a) has been variously described as the
'literalist', 'strict constructionist', or 'textualist' theory, and it
appears to have been this view to which (then) Chief Justice Brian
Dickson was expressing his opposition in *Big M Drug Mart* and
Hunter v. *Southam Inc.*[42] Position (b) is often referred to as the
'intentionalist', 'originalist' or 'original intent' approach. It has
found support in the United States from such legal figures as Robert
Bork and William Rehnquist.[43] It has also been roundly criticized
by many legal philosophers as being at best misguided, at worst
incoherent.[44]

Despite their differences, (a) and (b), the literalist and originalist
theories, are both frequently viewed as requiring judicial restraint in
the interpretation and application of constitutions. Each is thought
to require political and moral neutrality on the part of judges,

---

[41] The living tree metaphor was first applied to the BNA Act by Lord Sankey in
Edwards v. *A.-G. Canada*, [1930] AC 124 at 136. According to Lord Sankey, 'the
B.N.A. Act planted in Canada a living tree capable of growth and expansion within
its natural limits'. As Peter Hogg notes, 'The Supreme Court of Canada has approved
the living tree metaphor' in numerous cases. See Hogg, *Constitutional Law of Canada*,
340–1. Among these cases are *A.-G. Quebec* v. *Blaikie*, [1979] 2 SCR 1016 at 1029, and
Law Society of Upper Canada v. *Skapinker*, [1984] 1 SCR 357 at 365.

[42] *R.* v. *Big M Drug Mart*, [1985] 1 SCR 295, *Hunter* v. *Southam Inc.*, [1984] 2 SCR
14.

[43] See R. Bork, 'Neutral Principles and Some First Amendment Problems' and W.
Rehnquist, 'The Notion of a Living Constitution'.

[44] For critiques of the originalist position, see D. Lyons, 'Constitutional Interpretation and Original Meaning', 26–9; D. Brink, 'Legal Theory, Legal Interpretation,
and Judicial Review', 105; *Law's Empire*, 359–63. See also ibid. 318–34 which deals
with an analogous account of statutory interpretation.

something which is thought to be both possible and essential to the fulfilment of the judicial role within liberal democracies. Anything less than this amounts to the naked usurpation of the legislative function, a function properly fulfilled by elected political representatives. On each of these views, constitutional interpretation is, or at least should be, essentially a value-neutral activity, requiring nothing more than factual enquiry either into the meaning of words, as governed by linguistic conventions, or the historical intentions of a possibly long-dead group of founders. On this view, the existence and content of law are established by non-moral factors and it is to these alone that judges must repair in constitutional cases.

Position (c), by contrast, is commonly conceived to require a more activist, liberal approach. Calling this approach 'liberal' can be somewhat misleading, however, if only because a liberal approach to the interpretation of constitutional documents is often associated with a commitment to political liberalism. Yet as is plain from the history of the American Supreme Court in the early part of this century, that association amounts to a confusion. The American Court was notorious for employing a liberal approach to interpretation of the American *Bill of Rights* in an attempt to undermine the (politically) liberal policies of the Roosevelt administration. An example of a liberal approach to interpreting the *Bill of Rights* which led to the suppression of liberal legislation is *Lochner* v. *New York*[45] where the US Supreme Court struck down a state law forbidding employment in a bakery for more than sixty hours per week or ten hours per day. The Court held that this statute deprived the employer of his liberty of contract without 'due process of law', a violation of the fourteenth amendment.[46]

In any event, position (c) is commonly thought to require that judges take an active part in ensuring that the constitution is consonant with current trends in political morality. The metaphor commonly used in Canada is the 'living tree'. According to the defenders of this approach, reference to political morality is essential to determining what the constitution really means within a contemporary context. To use Dworkin's terminology, the constitution defines the concepts in terms of which questions of fundamental legal rights are to be argued: it is up to each generation to provide the

---

[45] 198 US 45 (1905).
[46] For further discussion of the misleading nature of the distinction between liberal and conservative judges, see *Law's Empire*, at 358–9.

best (or at least its own) constructive interpretation of those concepts. Judges take a leading role in reaching such understandings.[47]

According to critics of (c), on the other hand, the latter permits active meddling in the political process by unelected judges. It allows judges to subvert the real constitution—the real law—to be discovered, not in political morality, but within the 'four corners' of the document, or alternatively, the intentions of the framers. It permits judges unjustifiably to pursue their own, possibly idiosyncratic, visions of political morality at the expense of the law enshrined in a constitution properly adopted by appropriate political means.[48]

In very rough outline, then, these are the three basic approaches which have been taken in recent debates concerning constitutional adjudication and judicial review. Each is believed by its defenders to represent the only way to show fidelity to the constitution, to the law that is. One might reasonably wonder how the choice among these three adjudicative approaches could in any way be connected to the choice between theories of law like inclusive and exclusive positivism. But the connections, both theoretical and causal, are not difficult to see.[49]

Let us begin with an uncontroversial assumption: judges generally prefer to view and present themselves as always applying the law. Whether, on their own theories of law and adjudication they think this appropriate, or whether they are mainly concerned with how their activities will be viewed by the general public, judges do seem to prefer to conceive and characterize what they do as involving nothing but the application of pre-existing law. They are uncomfortable thinking of or talking about themselves as doing anything else.

[47] For Dworkin's view of constitutional interpretation, see *Taking Rights Seriously*, 106–7, 131–49 and *Law's Empire*, 355. For views generally sympathetic to this approach see Brink, 'Legal Theory, Legal Interpretation, and Judicial Review'; and Lyons, 'Constitutional Interpretation and Original Meaning'. See also D. Richards, 'Constitutional Interpretation, History and the Death Penalty: A Book Review', 1372–98.

[48] For a critique of the Canadian *Charter* and the licence it gives judges to decide legal issues on grounds of political morality, see Patrick Brode, *The Charter of Wrongs: Canada's Retreat from Democracy, passim.*

[49] One of Brink's principal aims in 'Legal Theory, Legal Interpretation and Judicial Review' is to establish similar connections between theories of law and theories or approaches to constitutional adjudication. Although there is much in this article with which I would take issue, the general themes pursued are similar to those advanced here.

Consider the following remarks by Lord Radcliffe, concerning the law-making activities of judges:

I do not believe that it was ever an important discovery that judges are in some sense lawmakers. It is much more important to analyse the relative truth of an idea so far reaching; because unless the analysis is strict and its limitations observed, there is a real danger in its elaboration. We cannot run the risk of finding the archetypal image of the judge confused with the very different image of the legislator.[50]

Consider also, the following advice offered by Radcliffe a few pages earlier:

[J]udges will serve the public interest better if they keep quiet about their legislative function ... [T]he judge who shows his hand, who advertises what he is about, may indeed show that his is a strong spirit unfettered by the past, though I doubt very much whether he is not doing more harm to general confidence in the law as a constant, safe in the hands of judges, than he is doing good to the law's credit as a set of rules attuned to the sentiment of the day.[51]

It is unlikely that many judges share Lord Radcliffe's desire to perpetuate this version of the noble lie. But his Lordship's comments do illustrate the obvious concern most judges have to be viewed, principally, as upholders of the law that already exists. There are of course notable exceptions to this generalization. An obvious example is England's Lord Denning, former Master of the Rolls, whose willingness to subvert the existing law whenever it failed to live up to Denning's sense of justice and fairness is legendary. That Denning was so roundly condemned by most English judges supports the view that judges are uncomfortable with anything which threatens Radcliffe's archetypal image.[52]

We may take as given, then, that judges prefer to apply, and to be seen as applying, pre-existing law. We may also take for granted that most people within Western democracies share this preference with the judges. Most are uncomfortable with the suggestion that judges may be up to something other than law application; hence Radcliffe's concern. People are generally willing to accept the odd hard case in which judges act as quasi-legislators. And everyone

---

[50] *The Law and Its Compass*, 14.   [51] Ibid. 11.

[52] On Lord Denning's propensity to 'seek justice despite the law', see P. Robson and P. Watchman, eds., *Justice, Lord Denning and the Constitution* and my review in 2 *Canadian Philosophical Reviews*, 294.

readily embraces the idea of judges sometimes being called upon to perform extra-judicial functions, say in federal inquiries like the Warren and Dubin Commissions.[53] But when they are acting as judges, concerning themselves with legal rights and obligations, their business, most think, is with the law, not politics or morality.[54]

If the existence of these preferences, and the normative beliefs upon which they are based, can be taken for granted, then it is clear that the choice between, say, inclusive and exclusive legal positivism can really have a significant impact upon which adjudicative approach (and the theory supporting it) is adopted in legal practice. According to exclusive positivism, any reference to political morality cannot be a reference to pre-existing law. It follows that whenever judges interpret a document like the Canadian *Charter* in terms of the rights of political morality it enshrines, they necessarily step beyond the application of law and are legislating. Adjudication in such cases amounts to the creation not the discovery of law. That's the theoretical connection. But there is a possible causal connection as well. If exclusive positivism were accepted as accurately reflecting the nature of law, then the tendency might be for judges to retreat from arguments of political morality in cases involving charter adjudication. Arguments of political morality could not be used to establish the existence or content of pre-existing valid law; and since judges wish to be seen as establishing the latter, they would shun arguments of political morality. But if political morality is excluded, we seem left with things like 'literal meaning', 'framer's intent', and so on. But these are the considerations which are associated with the adjudicative theories represented by positions (a) and (b) above, views which, in today's political climate, are used to argue for judicial restraint.

If, by way of contrast, a judge is thought to be discovering the existence or content of pre-existing valid law in a charter case involving appeal to considerations of political morality (because

[53] The Warren Commission, headed by Warren J., investigated the events surrounding the assassination of American President John Kennedy. Dubin, CJO, oversaw a Royal Commission concerning the events surrounding the disqualification from the Seoul Olympics of the Canadian sprinter Ben Johnson.

[54] Members of the Critical Legal Studies Movement are concerned to challenge this archetypal image as a sham. They also see it as representing a pernicious ideology masking the various contradictory and manipulative political forces at work in the law. See e.g. A. Hutchinson and P. Monahan (eds.), *The Rule of Law: Ideal or Ideology*.

there is nothing in the nature of law which precludes this possibility, as inclusive positivism suggests), then such a retreat seems far less likely. The judge and others will view his decision, not as one which encroaches upon forbidden territory reserved for legislators, but as one which is required by his normal legal-adjudicative obligation to discover and apply the law that exists and has institutional force over his decisions. There is nothing suspicious here requiring any special justification. There will be little danger that the archetypal image of the judge will be confused with the very different image of judge as legislator, politician, or moral reformer. So the judge will be more likely to follow adjudicative approach (c), as opposed to the more 'conservative' approaches represented by (a) and (b), if he accepts inclusive positivism.

If these reflections concerning the possible connections between legal theories, and theories about and approaches to, constitutional adjudication are even partly accurate, then we have reason for thinking that philosophical reflection concerning the nature of law is indeed an important activity for those engaged in, or who reflect upon, legal practice. I should like to add a cautionary note, however, one which will be more fully developed in the next chapter when we consider what I shall call 'causal/moral' arguments for theories of law. The fact that the acceptance of a theory of law like exclusive positivism may, given the archetypal image of judge as law-applier, have a tendency to lead causally to judicial restraint, is in no way a valid argument for or against it as a descriptive-explanatory theory of law. The causal effects of a philosophical theory's acceptance or rejection, application or misapplication have, with a few exceptions to be discussed later, no probative force at all when it comes to considering its truth or adequacy. The theory could be a good one, even though its effects are bad.

So a theory of law can have both causal and logical implications for a theory of adjudication. It is also clear that implications can go the other way round. Legal realists and members of the Critical Legal Studies movement are concerned, among other things, to point to what they think are the meagre effects which pre-existing, and supposedly authoritative, legal rules have for judicial decisions. In effect, they deny that laws have any institutional (or causal) force at all. John Chipman Gray said that the law is nothing but the rules laid down and applied by courts, and 'as the first change, so does the latter along with them. Bishop Hoadly has said:

"Whoever hath an absolute authority to interpret any written or spoken laws, it is he who is truly the Law-giver to all intents and purposes, and not the person who first wrote or spoke them." '[55]

On the view defended by Gray, adjudication can never amount to the application of authoritative rules with binding institutional force. Given that the judge necessarily must interpret whatever 'laws' seem applicable, he is subject to little if any institutional force. His decision creates the rule, which must then be 'interpreted' by a later judge who will himself, necessarily, find no binding institutional force in the first judge's interpretation. This 'rule-scepticism', if true, has important implications for the theory of law.[56] It rules out, for example, the model of rules. Conceiving of law as a system of valid rules which figure in guiding the conduct of citizens and the decisions of judges would be foolish and misleading if Gray's theory of adjudication were correct. If adjudication must proceed as Gray describes, a theory of law like Hart's would only serve to mask legal reality. And if proponents of Critical Legal Studies are right, this masking has nothing but pernicious effects. It permits us to hide the ideological forces really at work in law, forces which the false ideal of the rule of law only manages to obscure. It is no wonder, then, that Hart and other defenders of positivism are concerned to defeat the scepticism inherent in realist theories of adjudication. Once again, we see an important connection between the theory of law and the theory of adjudication. But again, this connection does not amount to an identification of the two.[57]

7. AN ALTERNATIVE

If we reject Dworkin's suggestion that law be identified as a scheme of institutional, moral rights to decisions before courts, then the question of an alternative naturally arises. Any successful candidate must, of course, be sensitive to the varying institutional forces that laws have in different courts without committing us to Dworkin's unattractive indexing options. It is essential to avoid a theory

---

[55] 'A Realist Conception of Law', cited in Feinberg and Gross (eds.), *Philosophy of Law*, 3rd edn. 50. The quotation from Bishop Hoadly is from his sermon preached before the king in 1717, p. 12.

[56] 'Rule-scepticism' is Hart's term. See *The Concept of Law*, ch. 7.

[57] See ibid. For a positivistic appraisal of Critical Legal Studies, see e.g D. N. MacCormick, 'Reconstruction after Deconstruction: A Response to CLS'.

which would force us to speak in terms of lower-court law and higher-court law. It should be possible to say simply what the law is with respect to one's rights, responsibilities, and so on, and to recognize that some judges are legally empowered to change that law in their decisions. It seems also important that we have a conception of law according to which most of our legal rights are held against fellow citizens not judges.

One obvious, though not necessarily the only, possibility, is to be found in legal positivism of the sort defended by Hart and Raz. My intention here is not to argue that their versions of positivism present the only theories of law which can accommodate the findings made above, nor that Dworkin's theory cannot somehow be modified in a way which would allow that theory to pass muster. My goal is the more modest one of illustrating how easily the form of positivism defended in this book can account for the features of law discussed above, e.g. its varying institutional forces. The ease with which it accounts for these features counts somewhat, even if not decisively, in its favour. It at least does so if the only plausible alternative is Dworkin's paradoxical theory of law and legal rights.

Although there is much in Raz's theory with which I disagree, he seems clearly on the right track when he follows Hart in identifying the law as a subset of the norms which the primary, norm-applying institutions (i.e. the courts) within a legal system are under legal duty to apply.[58] My only concern at this stage is with Raz's (apparent) suggestion that judges are always under duty to apply valid legal norms.[59] As we saw above, and as Raz in his more careful moments explicitly recognizes, this is not always the case. We might, then, usefully modify Raz's statement in the following way:

> Legal norms are a subset of the norms which the primary, norm-applying institutions (i.e. the courts) are under legal duty, via rules of recognition and adjudication, either to apply or to change in exercise of their legal-adjudicative power to do so.

The norms figuring in the subset of norms courts are under duty to apply (or change) are identified via Hartian rules of recognition. In Hart's early writings, rules of recognition seem to be identified as

[58] See Raz, *The Authority of Law*, chs 5 and 6.
[59] As we shall see shortly, Raz is of the view that one can be under duty to apply a norm and yet be at liberty, sometimes, to disregard or change it. My worry is not that Raz has missed this important point, merely that his wording misleadingly suggests that he has.

secondary, power-conferring social rules. Hart distinguishes between primary and secondary rules and between rules which impose duties and those which create and regulate powers. He also identifies primary rules with duty-imposing rules and secondary rules with rules which confer powers. Primary rules, he suggests, require that we act or forbear from acting whether we wish to or not, whereas secondary rules are 'parasitic' or secondary for they provide that people may 'by doing or saying certain things introduce new rules of the primary type, extinguish or modify old ones, or in various ways determine their incidence or control their operation'. Rules of the first type 'impose duties; rules of the second type confer powers, public or private'.[60]

As Raz has argued, Hart's rules of recognition are best conceived as duty-imposing, secondary rules requiring judges to apply a certain set of norms which are valid according to the criteria they contain.[61] In light of this, we cannot distinguish primary from secondary rules on the basis that the latter, unlike the former, confer powers. Some secondary rules impose duties, but they are presumably duties which take as their object or subject matter other norms which themselves either confer powers, impose duties, or grant rights and liberties. A secondary rule, then, is not necessarily a power-conferring rule but rather a rule about other rule(s). A primary rule, on the other hand, is not about other rules and what we may or should do with respect to them. It concerns other kinds of things and other kinds of activities. Some secondary rules are of course power-conferring, e.g., those which empower individuals to create, modify, or extinguish other primary and secondary rules. Legislators, presumably, are empowered to create binding primary and secondary legal rules by way of what we might call secondary rules of legislation. Judges too have certain powers arising from secondary rules, in this case, secondary rules of adjudication. As noted earlier in Chapter 2, the legal-adjudicative powers of judges to escape the institutional forces of existing laws vary depending on such factors as the level of court at which the judge presides and the circumstances of the case in question, e.g. whether applying the law in the instant case would lead to manifest absurdity or grave injustice. The varying institutional forces which laws have, and the corresponding legal-adjudicative powers of judges with respect to them, seem to be a function of secondary rules of adjudication prac-

---

[60] *The Concept of Law*, 79.   [61] See Raz, *The Concept of A Legal System*, 199.

tised by the judges. These play as crucial a role in determining the adjudicative duties of judges as rules of recognition. The importance of secondary rules of adjudication is seriously underestimated in *The Concept of Law*, where Hart seems more concerned with the conceptual work done by rules of recognition. But once we distinguish between the law and its variable institutional forces, the importance of these other fundamental secondary rules comes clearly into focus.

Another kind of important secondary rule is an interpretation rule, which determines not what counts as a law, but how laws are to be interpreted and understood in concrete cases. In effect, interpretation rules help determine the content of rules and other sorts of norms validated by rules of recognition. The question may not be whether rule R is valid according to a rule of recognition, nor whether R's institutional force for Judge Sally is such that Sally must apply R in case C, or is able, instead, to replace R with a different rule, R^1. The question may be, as it was in *Riggs* v. *Palmer*, how rule R, which is undeniably valid and cannot be changed or replaced, is to be interpreted, what its content is. As we shall see more fully in Chapter 8, the secondary interpretation rules practised by courts seem to vary. They also seem to include rules according to which moral factors can sometimes determine what a rule actually means. If so, then we have a further contingent fusion of law and morality sanctioned by inclusive positivism but rejected by exclusive positivism. But more on this later. The point to be made here is that determining that a rule is valid according to a rule of recognition is but one step to determining its proper effect on a legal decision. There are other secondary rules (rules about rules) which help to determine the institutional forces of these rules as well as how they are to be interpreted. And not all of these are power-conferring rules.

One final point of clarification concerns our rough characterization of the positivist's alternative theory of law. As Raz points out, courts are sometimes required legally to uphold standards in addition to the norms of their own legal system. 'Quite often the courts have an obligation to apply laws of other legal systems, rules of private associations, and so on, although these were not and do not become part of the legal system.'[62] It follows that we must think of laws as comprising only a subset of the norms which judges must

---

[62] *The Authority of Law,* 97

apply or change. In our terms, they constitute only a subset of the norms which have institutional force for judges. This is an important point: not all that the judges must (legally) apply is law validated by a rule of recognition; and, as we have already seen, not all laws validated by a rule of recognition must be applied by judges. Institutional force can be overcome in some instances, while in others it extends beyond the confines of legal norms. We run the risk of entirely missing these features of legal norms if, like Dworkin, we conflate a theory of law with a theory of adjudication and identify the law with whatever is binding on judges' decisions.

The positivistic theory we have sketched follows Dworkin in acknowledging the central role of courts in defining what law is. What the law is has something to do with what is enforceable within a court of law. Raz introduces and endorses what he calls the 'Basic Intuition', that 'The law has to do with those considerations that it is appropriate for courts to rely upon in justifying their decisions.'[63] This is an intuition shared by such diverse writers as Kelsen, Hart, Dworkin, and of course Raz himself. Where Raz and Hart would part company with Dworkin, however, is in their refusal to identify the law with our rights to decisions from courts. The law is instrumental, on their account, in determining what our adjudicative rights against judges are, if only because the judicial decision to which we have an adjudicative right is often the one which accords with existing law. But this is clearly not always true and so the law cannot be identified with adjudicative rights. Nor are legal rights necessarily co-extensive with adjudicative rights, as we saw earlier in our discussion of primary and secondary legal rights. To suppose that the law is to be identified with our rights to particular judicial decisions would, once again, be to confuse a theory of law with a theory of adjudication.

Although it has not been expressed explicitly in these terms, our positivistic theory can easily be made sensitive to the varying institutional forces laws can have in different courts. The suggestion that the law be identified with a subset of the norms which all courts within a legal system are bound to apply or change does not mean that the institutional force of law is one and the same for all judges, nor, obviously, that it is always strictly binding. To be bound by a norm is not necessarily to be absolutely bound. It makes perfectly good sense to say that one might be bound by a norm from which one

---

[63] 'The Problem About the Nature of Law', 207.

is sometimes free to depart, or which one has the power to change under certain defined conditions and for certain special reasons. Citing the parallel case of obligation-imposing promises, which one is none the less morally free to break under certain conditions, Raz notes that being legally bound by a norm is consistent with the power to change or expunge it. This is consistent so long as one is 'not at liberty to disregard it any time one finds that on the balance of reasons it would be best to do so'.[64]

So there is nothing in our positivistic theory which denies that the institutional force of binding law can be less than absolute and can vary from one court to the next. One can recognize, as law, only norms by which all the courts are bound (not just the highest court, as would be the case were we to follow the second of Dworkin's indexing options), while accepting that the legal-adjudicative obligations of judges with respect to that law will often be different; indeed, some may have the legal power to change that binding law. To be sure, each will be bound, but not necessarily in the same way or to the same degree. In short, one can accept that a norm is a norm of law only if (though not necessarily if) it has some degree of institutional force for all judges within the legal system, without thereby repudiating the important distinction between the law and its varying institutional forces.

8. CONCLUSION

In this chapter, I have attempted to make a case for distinguishing between theories of law (normative or descriptive), theories of adjudication, and theories of compliance; between law and its institutional and moral forces. I have used Dworkin's conception of law, as a scheme of rights to decisions before judges, to illustrate the importance of these distinctions. Whether, in the end, Dworkin is guilty as charged is perhaps of less importance than recognition of the fruitfulness of the distinctions herein defended. If the preceding arguments are sound, we have good reason not merely to acknowledge the 'separation of law and morals', i.e. the conceptual separation of law from its moral force; we have reason also to respect a conceptual separation between the law and the legal-adjudicative powers and obligations of judges, i.e. the conceptual separation of

[64] *The Authority of Law*, 114–15.

law and its institutional force over judges' decisions. These are important distinctions which are not at all easily accommodated by Dworkin's theory of law as a scheme of institutional moral rights to judicial decisions. We have, then, supported important conclusions concerning the manner in which jurisprudential theories should be fashioned, as well as sceptical conclusions concerning the viability of one particular candidate, Dworkin's integrity theory.

Finally, I have introduced a theory of law, modelled on the positivistic theories of Raz and Hart, according to which law is best conceived as a subset of the norms identified by a rule of recognition, and which have some degree of institutional force for all judges within the relevant jurisdiction. This proposal accommodates Dworkin's intuition that the identification of law is in some measure dependent on the obligations of judges, while respecting the important distinctions between law and its institutional and moral forces. That it so easily accommodates these fruitful distinctions is an important factor in its favour.

There are, of course, important questions which now arise. For instance, upon what kinds of factors can institutional force depend? Are moral factors a possibility, or is institutional force always, as Raz would want to insist, a function of non-moral considerations? It is to this important question that we turn in the next two chapters where inclusive positivism will be defended against Raz's exclusive positivism. As we shall see, the inclusive version of positivism offers a much better account of certain common features of law.

4

INCLUSIVE v. EXCLUSIVE POSITIVISM

1. THE FORMS AND LIMITS OF POSITIVISM

It is not easy to characterize natural-law theory in a way which captures what is more or less common to all theories going by that name. The same is true of positivism. Nevertheless, if pressed, one might reasonably identify natural-law theory as the view which affirms the proposition that there is a law, above (Augustine and Aquinas) or implicit in (Dworkin and Fuller) the explicit positive law in terms of which, necessarily, the existence and content of the latter can either be derived or challenged. It is no contingent accident that law and morality are connected: law just is a vehicle for the expression and enforcement of the moral law, or some particular element of it. Whether that element is to be identified with justice (as opposed to charity, benevolence, etc.) or with what Aquinas would have called 'exterior' as opposed to 'interior' movements,[1] the point remains: it is in the very nature of law to express moral demands and affirm moral rights, whether these are rights of political morality, as in Dworkin, or rights affirmed in or derivable from God's Eternal law, as in Aquinas. A law could no more fail to express (perhaps inaccurately) a moral requirement than could the making of a promise.

In contrast with natural lawyers, defenders of legal positivism are thought to deny anything but contingent connections between law and morality. Law is capable of expressing and affirming moral demands and rights: but it is not in its nature necessarily to do so.

---

[1] Exterior acts are 'observable' and subject to regulation by human law. Interior acts, e.g., coveting one's neighbour's goods, are 'hidden' and properly governed only by Divine Law. The latter is promulgated in, e.g., scripture or the pronouncements of authoritative figures like prophets or the Pope. See Aquinas, *Summa Theologica*, Question XCI (On the Various Kinds of Law) 4th Article (Whether There Was Any Need For a Divine Law).

Law, as the product of human activities, geared more or less successfully towards a multiplicity of human ends only some of which are
morally praiseworthy, is morally fallible. According to most defenders of positivism this feature of law is built right into our very
notion of it. The enactment of a law is not like an expression of
gratitude or an act of charity: it is not necessarily a morally good
thing, and one who makes a claim of legal right does not necessarily
express, or even attempt to express, a claim of moral right or duty.
Any connections between law and morality are contingent only,
dependent on whether, as a matter of fact, the right kinds of laws are
created in the right kinds of ways. It is this view which positivists
attempt to express when they affirm the separation of law and
morals.

Positivists are, of course, happy to acknowledge many contingent
connections between law and morality. Numerous laws, for
example those proscribing assault and theft, are quite clearly re-
statements of moral principle. But unfortunately there are all too
many examples of valid laws, such as those governing apartheid in
South Africa, which are incapable of moral defence.[2] Positivists are
also happy to say that judges sometimes decide hard cases by appealing to principles of morality when the law's guidance is insufficient to settle the question at hand: they will merely insist that these
legally binding decisions are sometimes also morally indefensible.
Judges are not infallible. In both instances, we see a connection
between law and morals, but one which is merely contingent.
Whether, in deciding a case on moral grounds, a judge necessarily
steps beyond positive law is, as we shall see shortly, a question
which divides legal positivists. But all are agreed that such appeals
are often made and that they serve to illustrate yet another close but
contingent connection between morality and law.

In recent years a controversy has arisen within the ranks of positivism over the possibility of one particular connection between
law and morals which some avowed positivists accept as possible
and indeed characteristic of modern legal systems, but others reject
as inconsistent with the very nature of law. Philosophers like Jules
Coleman, John Mackie, and David Lyons have suggested that
among the conceivable connections between law and morality that

[2] For a sustained analysis of law in South Africa and of how its existence bears on
debates among natural lawyers and positivists, see David Dyzenhaus, *Hard Cases in
Wicked Legal Systems*.

Inclusive legal posm:

a positivist might accept is that the identification of a rule as valid within a legal system, as well as the discernment of the rule's content and how it bears on a legal case, can depend on moral factors.[3] On this view, which we have called inclusive legal positivism, moral values and principles count among the possible grounds that a legal system might accept for determining the existence and content of valid laws. As an example, one might consider the possibility that a legal system's rule(s) of recognition could contain explicitly moral tests or criteria for the legal validity of Congressional or Parliamentary legislation. If it is possible for the rule of recognition to contain such criteria, then a law's validity might on some occasion not be determined by its pedigree alone, that is, by the fact and manner of its adoption. The simple fact of its enactment by a sovereign legislature, for example, would be insufficient to determine the rule's legal validity. We would be required to decide whether it violates a moral condition, say the due process clause in the American *Bill of Rights*, which is interpreted by most as specifying fairness as a (moral) condition for legal validity within the United States.

Despite a noticeable trend among positivists toward accepting that law and morality can be connected as inclusive positivism suggests, there are clear exceptions. Joseph Raz, as we have seen, advocates exclusive legal positivism, the view that the existence of a valid legal rule is solely a function of whether it has the appropriate source in legislation, judicial decision or social custom, matters of pure social fact, of pedigree, which can be established independently of moral factors.[4] In addition, the content of a legal rule can be determined, Raz believes, by establishing facts about human beings (e.g. their legislative actions and intentions) that can be ascertained without the use of moral arguments. Raz calls the union of these two views the 'strong social thesis'. We will continue to refer to

---

[3] See Jules Coleman, 'Negative and Positive Positivism'; David Lyons, 'Principles, Positivism and Legal Theory' and 'Derivability, Defensibility, and the Justification of Judicial Decisions'; John Mackie, 'The Third Theory of Law'; E. P. Soper, 'Legal Theory and the Obligation of a Judge: The Hart/Dworkin Dispute'; C. L. Ten, 'The Soundest Theory of Law'; W. J. Waluchow, 'Herculean Positivism' and 'The Weak Social Thesis'.

[4] It should be noted that Raz refuses to distinguish between the existence and validity of legal rules. If a legal rule exists it is valid and if it is valid, then it exists. So in talking of what is necessary to establish the existence of valid law we are referring to what is necessary for the very existence of law itself. There are no invalid laws according to Raz. See on this, *The Authority of Law*, ch. 8.

it as exclusive legal positivism and accept Raz as its principal and most powerful defender.

It is important to be clear from the start exactly what Raz means in asserting that the existence and content of laws are determined exclusively by social facts. Raz's intention is not to deny that legislation can be both motivated and justified by moral principles and values. Nor does he wish to dispute that judges sometimes engage in substantive moral reasoning when they decide cases, or that the law often contains reference to concepts and values which are recognizably moral in nature. His point is that once the appropriate social facts have been established, e.g. that a duly constituted legislature enacted such and such a statute and this is what it means, or that a higher-court judge by whose decisions I am strictly bound has decided that 'fairness' means such and such in this kind of case, the limits of existing law have been reached. Anything beyond a concern to establish social facts of the appropriate kind, where the appropriateness of a social fact is determined by Hartian rules of recognition, change, and adjudication, amounts to the creation of new law not the determination of the existence or content of what is already law. For example, the attempt to determine what is truly fair, so as to interpret a statute requiring employers to pay a fair wage, cannot amount to a determination of law. In asking the moral question 'What does fairness really require here?' a judge necessarily steps beyond positive law. He does so in a way licensed by law, by his legal duty to decide as the statute requires, but the law does not itself answer the question it poses. The law, via its statutory pronouncement, directs the judge to consult morality, to go beyond what Raz in an early paper called 'the limits of the law', and to fashion an answer on its behalf to the question of fairness it poses.[5]

In several key writings, Raz attempts to defend exclusive positivism against Dworkin and natural lawyers, as well as those positivists who embrace inclusive positivism and its claim that 'sometimes the identification of some laws turns on moral arguments'.[6] Not surprisingly, Raz has found an ally in Dworkin, who shares Raz's desire to undermine inclusive positivism. The latter, were it true, would strip Dworkin's interpretive theory of much of its appeal. Dworkin could no longer point to the fact that political morality is sometimes properly invoked in supporting claims to

[5] See Raz, 'Positivism and the Limits of the Law'.
[6] The Authority of Law, 49.

existing legal rights and duties as a reason to prefer his integrity theory to positivism.

The principal objective of this chapter is to begin defending the claim that inclusive positivism is superior to exclusive positivism as a general theory of law, where by 'theory of law' we mean a general, descriptive/explanatory theory of law of the sort characterized and defended in Chapter 2 above. We will do so by examining in detail a series of arguments which might be offered to support the contrary view, namely, that exclusive positivism is the superior theory of law. The main focus will of course be Raz, but it will be useful to consider other authors as well. In fact we shall begin by considering two central arguments found in the works of H. L. A. Hart who, along with Austin and Bentham, accepts inclusive positivism. Nevertheless, it might be thought that Hart's influential reasons for preferring positivism to natural-law theory could be extended to provide a sound basis for choosing exclusive over inclusive positivism. It will be instructive to consider these modified arguments, not only for the light they shed on our main question, but because of the more general lessons we can learn about the dubious validity of certain arguments one often encounters in jurisprudential debates about the nature of law. We shall be concerned, for example, with the question whether moral arguments for or against the adoption of legal theories are valid, and if so what specific kinds of moral arguments can properly be invoked.

Following our initial investigation of Hart's two arguments, we shall turn to our main concern, an examination of some of the many arguments entertained by Raz. In the course of this investigation reference will be made to related arguments offered by Dworkin. Throughout we will be pursuing a largely defensive strategy: that is, defending inclusive positivism against arguments which either have been or might be invoked against it. But a more positive case will emerge in our discussion of charter challenges, a case which we will examine further in the next chapter.

2. HART'S ARGUMENTS

In Chapter 9 of *The Concept of Law*, as well as in his classic paper 'Positivism and the Separation of Law and Morals', Hart assessed the merits of (what he understood to be) natural-law theory, distin-

guishing its excesses from its 'core of good sense'. He agreed with [Hart:
natural lawyers that in certain respects law and morality are more
than only contingently or coincidentally connected. Certain very
basic facts about human beings, in particular our almost universal
desire for survival, in conjunction with certain other contingent facts
about the environment in which we find ourselves, entail a 'natural
necessity' that morality and law share a certain 'minimum content'.
For example, each must include 'minimum forms of protection for
persons, property and promises'.[7] These minimum forms of protection might well be deficient morally in many instances, and there is
every reason to think that different legal systems will offer different
interpretations of what this minimum requires: Iranian property law
is not at all like its American or Canadian counterparts. There is no
natural necessity that there be a particular kind of property law,
only that there be property law of some kind or other.

Beyond recognizing this minimal overlap between the contents of
law and morals Hart was not prepared to venture. In his view,
human aims and circumstances are far too variable for us to derive
much more than must be shared between the two forms of social
regulation. He would certainly deny the robust theories of the good
one finds in natural lawyers like Aquinas and Finnis. For any
supposed universal human aims one might wish to posit, e.g. knowledge or friendship, there are far too many counter-examples to
suppose that we are all somehow united in our pursuit of these ends,
that they are in some sense 'natural', and that we must, if our laws
are to be valid, fashion our legal systems so as to promote and
protect these values.[8]

So Hart thought that classical natural-law theory rests on mistaken claims about our common, natural aims and ends. He also
thought it a mistake to accept Augustine's dictum, that a law which
is unjust is no law at all. This battle cry had experienced a revival,
following the Nazi holocaust, in the writings of legal theorists such
as Gustav Radbruch.[9] Concerned to find a respectable basis for
prosecuting war criminals whose actions were arguably sanctioned
by Nazi law, there were some who insisted that Nazi law had not
really been law after all. In violating the natural law so flagrantly,
Nazi 'law' lost all claim to validity, and the grossly immoral

[7] *The Concept of Law*, 195.
[8] See 'Positivism and the Separation of Law and Morals', 76.
[9] See Gustav Radbruch, *Rechtsphilosophie*.

actions taken in accordance with it were not therefore legally sanctioned by valid law. On the contrary, they were quite clearly illegal in so far as they violated what was and always had been truly valid law, the law of nature governing the affairs of all mankind. So went the line of thinking Hart was concerned to discourage. Nothing, he argued, is gained practically or philosophically in such attempts to deal with wicked regimes. Indeed, much is lost both in terms of intellectual clarity in the theoretical and scientific study of law, and in terms of its practical moral assessment. We are neither better philosophers nor better moral agents if we follow the lead recommended by Augustine and affirmed by Radbruch and the new natural lawyers.

3. BENTHAM'S CAUSAL/MORAL ARGUMENT

Hart's main concern about natural-law thinking was one he shared with Bentham and which has recently been reaffirmed by Neil Mac-Cormick: that the acceptance of Augustine's dictum, an unjust law seems to be no law at all, would render unlikely a healthy balance between respect for law and a morally critical attitude towards its many demands. In Bentham's view, failure to keep morality and law clearly distinct from one another leads to two forms of dangerous thinking. There is first the anarchist who, when faced with an apparently unjust law, reasons 'This ought not to be the law, therefore it is not the law and I am free not merely to censure and criticize the law, but to disregard it totally.'[10] Bentham's fear of the anarchist is best expressed in his 'Anarchical Fallacies' where he subjects the *French Declaration of the Rights of Man* to ridicule. After labelling the notion of imprescriptible natural rights 'nonsense on stilts', Bentham went on to describe it as 'mischievous nonsense' and 'terrorist language'.[11]

According to Bentham, the anarchist represents only one extreme view to which natural-law theory can lead. The reactionary represents the other. Natural-law thinking could just as easily lead one to reason as follows: 'This is the law, therefore it is what it ought to

---

[10] 'Positivism and the Separation of Law and Morals', 64–5.

[11] Jeremy Bentham, 'Anarchical Fallacies', in *The Collected Works of Jeremy Bentham*, Vol. 2, Article II.

be.'[12] Such reasoning, according to both Bentham and Hart, 'stifles criticism at its birth'.[13] We either end up dissolving law and its authority into a conception of what ought to be, or supplanting morality with law as a final test of conduct. MacCormick echoes Bentham and Hart when he suggests that natural-law theory enables states and governments to 'manipulate the idea of law'. 'The argument of last resort here is an argument for the final sovereignty of conscience, and how best to preserve it.'[14]

sovty of conscience argt.

It is not difficult to imagine how this moral argument for positivism might be modified in an attempt to provide support for rejecting inclusive positivism in favour of an exclusive version such as Raz's. The modified argument might run something like this.

If moral chaos, i.e. reactionary or anarchist thinking, as well as their morally undesirable side-effects, result from anything but a clear and total separation in thought between legal and moral validity, then inclusive positivism must be rejected. Granted it does not affirm a necessary union of legal and moral validity as natural-law theory does. But it accepts the possible union of the two. Indeed, many defenders of inclusive positivism acknowledge that this possible union is characteristically realized in Anglo-American legal systems. However, once we accept that law and morals can be and are related as inclusive positivism suggests, we will inevitably be led into thinking that they should and perhaps even must be so related. But if we begin to think that law and morality must be related as inclusive positivism says they can be, we will inevitably be led to reactionary or anarchist thinking: to sovereignty of conscience run wild, or to the utter suppression of moral autonomy. Our only safe bet, morally, is to insist that legal validity and moral validity be kept conceptually distinct from one another. We must insist on concepts of law and morals according to which it is not merely unnecessary but impossible for moral validity to serve as a condition of legal validity. We must insist on a concept of law according to which the existence of law will always be considered one thing, its moral merit something else entirely. We can do this only if we reject inclusive positivism in favour of exclusive positivism.

There are a number of reasons for questioning the moral argument in both its original and modified forms. They fall into two basic categories: those which question the validity of this kind of argument for legal theories and those which question the causal claims upon which this particular moral argument is based. We will consider reasons of both kinds.

[12] 'Positivism and the Separation of Law and Morals', 65.   [13] Ibid.
[14] 'A Moralistic Case For Amoralistic Law?', 10.

4. THE INVALIDITY OF CAUSAL/MORAL ARGUMENTS FOR LEGAL THEORIES

Bentham's moral argument for positivism and its cousin, the moral argument for exclusive positivism, are both causal arguments. By this I mean that they do not assert a logical, rational or theoretical connection between natural-law theory and inclusive positivism, on the one hand, and reactionary or anarchist doctrine on the other. The claim is not that, by the very logic of these two theories, we must accept one or the other of these two moral doctrines. Inclusive positivism and natural-law theory provide us with no good *reason* to be anarchists or reactionaries. Rather, their acceptance is said to lead, causally, to the acceptance of these moral positions. At the very least, the claim is that the tendency is towards one of the two positions. A person who adopts inclusive positivism will, the argument goes, confusedly and fallaciously arrive at a morally unacceptable stance towards law. That we are less likely to encounter this fallacious drift towards morally pernicious doctrines is offered as a good philosophical reason for rejecting inclusive positivism and natural-law theory in favour of exclusive positivism and legal positivism respectively.

There is, to say the least, something very odd in attempting to refute a descriptive-explanatory theory of law in this way. Why, to put the point bluntly, should we care, if our aim is philosophical understanding, whether people who adopt a jurisprudential theory will mess up morally? Whether a descriptive-explanatory theory of law, or of any other phenomenon, is true or philosophically enlightening seems independent of the practical moral consequences of its adoption and possible misapplication by people. For one thing, as Philip Soper notes,

The question is not whether it would be a good thing if morality and law were connected: the question is whether they are connected. The issue, in short, is not a matter for stipulation in either legal or political theory; it is a matter of deciding what is the case in terms of already existing concepts whose asserted connections we must test by ordinary, if controversial, political theory.[15]

Soper's point can be generalized beyond descriptive-explanatory theories of law. With a few exceptions to be considered below, the truth or adequacy of a philosophical doctrine, and the practical

[15] 'Legal Theory and the Claim of Authority', 214.

moral consequences of its attempted articulation or adoption, are two entirely separate matters, as David Hume seems clearly to have recognized:

> There is no method of reasoning more common, and yet none more blameable, than ... to endeavour to refute any hypothesis by pretext of its dangerous consequences. ... When an opinion leads to absurdity [i.e. contradiction or obvious falsehood], 'tis certainly false; but 'tis not certain an opinion is false because 'tis of dangerous consequences.[16]

In order to appreciate Hume's point and how it bears upon legal theory, consider the following useful parallel: the theories of scientific revolutionaries like Copernicus and Galileo. Copernicanism certainly shook the established order and the confidence Europeans had in the Catholic faith. Arguably it led to undesirable moral upheaval, possibly even to moral anarchism. The removal of the Earth from the centre of the known universe led some to question whether God and his moral authority should be similarly removed. Once sacred doctrine was seen to be fallible and subject to rational refutation by the new, developing sciences, its role as the touchstone of moral truth weakened. Yet science lacked the moral authority of religious doctrine and so morality became destabilized. It is essential to note that the rejection or questioning of morality in no way followed logically from Copernicanism, but it was arguably an important causal consequence of that doctrine's articulation and acceptance.

Whether Copernicanism really had the effects described above is an interesting historical question. But it is also one with which we need not be concerned here. Our question is philosophical not historical: if indeed Copernicanism did cause undesirable moral and social effects, would that have counted against the truth of what Copernicus had set out to prove? Surely not. But now the question arises: Why should the same not be true when the theory at issue is not a scientific theory but a descriptive-explanatory theory of law? As we saw earlier, the focus of such a theory can be influenced by moral considerations and by a variety of meta-theoretical evaluative factors concerning what makes for a good theory of law. But these are different from any morally undesirable effects caused by a theory's adoption and (mis)application. If law is as inclusive positivism suggests it is, and if recognizing this fact can sometimes lead

[16] Hume, *Treatise of Human Nature*, Book II, Part III, Sec. II, 409.

Consider: true that differences in intelligence levels / talents correlated with differences in race or sex.

90   INCLUSIVE V. EXCLUSIVE POSITIVISM

to morally dangerous, fallacious inferences, our move should not be to subvert the truth with a philosophically deficient but innocuous theory. It should be to adapt ourselves and our thinking so as to live better with its consequences.

One possible way of adapting might be to insist that non-moral, formal sources of legal validity always be employed within legal systems, even if they are not necessitated by the concept of law. This, in effect, is one of the two principal themes of MacCormick's 'A Moralistic Case for Amoralistic Law?' If allowing legal validity to depend on moral validity brings with it the dangers of anarchist or reactionary thinking, or the suppression of moral autonomy, then we might want to insist, as a matter of contingent legal practice, that only formal sources be employed within our legal system. In other words, we might wish to insist that the possibility envisaged by inclusive positivism, but ruled out by the exclusive version as inconsistent with the very nature of law, be ruled out in practice. We might accept that moral validity can condition legal validity but insist that it should not be allowed to do so. It is important to be clear, however, how different this line of argument is from causal/moral arguments for exclusive positivism. The latter seek to settle conceptual questions concerning 'what is the case in terms of already existing concepts'[17] by asking whether it is a good thing if morality and law are thought of as necessarily connected. The former asks which of two possible, and recognizably legal, practices ought we to adopt. In this case we are not trying to settle conceptual questions by way of moral argument. Rather we are trying to determine what we ought to do, where the logically possible options are determined by the concepts we now have in use and which are the main subject matter of general descriptive-explanatory theories of law.

Of course, there are at least two other lines of moral argument one might pursue without confusing conceptual analysis and moral argument. One could argue that law is a bad thing and should be abolished or permitted to 'wither away' in favour of less centralized and coercive forms of social regulation. Alternatively, one might suggest wholesale revision of our existing concepts of law and morality. In so doing one would be engaged in stipulative definition. But it is clear that none of the theorists with whom we are concerned in this book conceives himself to be offering stipulative definitions of law and morals. Each thinks he is providing an enlightening

[17] Soper, 'Legal Theory and the Claim of Authority', 214.

analysis of existing practices and the concepts through which we understand them. But if so, it is a fallacy to pursue this analysis by asking whether proposed answers lead causally to morally undesirable results.

It is perhaps worth pausing to consider the extent to which my complaint against causal/moral arguments depends on the assumption that the theories being defended or challenged are descriptive-explanatory in nature. It is clear that Bentham, Hart, MacCormick, and Raz have offered theories of precisely this character, and so the present question is in a sense moot. I should like, nevertheless, to consider briefly what we would have to say if their aim had been to defend a normative theory of some kind, possibly a Dworkinian interpretive conception of law. A Dworkinian conception, it will be recalled, is a constructive interpretation which seeks to put legal practice in its best moral light. Would the fact that the articulation and adoption of such a normative theory might lead causally to morally undesirable consequences count against it? Once again, the answer seems to be negative, unless the theory in question is of a very special sort.

Consider an analogous question: whether act utilitarianism is an adequate normative theory of ethics. Doubts are often raised over whether the principle of utility, as applied directly to our actions, successfully demarcates our moral duties. It is, of course, perfectly valid, though perhaps unsound, to argue against act utilitarianism by pointing out that it leads logically to patently unfair distributions of burdens and benefits, or to the punishment of the innocent. Here we test the theory by examining its logical implications for concrete cases. Such arguments have essentially the following form.

1. The principle of act utilitarianism, as applied to this particular set of factual circumstances, leads logically to the conclusion that such and such is our moral duty.

2. Such and such cannot be our moral duty in this set of factual circumstances. (It cannot, for example, be our duty to frame the innocent black to placate the angry mob.)[18]

3. Therefore we have good reason seriously to question the truth or adequacy of act utilitarianism as a theory purporting to demarcate our actual moral duties.

Here we have a valid argument of the form *modus tollens* in which

[18] This example was introduced and discussed by John Rawls in 'Two Concepts of Rules'.

the logical implications of a normative theory are drawn out and tested against our 'moral intuitions'. What distinguishes this case from causal/moral arguments for exclusive positivism is that the latter do not rest on valid deductions from a theory but rather the causal effects of its adoption. And of course most of these causal effects can be attributed to fallacious thinking. Neither anarchism nor reactionary thinking follows logically from natural-law theory or inclusive positivism. At best one might be led fallaciously to think they do. Those who think that anarchism is the logical consequence of natural-law theory might note Aquinas' insistence that unjust human enactments purporting to be law must sometimes be obeyed in order to 'avoid scandal and disturbance'[19] and the view of some medieval theorists that in 'temporal matters' the human sovereign enjoys an absolute authority and is answerable to God alone for his injustices.[20] This is hardly anarchist thinking.

True enough, it might be replied. But the above ignores one very important point. What is being offered, we are supposing, is not a descriptive-explanatory theory but a normative theory, and the latter, unlike the former, is supposed to be concerned directly with right and wrong actions and decisions. If people are led in adopting a normative theory to act badly or to make the wrong decisions, then that theory, which purports to tell them which actions and decisions are morally correct, is at the very least highly suspect.

This objection does have limited validity against one kind of normative theory: a theory purporting to provide action-guides or decision-rules to be utilized in everyday living. If what we are interested in is a set of principles which can be consistently and easily applied without mistake in our everyday affairs, then a theory which leads causally, even if not logically, to wrong decisions is unacceptable. If our aim is a set of principles to be utilized at what R. M. Hare calls the 'intuitive level' of everyday moral thinking, where our concern is to do the right thing (not necessarily for the right reasons) then the kinds of considerations to which causal/moral arguments appeal are indeed relevant.[21]

But why should we suppose that the provision of workable action guides is necessarily the only reason for offering a normative theory

---

[19] Aquinas, *Summa Theologica*, Part II, Question XCVI, 4th Article.

[20] For a useful survey of the considerable range of medieval theories of natural law, see W. Ullmann, *The Medieval Idea of Law*.

[21] On the 'intuitive level' of moral thinking, see R. M. Hare, *Moral Thinking: Its Levels, Method and Point, passim.*

of ethics? The philosopher's normative ethical theory may be directed to other philosophers and scholars whose interests are not directly practical but revolve around the desire to develop a coherent and enlightening theory which systematizes our moral dispositions and beliefs in ways sanctioned by the philosophers' meta-theoretical evaluative judgments. That such a philosophical theory, designed for this purpose and with these considerations in mind, might be misapplied or practically unworkable if applied for other purposes seems quite beside the point. It's as if we were being asked to reject quantum mechanics because they fail to inform Tony, our neighbourhood mechanic, how best to fix our carburettor.

A philosopher whose aim was clearly not the provision of action guides was G. E. Moore who was happy to concede that his 'ideal utilitarianism' seldom tells us, with any degree of certainty, whether our actions are in fact morally right. The consequences of our actions, Moore thought, are numerous, unpredictable and in many instances, unknowable. But this was of little concern to Moore because his theory was not designed to offer decision-rules, as arguably Bentham's was. It was enough, for Moore, that the theory correctly identifies what it is that makes actions morally right when they are in fact so. The epistemological problems surrounding attempts to calculate the actual effects of our actions were thought worthy of note but of no particular concern. Again, Moore's aim was not a set of workable prescriptions, but a philosophically enlightening account of what factors determine our moral duties.[22]

So a normative theory of ethics designed, not as a set of action guides but as a philosophical account, is untouched by objections which point to the morally undesirable results of the theory's adoption and (mis)application in practical contexts. There seems no reason to think the same is not true if one's concern is to articulate a theory of law which is normative in character. Once again, the question arises: What is the goal in offering such a theory and for what purposes is it to be employed? If we're interested, e.g., in a workable set of prescriptions for judges about how they should decide cases, then perhaps causal/moral consequences are of interest and have probative value. Here we would have the analogue of Hare's intuitive level, where the aim would be to ensure that correct decisions are made, not that the judges actually follow explicitly the right rules and principles in arriving at those decisions, or that they con-

---

[22] Moore's theory is sketched and defended in *Principia Ethica*.

ceive their adjudicative role and its demands in the philosophically correct manner. But there is no reason to think that
a normative theory of law, say a Dworkinian interpretive
conception, is designed with such directly practical goals in
mind.

But suppose that it is. Causal arguments still seem suspect. If,
in offering a normative theory of law, we are really out to
justify the use of coercion by the state, it hardly seems appropriate to let the possible misapplication of the theory count
against it. Surely what is required in a Dworkinian conception is
an honest account of what people's moral/legal rights actually
are. Anything less would seem to violate the integrity that
Dworkin sees as so crucial in legal practice. Suppose that interpreting legal rights in such and such a manner really does put
the use of coercion against individuals in the best moral light.
Suppose further that adopting this justificatory interpretation
might in practice lead causally to morally undesirable results
because, for example, the interpretation is likely to be misapplied by judges or misunderstood by litigants and other citizens.
Would Dworkin really want us to reject this philosophically
best interpretation of our legal rights on these grounds? Would
he wish to accept this kind of argument as having force against a
lawyer's attempt to invoke the 'dangerous' interpretation in supporting his client's claim of legal right? Presumably not. To
allow people's rights to be determined in this way would surely
be to flout one of Dworkin's most fundamental concerns: that
the law take rights seriously.

In light of the above arguments, we have good reason to draw
the following conclusions. Unless moral arguments of the sort
offered by Bentham, Hart, and MacCormick are designed to
challenge a theory whose aim is practical application in everyday
life, they are invalid. They appeal to considerations which fail
to touch the relevant issues of philosophical adequacy or, if
Dworkinian conceptions are in play, the actual moral justification of state coercion and the related issue of the enforcement of
actual moral rights. The causal/moral arguments of Bentham,
Hart, and MacCormick give us no reason, therefore, to prefer
exclusive over inclusive positivism. We do well to head Hume's
cautionary note: ''tis not certain an opinion is false because 'tis of
dangerous consequences'.

5. A DUBIOUS CAUSAL CONNECTION

Suppose, however, that the arguments of section 4 are all off track, that the causal/moral arguments of Bentham, Hart, and Mac-Cormick are indeed valid. We still have reason to reject them because they rely on false premises concerning the causal effects of inclusive positivism and natural-law theory. Why should we suppose that failure to keep legal and moral validity conceptually distinct from one another will lead to either of Bentham's extremes, to anarchism or reactionary thinking?

Lon Fuller certainly thought otherwise. In fact he followed Radbruch in believing that it is positivism which leads to Bentham's second extreme. As Robert Summers observes, Fuller believed that (exclusive) positivism not only misrepresents legal reality, it is unhealthy as well. 'In his view, purportedly descriptive general conceptions of theorists, legal personnel, and citizens about what counts as valid law may ultimately shape what the law actually becomes.' Thus, if a society adopts exclusive positivism as its theory of law, 'it runs the risk of falling into a "law-is-law" formalism. To the extent that this eventuates, it may also influence moral ideas, which thereafter reinforce the law.'[23]

Whether the beliefs of Fuller and Radbruch concerning the moral dangers inherent in (exclusive) positivism are plausible, or whether, as Hart thought, they amount to 'hysteria'[24] is not our main concern. I have drawn attention to these beliefs only because they indicate that the very same causal effects which Bentham ascribed to natural-law theory have been ascribed to positivism as well. This itself should cause us to look suspiciously upon Bentham's argument. In any case, our interest is not in the consequences of adopting exclusive positivism but the supposedly pernicious effects of accepting inclusive positivism. Why should we suppose that accepting the possible connections between law and morality posited by inclusive positivism leads to either of Bentham's extremes? In fact we have very little reason to think that at all.

Consider a nation which, like Canada, has formally adopted a constitutionally entrenched charter of rights recognizing, and giving legal effect to, certain rights of political morality. These are rights

---

[23] Summers, *Lon L. Fuller*, 53, referring to 'Positivism and Fidelity to Law', 637, *Harvard LR* version.

[24] Hart uses this term in 'Positivism and the Separation of Law and Morals', 74.

the unreasonable infringement of which by legislation, or administrative or judicial decisions, renders the latter legally invalid.[25] We
will call such a society a 'charter society' and its legal system a
'charter system'. Let us assume that it is generally understood within
such a charter society that the violation of a charter right is not
merely a legitimate reason for a court's declaring that a law or
decision shall henceforth be invalid, but rather a ground for the
claim that it already is invalid, and that a court therefore has a
legal-adjudicative obligation to declare it so.[26] In other words, we
will assume that it's the conflict with the constitutionally recognized
moral right that makes a law or decision legally invalid, not the
(morally-neutral) fact that a judge has declared it to be invalid in a
trial testing its validity. Assume further that the rights of political
morality specified in the charter are to a degree abstractly described
and have been subject to few, if any, judicial attempts to define their
boundaries, and that an important measure of moral argument is
therefore required to substantiate their infringement by offending
legislation or judicial decisions. Interpretations with precedential
effect are few and far between. Now comes our question: Why
should we suppose that people within such a charter society will be
led to either anarchist or reactionary thinking, to sovereignty of
conscience run wild or moral autonomy suppressed, as Mac-
Cormick might put it?

If anything, reactionary thinking seems very unlikely within such
a society, where citizens have a publicly recognized platform from
which to challenge the legal validity of decisions made by their
legal authorities. It is generally accepted not merely that fallible
authorities sometimes make decisions which are morally indefensible, but that some of these decisions, because they violate important rights of political morality recognized in and validated by the
charter, lack legal validity. It is also recognized that citizens are
empowered by law to point this out in court and to have their arguments accepted as legally sound and determinative.

[25] There is considerable controversy concerning how best to interpret the legal
effect of documents like a charter of rights and freedoms. In the next chapter I shall
defend the view that such documents recognize legal rights whose content depends on
moral argument in the way sanctioned by inclusive positivism but denied by exclusive
positivism.

[26] We will discuss later the important differences between these two interpretations. The first, as we shall see, is the one to which defenders of exclusive positivism
are driven. The second is consistent with inclusive positivism and preferable as an
interpretation of 'charter challenges'.

Compare a non-charter society where legislative authorities enjoy powers of enactment considered morally unlimited in scope and extent, where formal source or pedigree is all that matters in determining whether a decision or law is valid legally. In this second society, where far greater faith has presumably been put in the good moral sense of legislators and judges, one can well imagine the possibility of reactionary thinking. The thinking might be: 'We trust our legislators and judges to do the right thing, otherwise we would restrict their powers. Hence, this is the law; therefore it is what it ought to be, and I should obey.' The inference is of course invalid in so far as well-intentioned legislators and judges can still get things wrong, and so a morally sensitive citizen will always be sceptical whether a law is in fact morally acceptable. But it is easy to see how the invalid inference might be made nevertheless, how people just might, as Fuller observed, lapse into a 'law-is-law' formalism.[27] But in a charter society, where moral constraints upon legislative power are officially and publicly recognized, it would seem less, not more, likely that people would lapse into this easy but fallacious type of inference. The only possible exception is a society in which deference to authoritative interpretations of moral rights is for some reason the norm. But there is little reason to think that such deference will be common within a charter society which accepts moral limits upon legislative, administrative, and judicial power and accords citizens a public forum within which to affirm such limits.

Yet the real worry may not be the reactionary but the anarchist. Perhaps recognition of moral limits upon legislative power inevitably leads to a kind of disrespect for the law's authority which is both morally and politically dangerous. It may lead citizens to become laws unto themselves, as Hobbes seemed to think it would. Yet once again it is difficult to accept the proposed causal connection. A system which formally recognizes its own limitations, which recognizes that its legislators and judges may legally err by violating important rights of political morality, seems one which will command the respect of a morally enlightened and sensitive citizenry. Compare once again the alternative system which recognizes no moral restraints upon the legislative powers of its authorities and denies citizens the legal power to challenge the validity of its directives on grounds of political morality. Surely it is this second system

[27] Summers, *Lon L. Fuller*, 53.

which contains the seeds of anarchism. When faced with a claim to unrestricted authority most people are inclined to reject that claim and to assert their moral autonomy instead, just as children lean toward rejecting parental authority when its reins are held too tightly. People are prepared to accept the authority of others, but only on terms which recognize its reasonable and rightful limitation. Authorities which recognize legal/moral limitations on their own legislative and adjudicative powers are far more apt to commend themselves to us, to be accepted as legitimate legal authorities. We will see the existence of such authorities as far less threatening to our moral autonomy than the alternative. As Summers observes, this is a point well recognized by Fuller, though Fuller fallaciously thought it argued against positivism. 'A system of law sufficiently open to moral argument is more likely to be morally acceptable and thus capable of serving the cause of peace and order.'[28]

We must conclude, then, that there is little merit in the causal/moral arguments of Bentham, Hart, and MacCormick. They are invalid and rest on false premises concerning the causal effects of accepting inclusive positivism or natural-law theory. They therefore provide us with no grounds for rejecting either view.[29]

6. THE ARGUMENT FROM INTELLECTUAL CLARITY

Hart's second set of reasons for preferring positivism to natural-law theory lies in the latter's apparent tendency to obscure and oversimplify a number of complex practical issues, such as the question which confronted the post-war German courts, 'Are we to punish those who did evil things when they were permitted by evil rules then in force?'[30] This question, Hart wrote, cannot be answered by a simple refusal to recognize evil law as valid. 'This is too crude a way with delicate and complex moral issues ... A case of retroactive punishment should not be made to look like an ordinary case of punishment for an act illegal at the time.'[31] According to this argu-

---

[28] Ibid. 59.
[29] In private correspondence, H. L. A. Hart has revealed that he no longer accepts the validity of causal/moral arguments for positivism. He now wishes to employ only arguments which rely on meta-theoretical evaluative, not moral-evaluative considerations.
[30] *The Concept of Law*, 206.   [31] Ibid. 206–7.

ment, positivism, with its insistence that legal validity fails to entail moral validity, allows us better to conceive and appreciate such practical moral dilemmas.

A related reason for preferring positivism is the clarity it furnishes in the theoretical study of law. According to Hart, we make no gains in the theoretical or scientific study of law as a social phenomenon if we follow natural-law theory in denying the label 'law' to evil enactments. This would lead us to exclude such enactments from our analysis of law, 'even though they exhibited all the other complex characteristics of law'.[32] Nothing but confusion would follow from such a proposal. 'Study of [law's] use involves study of its abuse.'[33]

So according to Hart, both theory and practice find strength in the doctrines of legal positivism. The theory is superior to natural-law theory in so far as its adoption 'will assist our theoretical inquiries' and 'advance and clarify our moral deliberations'.[34] There are two questions for us to address here. First, has Hart provided sound reasons for preferring positivism to natural-law theory, and second, could similar reasons be utilized to support our choosing exclusive over inclusive positivism? To both questions we must answer No.

Let us begin with the first question. What are we to make of Hart's claim that clarity in theoretical inquiry and moral deliberation are advanced if we adopt positivism as opposed to natural-law theory? Our first point must surely be that Hart has come perilously close to begging the question. If moral validity is indeed conceptually independent of legal validity, then dealing with 'the German informers, who for selfish ends procured the punishment of others under monstrous laws'[35] by claiming that the informers' acts were illegal simply because they were monstrous, does invite confusion. But if legal validity is not conceptually independent of moral validity, then perhaps it is the positivist's approach which threatens moral deliberation. If, as is arguably the case, most people believe that there is an obligation to obey the law as such, and if the positivist insists that evil law is still law so long as the legal system's recognized tests for validity have been satisfied, then it is positivism which obscures matters. It will sometimes lend an unwarranted aura of moral authority to evil laws and incline people away from serious moral reflection about whether to obey them.

[32] Ibid. 205.   [33] Ibid.   [34] Ibid. 204–5.   [35] Ibid. 207.

Now it may be that the above response to Hart's Argument From Intellectual Clarity is no more persuasive than the argument itself. My point is not that it is, merely that each side will undoubtedly accuse the other of begging the question in claiming that his theory promotes clear thinking. Moral confusion and obfuscation will be identified in different lines of moral reasoning depending on one's views concerning the nature of law. How one conceives a moral dilemma posed by law, and indeed whether one sees a dilemma there at all, are largely dependent on whether one adopts positivism, natural-law theory, or some other philosophical view about law.

So at this point we seem to have a stand-off, a point well recognized by Leslie Green who offers the following comment on Hart's argument that positivism promotes clarity of thought about the complex moral character of law, in particular the central question of the citizen's duty to obey. 'If anyone doubts that this is necessary to being clear-headed about political obligation he should consider the muddle Kant ends up in by subsuming law in Recht; anyone who thinks that it is sufficient should remember that Hobbes's positivism also led directly to an absolute duty to obey.'[36]

But what about Hart's more specific complaint against natural-law theory: that in the case of the German informers, 'A case of retroactive punishment should not be made to look like an ordinary case of punishment for an act illegal at the time'? With positivism, he would argue, we say that the informers acted legally but monstrously, and that in punishing them for their wicked actions we violate an important principle: *nulla poena sine lege*. With natural-law theory, on the other hand, we have to say that the informers acted illegally because their actions were monstrous, and so we were merely bringing criminals to justice, something we do all the time and which requires no special justification. Surely, Hart might say, that natural-law theory leads us to conceive the infliction of punishment in this way in such cases gives us very good reason to adopt positivism instead.

We do, of course, have reason to prefer positivism on this score if the defender of natural-law theory is truly forced to accept the view Hart attributes to him. But surely the above is not how such a theorist will wish to characterize the situation. He too will recognize that the German informer case is not an ordinary case of punishment

[36] Leslie Green, 'The Political Content of Legal Theory', 1.

for an act illegal at the time. He may say that it is a case of punishment for an illegal act, but there is nothing to stop him from viewing the case as highly unusual, as one which infringes an important, though not absolute, principle of the natural-law: that secular legal authorities should punish only those who, in doing evil, did what the state at the time explicitly forbade. In other words, there is no reason to think that a defender of natural-law theory would not wish to embrace the principle of *nulla poena sine lege* and accept that its infringement can be justified only in exceptional cases where violation of other principles of the natural-law is both clear and profound. A tradition of legal thought which is willing to embrace the proposition that unjust laws must be obeyed if failure to do so promotes 'scandal and disturbance',[37] will surely be happy to see Hart's moral dilemma for what it is. He will be happy to say that this is not an ordinary case of punishment for acts illegal at the time.

So it is far from clear that Hart's Argument From Intellectual Clarity, as applied to cases like the German informer case, provides much support for positivism. What about his claim that positivism advances clarity in our theoretical inquiries about law? According to Hart, positivism does not force us misleadingly to exclude certain rules, the immoral ones, even though they exhibit all the other complex characteristics of law. The obvious reply is that there is also nothing in natural-law theory which compels the exclusion of immoral rules from the scope of theoretical inquiries about law. As Neil MacCormick notes, such rules both can and should be studied as pathological specimens of law, 'and the grounds for their exclusion from the true category could and should be expounded and addressed within the discipline of law, even if a natural lawyer's criteria of legality [are] adopted'.[38]

There is no reason, then, to think that a defender of natural-law theory must deny that the study of law's use should involve study of its abuse. We might note at this juncture John Austin's discussion of 'laws not properly so-called'. Austin did not banish such non-laws from the scope of jurisprudential inquiry, indeed he talked about them extensively. He merely wished to separate non-laws, e.g., 'imperfect', 'permissive', and 'declaratory' laws, from the category of 'laws properly so called', thereby highlighting what was essential

---

[37] Aquinas, *Summa Theologica*, Question XCVI (On the Power of Human Law), 4th Article (Whether Human Law Binds a Man in Conscience?), emphasis added.

[38] 'A Moralistic Case For Amoralistic Law?', 9.

(he thought) to what is truly law: the command element. The natural lawyer's basis for dividing the province of jurisprudence into Austin's two categories, laws and non-laws, will of course be very different from Austin's, but there is no reason to deny him the same theoretical privileges as Austin. Immoral laws could, for the natural lawyer, easily be conceived as 'laws not properly so called' and studied on that basis.

We must conclude, then, that Hart's arguments from moral and theoretical clarity are weak at best. They appear to provide little reason for choosing positivism over natural-law theory. Yet even if they did support this choice, it is clear that they could not be re-utilized to support exclusive positivism. An appeal to moral clarity concerning the demands of morally dubious law would not be open because inclusive positivism also acknowledges the conceptual possibility of morally iniquitous, yet legally valid, rules. It too recognizes and stresses the possibility of an evil system of law, incorporating little or no moral constraint upon legal validity in which the dilemmas, as Hart describes them, would clearly exist. From the fact that moral and legal validity can be related to one another, it does not follow that they are or must be. Unlike exclusive positivism, however, inclusive positivism also recognizes another important fact which is seriously obscured by the former theory: there are systems of law, e.g. charter systems, in which the accepted tests for legal validity do appear to include a distinctly moral dimension. Of course in a charter system the dilemmas discussed by Hart might not be the ones with which judges are typically faced. The dilemma might not be whether to punish people for evil actions permitted by valid law, though this possibility would still exist because recognized moral tests for law may not always be sufficient, even when properly applied, to exclude every wicked law. Rather the dilemma might be the one we fashioned earlier in discussing natural-law theory: whether to hold people responsible for relying, reasonably or not, on the validity of laws which are later declared to have been invalid because they violated (recognized) moral tests for law. Such a dilemma would be particularly acute in cases where reasonable people disagreed about whether the relevant moral criteria had been violated. Here we would encounter dilemmas similar to those found within contract law, which involve reasonable but mistaken reliance on the undertakings of others.

It would seem that superior moral clarity is not a basis upon which we can choose exclusive over inclusive positivism. What about clarity in the theoretical study of law? Here too we find little warrant, as Raz himself seems to acknowledge. Positivism is often recommended on the ground that it clearly separates the description of law from its evaluation. 'This, it is alleged, prevents confusion and serves clarity of thought.'[39] By parity of reasoning it could be argued that there is reason to accept exclusive positivism which renders this useful separation not merely possible but conceptually necessary.

Raz's reply to this line of argument is similar to our first response to Hart's moral clarity argument. He acknowledges and applauds the alleged virtues of clarity inherent in positivism (at least in its exclusive version) but adds that these can hardly be used to defend its adequacy as a general theory of law. To do so, Raz suggests, would be to presuppose the thesis rather than support it.[40] In other words, this line of defence begs the very issues in question. The same is true if the intention is to defend exclusive positivism against inclusive positivism. To be sure, if the law truly must be identified in terms of social sources alone, then any attempt to identify it which fails to distinguish clearly between legal and moral factors will be highly misleading and probably wrong. We will inevitably find ourselves with an unacceptable mixture of views about what the law is and what it ought to be. However, if the identification of a law or its content sometimes does involve moral considerations, then any attempt to separate law and morality conceptually in the manner required by exclusive positivism is what will be misleading and incorrect. At best, only a part of what it is we are after would have been successfully identified.

We must conclude, then, that neither the causal/moral arguments of Bentham, Hart, and MacCormick, nor Hart's arguments from moral and theoretical clarity can be adapted successfully to provide support for exclusive positivism. If sound arguments are to be found we must look elsewhere.

7. THREE POPULAR ARGUMENTS

It is now time to turn to our main concern: an assessment of Raz's arguments for exclusive positivism. As before, we will be asking whether any of these arguments, perhaps in a slightly modified form,

[39] *The Authority of Law*, 42.   [40] See ibid.

provides good reason to reject inclusive positivism in favour of Raz's exclusive theory. Once again, our conclusions will be negative.

(i) The Linguistic Argument

The first popular argument considered by Raz claims that positivism 'correctly reflects the meaning of "law" and cognate terms in ordinary language'.[41] It is part of our understanding of these terms that a law can be morally unacceptable but legally valid none the less. Indeed, the fact that we fully understand what it means to say that 'an unjust law seems to be no law at all', suggests strongly that the meaning of 'law' excludes any essential reference to its justice or wider moral merit. Thus, it might be argued, an appeal to ordinary language supports exclusive positivism because the latter makes the existence and content of laws depend exclusively on non-moral issues concerning social sources.

Raz views such appeals to linguistic usage as having some probative force but rightly questions whether that force is sufficient to settle issues of substance. We do not, he writes, 'want to be slaves of words. Our aim is to understand society and its institutions. We must face the question: is the ordinary sense of "law" such that it helps identify facts of importance to our understanding of society?'[42] If it is not, then so much the worse for our 'ordinary' understanding of the word 'law'. It can not be used to support exclusive positivism. The desire to avoid being a slave of words is one shared by many legal philosophers including Hart who, in defending positivism against natural-law theory, noted that we cannot base our choice between these two on 'the proprieties of linguistic usage. If we are to make a reasoned choice between these concepts, it must be because one is superior to the other in the way in which it will assist our theoretical inquiries, or advance and clarify our moral deliberations, or both.'[43] We have seen reason to doubt Hart's grounds for preferring positivism, but one cannot quarrel with his desire to avoid settling matters on linguistic grounds.[44]

[41] Ibid. 41.   [42] Ibid.   [43] *The Concept of Law*, 204–5.

[44] For further discussion of the role of linguistic appeals in defending theories of law, see Raz, 'The Problem About the Nature of Law', 203, and Leslie Green, 'The Political Content of Legal Theory'. See also *Law's Empire*, ch. 1, especially 31–7 where Dworkin dismisses 'semantic' theories of law which purport, Dworkin thinks, to expose the implicitly accepted linguistic criteria governing the use of such terms as 'law' and 'legal'. Whether many philosophers have ever seriously viewed their theories as 'semantic' in this sense is highly questionable. Austin did suggest that the central claims of his theory were 'identity propositions', by which he meant analytic

(ii) The Argument From Bias

A second reason sometimes given in favour of positivism, which by extension might be invoked to support the exclusive version of that theory, is that it eliminates investigator bias. Since exclusive positivism entails that the existence and content of laws are entirely matters of social fact, the theories and descriptions of a legal scholar like Sir Rupert Cross, who sets out to describe the state of the law within a particular legal jurisdiction, will be less likely to be influenced by moral presuppositions and biases if he adheres to exclusive positivism as his guiding philosophy of law. His will be as close as one can get to what Kelsen thought essential, namely, a pure theory of law. His pure descriptions of law will be uncontaminated by his impure evaluations of it. Should a legal commentator follow the lead recommended by inclusive positivism, however, and view the state of valid law as sometimes conditioned by moral considerations, then the investigator's moral bias will inevitably creep in to a much larger degree. His theoretical neutrality will be seriously compromised.

This argument quite obviously begs the questions at hand too. If the existence or content of law within a jurisdiction is sometimes partly a function of moral considerations, then any description purporting to articulate the state of valid law within that legal jurisdiction which neglects moral factors altogether will be misleading and wrong. What good is a 'pure' theory if the phenomenon under investigation is altogether 'impure'. A commentator's moral sense may be required in some instances if an adequate account of the phenomenon he sets out to describe is to be possible. Commentators should strive for impartiality and objectivity. But if the very existence of what they are investigating depends crucially on its satisfying

truths. But very few others see themselves as exposing the semantic ground rules governing the use of legal terms. Contrary to Dworkin, Hart most certainly did not. As he makes plain, his project in *The Concept of Law* is to offer what he terms an 'essay in descriptive sociology' (p. vii). His purpose is 'not to provide a definition of law in the sense of a rule by reference to which the correctness of the use of the word can be tested'. It is rather 'to advance legal theory by providing an improved analysis of the distinctive structure of a municipal legal system and a better understanding of the resemblances and differences between law, coercion, and morality as types of social phenomena'. (17) See also his dismissal in 'Positivism and the Separation of Law and Morals' (81) of the 'arid wastes' of attempts to define the word 'law'. Michael Bayles has recently argued that it is Dworkin himself, not his opposition, who tries to provide a 'semantic' analysis of law. On this see 'What Is Jurisprudence About? Theories, Definitions, Concepts, or Conceptions of Law?', 23–40. See also, 'Hart vs. Dworkin'.

moral conditions, then full moral impartiality may not be possible. If an enacted rule is valid within a legal system only if it satisfies a legally recognized moral condition, then a commentator who wishes to describe the content of valid law within that jurisdiction may have no choice but to ask the moral question: Does the rule satisfy the moral condition? It may be true that the asking of such a question brings with it more risk of moral bias than the asking of questions like: Has the rule been passed by the House with at least a two-thirds majority? How has the Supreme Court interpreted the relevant moral condition? or How is the Supreme Court likely to interpret that condition in future cases? But that just may be a risk one must run if one wants an adequate account. Again, what good is a 'pure' account if the phenomenon under investigation is altogether 'impure'?

(iii) The Institutional Connection Argument

A more plausible argument for exclusive positivism rests on the undeniable fact that in some sense human law is a social institution. That he brought this fact forcefully to our attention is sometimes said to be one of John Austin's greatest achievements. Austin stressed that positive law is not an ideal but a social construct. It is, as Gray put it, 'not that which ought to be, but that which is. To fix this definitely in the Jurisprudence of the Common Law, is the feat that Austin accomplished.'[45]

According to Austin and Gray law is not an ideal to be discovered in religious teachings, nature, or morality, but in the activities of a complex social institution. It is the product of these activities, and nothing which fails to be connected to these activities can properly be considered law. This view is shared by Raz who insists that law has socially constituted sources and limits. It is necessarily not comprised of all social rules and conventions, nor does it contain all the demands of positive or ideal morality. Rather, law is a social institution with its own institutional limits. The content of law is defined by the law itself: it creates its own boundaries through the law-creating and law-defining activities of authoritative individuals like legislators and judges. Legal systems have their own individual sets of standards, offices, procedures, rules of recognition, and so on, which they bring into existence as social phenomena and which they enforce effectively within their communities. '[I]t is a consequence of

[45] J. C. Gray, 'A Realist Conception of Law', 47.

the institutional character of law that it has limits', limits which are defined by the 'operations of the relevant adjudicative institution'.[46]

Unlike the preceding arguments, the institutional connection *too mild? concession...* argument does seem to provide some reason for preferring positivism to classical natural-law theory. Aquinas, for instance, posits (natural) laws and criteria for valid human laws existing independently of any and all acts of official recognition within particular human legal systems. These laws and criteria are not necessarily endorsed officially by all legal systems, but they are imprinted on the consciousness of all rational creatures whose knowledge of them is characterized as their 'participation of' God's eternal law.[47] So it would appear at first glance that Aquinas' theory is incompatible with the institutional character of law. But we must be careful here. A closer look reveals that the degree of incompatibility is far less than one might initially have supposed.

Aquinas stresses the need for positive human law as a means of furthering natural human aims and ensuring compliance with the natural law. He also recognizes that the natural law is sometimes indeterminate with respect to its demands in particular sets of circumstances and that authoritative decisions emanating from social institutions are required to settle issues 'left open' by the natural law. Those who neglect these important points about Aquinas concentrate on passages such as the following, where the institutional nature of human law seems to be missed, or at least ignored.

As Augustine says, that which is not just seems to be no law at all. Hence the force of a law depends on the extent of its justice. Now in human affairs a thing is said to be just from being right, according to the rule of reason. But the first rule of reason is the law of nature. Consequently, every human law has just so much of the nature of law as it is derived from the law of nature. But if at any point it departs from the law of nature, it is no longer a law but a perversion of law.[48]

In this important passage, Aquinas has expressed two crucial points: (1) that the (moral) force of law depends, in the end, not on its enactment and enforcement by human authorities but on its justice, where justice is an ideal, not something that might exist in

---

[46] *The Authority of Law*, 44.
[47] Aquinas, *Summa Theologica*, Question XCI (On the Various Kinds of Law), 2nd Article (Whether There Is in Us a Natural Law?).
[48] Ibid., Question XCV (Human Law), 2nd Article (Whether Every Human Law is Derived from the Natural Law?).

social conventions or what Austin called 'positive morality'; and (2) that a human law, i.e. one created by the activities of legislative or adjudicative authorities, derives its very status as law, not from these creative, social-institutional activities alone, but from the law of nature of which it is an expression. The question now arises: Do we not have here a denial that it is in the nature of human law necessarily to be the product of social-institutional activities? Do we not have a denial of what Raz's argument asserts to be a necessary feature of human law: institutional connection? Not entirely. Immediately following the passage quoted above, Aquinas goes on to describe two different ways in which human laws may be derived from the natural law. It is here that he shows appreciation for the social-institutional nature of human law.

it must be noted that something may be derived from the natural law in two ways: first, as a conclusion from principles; secondly, by way of a determination of certain common notions. The first way is like to that by which, in the sciences, demonstrated conclusions are drawn from the principles; while the second is likened to that whereby, in the arts, common forms are determined to some particular. Thus, the craftsman needs to determine the common form of a house to the shape of this or that particular house. Some things are therefore derived from the common principles of the natural law by way of conclusions: e.g., that *one must not kill* may be derived as a conclusion from the principle that *one should do harm to no man*; while some are derived therefrom by way of determination: e.g., the law of nature has it that the evil-doer should be punished, but that he be punished in this or that way is a determination of the law of nature.

Some natural laws are universally applicable to all situations and times and are known to all reasonable persons as lawful requirements. It is a law of England, Canada, and Hungary that one must not kill (except under certain defined conditions); and, more importantly, the law of these three countries would necessarily include that injunction even if their legislatures and courts failed to recognize it explicitly, or even declared that it is lawful always to kill another human being. Here we clearly have a denial of the necessary institutional nature of some human laws. Some laws which not only ought to but do govern the affairs of state, and are properly enforceable in human courts of law, derive their legal status from something other than their being 'connected in certain ways with the operation of the relevant adjudicative [and legislative] institutions'.[49] They are

[49] Raz, *The Authority of Law*, 44.

human laws because and only because they are common principles of the natural law which 'exist' within all legal systems. They exist even within legal systems which fail to recognize them. Recognition is not, in the case of these laws, a necessary condition for existence.

But there are some human laws with respect to which recognition is indeed necessary for existence. They derive their status as human law from two sources: the natural law and the activities of the appropriate social institutions. According to Aquinas one and the same principle of the natural law may yield different laws in different communities. One reason for this is that circumstances may vary from one place to another. '[L]aws imposed on men should ... be in keeping with their condition, for, as Isidore says, law should be possible both according to nature, and according to the customs of the country.'[50] Given conditions, C1 in society S1, it may be in accordance with the eternal, unchanging, and universally binding natural law that the penalty for perjury in S1 be a year in prison. Should the sovereign (or a presiding judge) within S1 see that this is so, and fulfil his legislative (or adjudicative) duties, he will create (or recognize) human law L1 which derives its status as law from both the natural law and the decision of the sovereign (or a judge) in S1. Before the decision to create L1 (in a court or legislature), L1 did not exist within S1. Given conditions C2 in society S2, however, it may be in accordance with this same eternal, unchanging and universal natural law that the penalty for perjury in S2 be two years in prison. Should S2's sovereign (or a presiding judge) see his duty and perform it, he will create (or recognize) human law L2 which also derives its status as law both from the natural law and the sovereign's (or the judge's) decision. Much of what we think of as human law gains its existence in this way, according to Aquinas, and to that extent his theory does reflect the institutional nature of law.

The role of human social-institutional activities in determining the existence of human law does not end here however. According to Aquinas, some principles of the natural law fail to yield concrete results in specific cases, either (a) because superior knowledge and experience, together with knowledge of the natural law, is required in order to derive these results; or (b) because an arbitrary decision among alternatives left open by the natural law must be made. If it is (b) which Aquinas means to suggest, then he has recognized the

[50] Aquinas, *Summa Theologica*, Question XCV (Human Law), 3rd Article (Whether it Belongs to Human Law to Repress All Vices?).

necessity of what in recent times has come to be known as 'discretion'.[51] Human reason, guided by the precepts of the natural law and knowledge of a society's particular circumstances, will only get us so far in deriving human laws. At some point a choice will have to be made between alternatives, all of which are compatible with the natural law but only one of which can be adopted and followed. It is the function of legislative or adjudicative authorities, on this view, to make rationally unrestrained choices among these alternatives, their choices being sanctioned by but not strictly derivable from the natural law. No reason can be given for choosing A over B, except that both are consistent with the natural law and a choice must be made.

The necessity for discretionary choices seems to be what Aquinas has in mind when he entertains the fourth objection to his claim that every human law is derived from the natural law.

OBJ. 4. Further, it is possible to give a reason for things which are derived from the natural law. But it is not possible to give the reason for all the legal enactments of the lawgivers, as the Jurist says. Therefore not all human laws are derived from the natural law.[52]

Earlier he considers a similar objection.

OBJ. 1. It would seem that not every human law is derived from the natural law. For the Philosopher says that the legal just is that which originally was a matter of indifference. But those things which arise from the natural law are not matters of indifference. Therefore the enactments of human laws are not all derived from the natural law.[53]

In reply Aquinas does not deny that the choice of the 'legal just' is a matter of indifference, but restricts these arbitrary choices to 'those enactments which are by way of determination or specification of the precepts of the natural law'.[54] What Aquinas seems to have in mind is this. In one and the same society, S1, and given one and the same set of circumstances, C1, there is nothing to choose between human law L1 (all should drive on the right) and human law L2 (all should drive on the left). Either is consistent with the natural law—it is a matter of indifference which is chosen—but only one can be

---

[51] We will later examine theories concerning the existence, necessity, and desirability of judicial discretion in hard cases. Dworkin's early critique of positivism centred on what he took to be the positivist's theory of (strong) judicial discretion.

[52] Aquinas, *Summa Theologica*, Question XCV (Human Law), 2nd Article (Whether Every Human Law is Derived from the Natural Law?).

[53] Ibid.   [54] Ibid.

adopted. It is the role of the relevant adjudicative or legislative authority to make the choice between L1 and L2. The law determining on which side of the road we must drive in S1 does not exist before this choice has been made. Unlike the common principles of the natural law which exist within all legal systems regardless of the activities of the relevant adjudicative and legislative authorities, L1 or L2 cannot, logically, exist as law within S1 unless one of these is 'connected' in the right way with the activities of the appropriate social institution(s). Existence is here a function of both the natural law and recognition by the relevant human authorities.

Whether my 'discretion' interpretation of the method of determination is correct is, admittedly, open to question. Aquinas sometimes writes as though he thought there are always grounds for choosing one law over another in a given set of circumstances, but that these grounds are not rationally demonstrable. On this alternative interpretation, the limitation is epistemic, not logical. It is not that there is more than one option consistent with the natural law which would be lawful if recognized by the appropriate authority; there is one and only one option but we cannot demonstrate what it is and must therefore depend on the enlightened (we hope) determinations of human legislators and judges. In responding to the objection that it is not always possible to give a reason for a legal enactment by a human lawmaker, Aquinas suggests that in determining particular points of the natural law, we must defer to 'the judgment of expert and prudent men'. Invoking the authority of Aristotle, he adds that 'in such matters, we ought to pay as much attention to the undemonstrated sayings and opinions of persons who surpass us in experience and prudence, as to their demonstrations'.[55]

It is not entirely clear whether the determinations of Aquinas' persons of experience and prudence are rationally justifiable in ways known only to them, or whether there is an element of pure fiat even in their choices. If it is the latter, then we are still left with the discretion interpretation. If it is the former, then presumably all laws, natural, divine, eternal, and human, are fully rational and their grounds discoverable by a sufficiently intelligent and experienced rational agent. The only limitations on deriving human from natural laws are epistemic in nature.

But these difficult questions in Thomistic exegesis need not con-

[55] Ibid.

cern us here. It is clear that, on either interpretation of Aquinas' view, a good portion of human law is the (partial) product of authoritative human decisions incapable of pure deduction from the natural law. They derive their status as law not exclusively from the natural law but from their social-institutional recognition, by their being, as Raz puts it, 'connected in certain ways with the operation of the relevant adjudicative [and legislative] institutions'.[56] So Aquinas seems not to have completely ignored the institutional nature of human law.

Having said all that, it is nevertheless important to stress once again that, in Aquinas' view, not *all* (human) laws are of necessity connected with appropriate social-institutional activities. He will continue to insist that there are laws and criteria for validity whose existence cannot be traced to the operations of adjudicative or legislative institutions. They are said to 'exist' within, and be binding upon, all human communities and all human legal systems, even when no institutional acts of recognition with respect to them have been performed. To this extent at least, Aquinas does depart from Raz and other legal positivists.

Despite its apparent, if limited, force against traditional natural-law theories, it is clear that Raz's Institutional Connection Argument offers no reason to prefer exclusive to inclusive positivism.[57] The explanation for this should be fairly clear at this point. A consequence of inclusive positivism is that moral considerations can be relevant to the identification of the existence and content of law only if the legal system itself has in some way recognized them as serving that role. And the accepted rule of recognition might be as simple as 'Whatever the Queen in Parliament enacts is law', in which case moral considerations would have no bearing at all on questions of validity. Alternatively, a rule of recognition might specify principles of liberty and equality as grounds of legal validity, in which case morality would be seriously implicated; or there might be secondary interpretation rules according to which certain moral factors help determine the very content or meaning of rules validated by a rule of recognition, a possibility for which I shall argue in Chapter 8. So inclusive positivism, unlike the natural-law

---

[56] *The Authority of Law*, 44–5.

[57] I do not mean to suggest that Raz thinks it does offer such a reason. His aim in offering the argument seems to be to provide reasons for subscribing to some version or other of positivism instead of some version or other of natural-law theory.

theory of Aquinas, is fully compatible with the institutional nature of law. Morality counts, on this theory, but only if it has the right connections.

8. THE ARGUMENT FROM EXPLANATORY POWER

In Chapter 3 of *The Authority of Law*, Raz considers two arguments which are explicitly designed to defend exclusive positivism against inclusive positivism. As a result, no extrapolation or modification on our part is necessary: we may tackle the arguments directly.

According to Raz's first argument, exclusive positivism is to be recommended because it 'reflects and explicates our conception of the law'.[58] It 'explains and systematizes' a number of pre-theoretical distinctions often made in relation to law. These include the difference between the legal and the moral evaluation of judges and their decisions; the distinction between settled and unsettled law; and the contrast often drawn between applying the law and creating, modifying, or developing it. It 'is our normal view that judges use moral arguments (though perhaps not only such arguments) when developing the law and that they use legal skills when applying the law.'[59]

According to this Argument From Explanatory Power, exclusive positivism 'coincides with the way these distinctions are generally applied', and to that extent it has 'explanatory power and is supported'. It follows from exclusive positivism that 'the law on a question is settled when legally binding sources provide its solution. In such cases judges are typically said to apply the law, and since it is source-based, its application involves technical, legal skills in reasoning from those sources and does not call for moral acumen.'[60] Similarly, if the appropriate valid sources fail to determine an answer to a legal question, then it will be thought unsettled and courts will be viewed as breaking new ground. And in breaking this new ground, judges will naturally base their decisions partly on moral and other extra-legal considerations. They will have to. They can no longer apply pre-existing law.

There are at least two responses to be made to Raz's argument. First, it might be questioned whether the features of legal practice cited by Raz truly do amount to pre-theoretical data which any

---

[58] *The Authority of Law*, 48.   [59] Ibid. 49.   [60] Ibid. 49–50.

successful theory of law should be able to explain and systematize, or whether they are (at least as they are described) consequences of exclusive positivism and therefore of no embarrassment to inclusive positivism or any other theory of law with which they might be incompatible. Stephen Perry raises this important question when he suggests that the distinctions to which Raz draws attention are not so much systematized by exclusive positivism as they are implied by it. They are not theory-independent, empirical facts which any successful theory of law must accommodate, but rather 'claims about the theoretical character of the legal process which presuppose the acceptance, explicit or implicit, of a certain philosophical interpretation of that process'. In other words, '[o]ur pretheoretical conception of law does not ... draw Raz's distinctions in such a sharp and unequivocal way that we have no choice but to accord them theoretical recognition'.[61]

But suppose Perry is wrong, that the distinctions as drawn and discussed by Raz are indeed ones which any successful descriptive-explanatory theory of law must accommodate and explain. There is no reason to think that inclusive positivism cannot measure up to the task.

Consider again a charter society in which moral criteria for law have been explicitly incorporated into a rule of recognition or the constitutional law it recognizes. Here the various distinctions noted by Raz will still hold good, though they may be interpreted or understood in slightly different ways. Judges will still be evaluated on the basis of their technical abilities and their moral acumen, because both will be instrumental in identifying valid law. A judge who is asked to determine the legal standing of legislation claimed unreasonably to infringe a charter right to equality, but who lacks moral insight entirely, will be unable to fulfil a crucial part of her appointed task. She will be unable fully to identify the valid law of her jurisdiction.[62]

The distinction between settled and unsettled law will also be preserved within a charter society. It is important to be clear that not all questions having to do with source-based rules and decisions are settled. 'That the existence and content of the law is a matter of social

[61] Perry, 'Judicial Obligation, Precedent and the Common Law', 228.

[62] Again, we are presupposing here that some of the rights recognized in charters are rights of political morality, and that they require moral understanding and argument to determine their nature and scope. Sustained argument for this claim is deferred till later.

fact which can be established without resort to moral argument does not presuppose nor does it entail the false proposition that all factual matters are non-controversial nor the equally false view that all moral propositions are controversial.'[63] Often questions of interpretation or proper jurisdiction, as well as questions having to do with conflicts in the law, will render an issue surrounding a source-based rule as indeterminate as the most intractable of moral dilemmas. It is equally important to be clear that not all moral questions are inherently unsettled. Some moral questions receive the same answers regardless of whatever remotely plausible moral theory, meta-ethical or normative, one happens to accept. In other words, some moral questions are quite easily answered and subject to (virtually) unanimous agreement. A statute purporting to enslave all Canadian citizens of Russian descent would undeniably flout sections 7 (life, liberty, and security of the person) and 15 (equality) of Canada's *Charter of Rights and Freedoms*. However one chose to interpret or understand these moral notions, one would be forced to accept that sections 7 and 15 are violated by such a monstrous statute. It is hardly an objection to the present argument that no provincial or federal legislature would ever attempt to enact such a law. The obvious fact that a perversity of this kind could never pass a charter challenge would be counted among the principal reasons why no such legislation would ever be contemplated.

It follows, then, that some questions of legal validity whose answers depend on moral considerations can (and do) fall squarely within the province of settled law. Thus we have no need to suppose that the existence of the latter is explicable only by supposing that the answers to some legal questions, i.e. those easily settled, are determined by source-based rules and decisions alone. To be sure, settled law in charter societies will not be equated with law whose existence and content are exclusively a function of social sources alone. But to consider this an objection would be to beg the question at hand in favour of exclusive positivism, to mistake an implication of that theory for a pre-theoretical datum to be explained.

Similar considerations apply to the distinction between the legal and moral evaluation of judicial decisions. Charters and rules of recognition typically do not incorporate all the possible moral grounds for objecting to judicial and legislative decisions. It follows that a valid decision which violates none of the moral

[63] Raz, 'Authority, Law and Morality', 9.

conditions specified in a charter or rule of recognition might yet be morally unacceptable, might yet betray gross moral insensitivity and so on. It is also worth noting that courts will often overturn legislation only if the offending legislation infringes a charter right to a significant degree. In *Regina v. Morgentaler, Smoling and Scott*, the Ontario Court of Appeal ruled that substantive review of legislation on grounds of fundamental justice 'should take place only in exceptional cases where there has been a marked departure from the norm of civil or criminal liability'.[64] In the view of the Court, any injustices to pregnant women arising from section 251 of the Canadian *Criminal Code* (which made it an offence to procure an abortion except under certain clearly defined conditions) were not 'exceptional' enough to warrant a judicial declaration of invalidity under section 7 of the *Charter*. The Supreme Court of Canada thought otherwise, ruling 5–2 that section 251 was sufficiently unfair to warrant such a declaration. As this example shows, a law which is perfectly valid according to a charter system's criteria for validity may nevertheless be subject to moral criticism. In some instances we might still wish to condemn the law morally even though one would be forced to acknowledge that the system's accepted moral criteria had been satisfied.

The difference of opinion between the two courts in *Morgentaler* reveals yet another factor of some importance for our main question. Moral conditions contained within constitutional charters of rights are no less subject to misinterpretation than pedigreed, source-based laws. Some of these misinterpretations may even betray moral insensitivity. This was certainly how the Ontario Court of Appeal's decision in *Morgentaler* was viewed by members of the 'pro-choice' movement. They thought the decision betrayed gross moral insensitivity to the needs of Canadian women and to the violation of autonomy which they believed section 251 represented. Many who objected to President Reagan's nomination of Judge Robert Bork for the American Supreme Court had related worries. They were concerned that his attempts to determine the existence and content of valid law within the United States would be based on misguided moral, political, and jurisprudential views on such matters as equality, liberty, and due process.[65] In both cases, then, there was ample room for the

---

[64] *R v. Morgentaler, Smoling and Scott* (1986), 2 OR (2d) 353 (CA, aff'd [1988] 1 SCR 30 (SCC).

[65] For an enlightening account of the jurisprudential significance of the Bork defeat, see Ronald Dworkin, 'From Bork to Kennedy'.

non-legal, moral evaluation of judicial decisions, despite the fact that Canada and the United States are charter societies.

Whether, in the end, Judge Bork and the Ontario Court of appeal were guilty of moral insensitivity, the point remains that moral provisions within charters and bills of rights are subject to 'insensitive' misinterpretation. They are also subject to attempts by judges to read into such documents their own peculiar visions of political morality. Some of these attempts can be motivated by jurisprudential views concerning the strategies of interpretation appropriate to the judicial role. For a variety of reasons, judges sometimes seek to follow very traditional lines in interpreting the moral provisions of charters. They may even seek to find, in the past legal history of a moral concept like equality or fundamental justice, a 'neutral' meaning which can be used to settle a substantive question of legal validity. They may seek to discover a technical meaning, or the original intent of the framers, things which they believe can be discovered and implemented independently of their own substantive moral views. Decisions based on such interpretive strategies may well be, and often are, criticized as legalistic, formalistic, overly technical, and above all else perhaps, insensitive to the real issues of political morality which a charter of rights requires judges to explore. All of this can be accounted for and explained without accepting exclusive positivism. As before, we have no need of that thesis to explain the aspects of legal practice to which Raz draws our attention. Exclusive positivism is not necessary if we are to find theoretical space for the moral evaluation of judging and judicial decisions.

9. THE ARGUMENT FROM FUNCTION

According to Raz, exclusive positivism is stronger than its competitors not only because it reflects and explicates our conception of law, i.e. because of its explanatory power, but also because there are 'sound reasons for adhering to that conception'.[66] The thesis 'captures and highlights a fundamental insight into the function of law', which is to designate in an accessible way the standards of behaviour required for social co-operation. A fundamental function of the law is to provide 'publicly ascertainable standards' by which

[66] *The Authority of Law*, 48.

individuals are held bound 'so that they cannot excuse non-conformity by challenging the justification of the standard'.[67] It is for this reason, Raz writes, that we 'differentiate between the courts' applying the law, i.e. those standards which are publicly ascertainable and binding beyond a moral argument open to litigants', and other activities of the courts whereby they develop and change the law relying on 'moral and other rational grounds'. In making this the sole test for identifying law, exclusive positivism 'identifies it as an example of a kind of human institution which is of decisive importance to the regulation of social life'.[68]

D's
conception
of posm.
+ its
weaknesses

Raz is not alone in viewing an appeal to the functions of law as a key plank in the positivist's platform. An argument based on just such an appeal is attributed to legal positivists by Dworkin in his critique of their views. According to Dworkin, all positivists ultimately conceive of law as a public institution whose primary, defining function is to provide 'a settled, public and dependable set of standards for private and official conduct'.[69] Owing to the fact that they view the law this way, Dworkin argues, positivists are unable to account for certain key facts about law as it is practised within modern legal systems. At the very least they give the wrong story or description of the relevant facts, which include frequent judicial appeals to inherently controversial principles of political morality as grounds for asserting the existence of legal rights. Judges do not, as positivism (supposedly) demands, always appeal to these principles as reasons for creating and developing new law. Sometimes reference is made in arguments purporting to establish pre-existing legal rights and duties. Yet given their views about the law's primary, defining function, Dworkin adds, positivists are barred from accepting this latter possibility and seek to establish an alternative account in their misguided theory of judicial discretion. Appeals to inherently controversial principles and concepts of political morality must, conceptually, be discretionary and creative, not declaratory of pre-existing law. Were the existence and content of law to depend on inherently controversial and contestable questions of political morality, then, according to positivism, the whole point of law would be lost. It would be like having a toaster into which no slices of bread could possibly fit. We would not in such a case have a bad toaster: we would not have a toaster at all. Similarly, were legal rights to depend on political morality, we would not have a

[67] Ibid. 50.   [68] Ibid. 50–2.   [69] *Taking Rights Seriously*, 347.

bad legal system: we would have nothing which we could reasonably recognize as law. The only way in which law can fulfil its defining function, according to positivists, is if its existence and content are fully determined by pure pedigree, by social sources. Thus the positivist's theory concerning the functions of law commits him to exclusive positivism. But, Dworkin argues, that thesis (and hence positivism itself which Dworkin identifies with exclusive positivism) is refuted by the above-mentioned judicial appeals to controversial principles and concepts of political morality.

We will consider Dworkin's Argument From Function more fully in Chapter 6. As will be seen, some of the objections to Raz's version of the argument apply equally well to Dworkin's rendition. Our concern in this chapter, however, is Raz's use of the argument to challenge inclusive positivism. There are a number of objections to consider, but first a few words of clarification are in order.

As it has been sketched above, the Argument From Function fails to distinguish adequately between what we might, following our earlier discussion in Chapter 2, call 'moral-evaluative' versus 'descriptive' ascriptions of function. Consider these examples. One can sensibly suggest that the function or purpose of offensive nuclear weapons is either to kill or to threaten to kill people, and do so without thereby suggesting or implying that this function should be served or that offensive nuclear weapons are good things to have. Similarly, one can suggest that the function of legally sanctioned apartheid is to maintain the existing racial power structures within South Africa without suggesting or implying one's commitment to this morally intolerable doctrine. And this is because such ascriptions of function are descriptive in nature. They offer explanations for why certain things exist in the forms that they do, and often articulate the purposes which other people believe they justifiably serve. But these articulations in no way commit the speaker to those very same evaluative beliefs. This is so whether the evaluative beliefs in question are prudential, moral, or something else entirely. Contrary to Dworkin's apparent suggestion, one can offer an enlightening account of how others view human creations like bombs, political regimes, and legal systems without oneself adopting the viewpoint of an engaged participant. Just as one can offer a descriptive theory of law which is not a moral theory of adjudication, one can offer an account of apartheid without seeking (unsuccessfully) to justify its existence and its use against South African Blacks.

We should not think, of course, that descriptive ascriptions of function are always evaluatively neutral or uncommitted. As we have seen in Chapter 2, 'evaluative' and 'moral' are not equivalent terms, and descriptive ascriptions are guided by various meta-theoretical evaluative considerations. As Raz says, 'any good theory of [law] is based on evaluative considerations in that its success is in highlighting important social structures and processes, and every judgment of importance is evaluative'.[70] Descriptive legal theory engages in evaluative judgment for such judgment is 'inescapable in trying to sort out what is central and significant in the common understanding of the concept of law'.[71] For Raz, then, even descriptive-explanatory ascriptions of function would have to be partly evaluative in so far as these depend on judgments about which features of law, e.g. the authoritative, public settling of social issues with a measure of finality and certainty, are worth highlighting. They depend on the meta-theoretical evaluative judgment that certain features of legal practice, if explained and related to other features of social life, will help us conceive and coherently deal with a wide variety of social and intellectual issues with which we are concerned as citizens and philosophers. They might even help us to deal with issues of practical moral concern. But as we saw earlier, we can ascertain moral significance and relevance without thereby committing ourselves to the view that what is seen as morally relevant is necessarily morally justified or a morally good thing.

Once we acknowledge the distinction between moral-evaluative, and meta-theoretical evaluative but descriptive, ascriptions of function, the question naturally arises: How are we to interpret the ascriptions of function made by Raz and attributed to positivists by Dworkin? We will discuss Dworkin's ascriptions later in Chapter 6, resting content at this stage with the simple observation that Dworkin seems clearly to characterize positivism as a theory revolving around moral-evaluative ascriptions of function to law. On his account, positivism is a 'conception' of law and, as we observed above, conceptions of law purport to provide legal practice with morally worthy purposes. As for Raz, it is clear that his ascriptions of purpose are descriptive in nature and based not on moral-evaluative ascriptions of worthy purposes but meta-theoretical judgments of importance. According to Raz, exclusive positivism is to be commended, not because it invests law with a morally worthy

[70] Raz, 'Authority, Law and Morality', 320.   [71] Ibid. 322.

purpose, but because it helps us in 'highlighting important social structures and processes', in 'trying to sort out what is central and significant in the common understanding of the concept of law'. What is central and significant might be thought to be so because of our moral concerns, but in Raz's view it is obviously not necessarily of moral worth.

We now come to our main question: Does Raz's Argument From Function, understood in light of the above, give us reason to reject inclusive positivism? There are at least two reasons for thinking that it does not.

First, the argument appears to exaggerate the extent to which defenders of positivism are or need be concerned to stress the law's capacity to resolve social issues in ways which render them invulnerable to the unsettling influences of moral argument. Positivists neither do nor need to conceive of the relative certainty, determinacy and predictability which law can sometimes create as its sole or overriding purpose. Nor need they conceive of this as a *sine qua non* of legality, as a purpose which must be fulfilled if law is to exist. Consider Hart, for example, who insisted that laws should sometimes remain flexible in their application. He argues, quite convincingly, that the possibility of blindly committing ourselves to undesirable results in unanticipated cases is often a sufficient reason for framing legal standards in loose, open-textured terms like 'fair', 'reasonable', and 'foreseeable'. We thereby allow considerable room for manœuvring when these standards come to be applied in actual cases. We no doubt pay a price in terms of predictability and the like when this route is taken. For instance, we might not ever be certain, until we come to court, whether our use of force to defend ourselves will be thought 'reasonable' in the circumstances. But clearly in this and many other cases, the absence of clearly defined boundaries is of no unreasonable hindrance to the effective working of law. Better that we be required to use our own judgment and be judged after the fact than to have clear, but in the circumstances, wholly unreasonable guidance from the law.[72]

[margin handwritten note: Hart not committed to absolute implementation of certainty, determinacy of law.]

Now if the avoidance of unreasonable, unintended results serves in the minds of positivists like Hart as a sufficient reason to recommend the deliberate framing of rules which are relatively indeterminate when they might have been far more determinate, then it is clear that not all defenders of positivism view certainty, predic-

[72] For Hart's detailed arguments on these matters, see *The Concept of Law*, ch. VII.

tability, and the related values as of total or overriding importance. That the set of public standards for private and public conduct should not commit us to highly unreasonable results, or that they should not violate certain fundamental rights of political morality enshrined in a constitutional charter, are aims, along with certainty and the like, which a positivist might, and indeed should, recognize as ends towards which law often does and ought to strive. A legal positivist need not support 'mechanical jurisprudence', nor need she be a 'rule fetishist'.

A second objection to Raz's Argument From Function is that its plausibility appears to rest on an exaggerated contrast between the certainty obtainable from rules whose validity is solely a function of pure pedigree or social source, and the supposed instability encountered if, e.g., the validity or content of a law is sometimes partly based on its conformity with standards of political morality. As noted earlier, it is a commonplace that pedigreed rules, whose validity and content are a function of non-moral factors, are nevertheless often subject to considerable controversy over their proper interpretation, indeed over the very procedures to be used in trying to understand them and what they imply for legal cases. Pedigreed rules sometimes conflict with one another and have 'gaps'. It is also beyond dispute that moral questions sometimes admit of easy resolution. It is no less difficult to determine whether 'a shell of a car with a rusty engine, no gear box, a roof like a sieve, and several tires missing'[73] is really a car for purposes of a rule prohibiting the parking of cars on city streets than it is to determine whether a law requiring all practising lawyers in British Columbia to be Canadian citizens amounts to the unreasonable infringement of a right against discrimination.[74] It follows that allowing some questions concerning the validity and content of putative laws to depend on factors in political morality need in no way conflict with the assertion that an important function of law is to serve as a dependable public standard. Questions of political morality do have considerable penumbras of uncertainty, but this fact should not be exaggerated. Neither should we ignore the fact that questions surrounding the existence and interpretation of pedigreed sources have similar penumbras.

[73] *Smart* v. *Allan & Another* [1963] 1 QB 291.

[74] *Andrews* v. *Law Society of BC*, [1986] 4 WWR 242 (BCCA). The decision was later upheld (3 to 2) by the Supreme Court of Canada in *Law Society of BC* v. *Andrews*, [1989] 56 DLR (4th) 1. This case will be discussed in some detail in the next chapter.

I conclude that Raz's Argument From Function provides no reason to reject inclusive positivism. Of course there is nothing to prevent a defender of positivism from going beyond the argument as stated to suggest that it would be a morally good thing were the existence and content of laws always to depend on pure pedigree. But as we saw earlier in this chapter, pursuing such a strategy amounts to offering a moral theory about what kinds of laws we should adopt. It is a theory not about the very nature of law itself but about which possibilities left open by the concept of law we should pursue as a matter of variable legal practice. Offering such an account amounts to making a moral recommendation, not proposing a descriptive-explanatory theory of law. But it is a descriptive-explanatory theory in support of which Raz's Argument From Function purports to be offered.

10. THE AUTHORITY ARGUMENT: AN OUTLINE

In a variety of his essays on the nature of law, Raz attempts to support exclusive positivism by showing that it alone is consistent with the authoritative nature of law. It is in these ingenious attempts that we find Raz's most powerful argument.

According to Raz it is in the very nature of legal systems that they necessarily claim justified authority over a population. This claim is, somewhat paradoxically, almost always false, but it must be made by those who represent the legal system, if what they represent is truly to count as law.[75] From this proposition Raz infers that a legal system must at least be the kind of thing which is logically capable of possessing authority.[76] It would be wildly implausible to suppose that all legal systems are conceptually confused about their capacity to command authority, claiming to have that capacity when they are the kinds of things, like trees and planets, of which this is logically impossible.

So law must at least be capable of bearing practical authority. It

---

[75] Raz is among those contemporary writers who think that there is seldom, if ever, ← NB an obligation to obey the law upon which a claim to legitimate authority might be based. See e.g. *The Authority of Law*, part IV and *The Morality of Freedom*, chs. 2–4. According to Raz, the proposition that there is even a prima-facie obligation to obey the law has been 'refuted by various writers in recent years'. (*The Authority of Law*, 97.)

[76] For details, see 'Authority, Law and Morality', 300–2.

must at least make sense to think that it could enjoy this normative property. From this proposition Raz infers that legal directives, e.g. laws and judicial decisions, must be intended to have, and be widely accepted as having, a special 'peremptory status'. Legal directives, as authoritative, serve a mediating role 'between people and the right reasons which apply to them'.[77] They 'must occupy, as all authority does, a mediating role between the precepts of morality and their application by people in their behaviour'.[78]

Since it is of the very essence of [an] alleged authority that it issues rulings which are binding regardless of any other justification, it follows that it must be possible to identify those rulings without engaging in a justificatory argument, i.e. as issuing from certain activities and interpreted in the light of publicly ascertainable standards not involving moral argument.[79]

In illustration of these important points about authority (as he understands it) Raz has us consider an arbitrator whose role is to issue an authoritative directive which is binding on the parties to a dispute. In this case the directive should be based on the reasons for action which apply to the disputants and over which the controversy has arisen. Raz calls these 'dependent reasons'. If the issue is which of two final offers is most fair to both the company and the union, then the arbitrator's role is to consider the dependent reasons of fairness in deciding who has the better case. It would be wrong for him to decide on reasons other than those dependent reasons which apply to the disputants.

Not only is the arbitrator's ruling to be based on the applicable dependent reasons for action of the disputants, it is intended to replace those reasons in the disputants' practical deliberations. If the arbitrator rules that offer A is fairer than offer B, then the ruling is meant to serve two functions. First, it is intended to be a (binding) reason for both parties to accept A. Second, its binding, authoritative nature means that it is also expected to exclude from their consideration all the disputed dependent reasons which applied before the ruling was issued. That A exceeds B in fairness is no longer a relevant (if contested) reason for their accepting A: that the arbitrator ruled that A is the fairer of the two is the only relevant

---

[77] Ibid. 299.   [78] Ibid. 310.   [79] *The Authority of Law*, 51–2.

consideration. The first is excluded by the second.[80] So the arbitrator's authoritative judgment concerning which side's case accords best with the balance of relevant dependent reasons is meant to replace those reasons in the disputants' practical deliberations. If the disputants do not reject the pre-empted dependent reasons for action, 'they defeat the very point and purpose of the arbitration'[81] *(challenge this reasoning)* which is 'to settle the dispute', to 'settle for them what to do'.[82]

According to Raz, legal directives are like the arbitrator's decision in so far as they too are meant to serve a mediating, exclusionary role. They are to settle what to do, in part by excluding contested dependent reasons for action. In other words, legal directives are also presented as being authoritative, as having a pre-emptive status. That a legal directive requires X is intended not only to be a good reason to do X, it is also meant to exclude all other (dependent) reasons we might have either to do X or to refrain from doing X. The fact of law is itself supposed to provide an exclusionary reason which makes irrelevant in our practical deliberations any other reasons we would otherwise have. From this supposedly defining feature of law, Raz attempts to derive support for exclusive positivism over its rivals, inclusive positivism and natural-law theory. But before we get to that stage in the argument a few cautionary comments are in order.

In saying that the very point of law and arbitration is to settle disputes by excluding controversial dependent reasons and replacing them with authoritative rulings, Raz is clearly making what we earlier termed a descriptive-explanatory ascription of function. He in no way intends us to view his ascriptions as moral-evaluative in nature, for example as part of a Dworkinian conception which seeks to understand law and its authority by trying to impose a morally worthy purpose on it. It is perfectly consistent with Raz's descriptive ascriptions of purpose to deny that the social institutions he discusses, i.e. law and arbitration, are morally worthy of our support or allegiance. Just as one can say that the morally pernicious purpose of apartheid is to sustain racial inequality, one can intelligently claim that the whole point of law, which is to issue

---

[80] H. L. A. Hart has recently defended the very similar view that law typically provides 'peremptory' reasons for action. See for example, 'Commands and Authoritative Legal Reasons', in *Essays on Bentham*, 243–68. For critical discussion of Hart's theory see Lyons, 'Comment'; MacCormick, 'Comment'; and Postema, 'The Normativity of Law' in Gavison (ed.), *Issues in Contemporary Legal Philosophy*.

[81] 'Authority, Law and Morality', 298.   [82] Ibid. 297.

a descriptive attribution of function =? not in any way endorsed by speaker.

Is it not a valuable function acc to Raz - ? whether n not it has moral value?

but this leaves out R's justification thesis, which explains (when) such peremptory exclusionary reasons for action can be justified...

126   INCLUSIVE V. EXCLUSIVE POSITIVISM

peremptory, exclusionary reasons for action, is something to be morally condemned. One might argue that moral autonomy is unjustifiably compromised unless we always consider, in relation to each and every one of our actions, what the relevant dependent moral reasons require, and that a social institution such as law, which necessarily requires that we exclude such factors from our deliberations, and is prepared to back its requirements with coercive force, cannot be tolerated. On the other hand, one might, in pursuance of a theory like Hobbes', argue that a virtually complete surrender of our capacity to judge dependent moral reasons is just what morality requires if the state of nature is to be avoided. There is nothing in Raz's descriptive-explanatory account of the point of law which is at all inconsistent with either of these two lines of argument.

There are some, however, who seem to view Raz's ascriptions of purpose as moral-evaluative in nature. David Lyons, for example, attributes to Raz the following argument, reminiscent of Bentham's Causal/Moral Argument for positivism. 'The social order is liable to break down if substantive moral arguments used in adjudication are counted in helping to interpret the law because that would encourage members of the society to break the law in hope of avoiding the legal consequences by challenging the justification of the standard.'[83] To this, Raz offers the following reply: 'I am happy to say that nothing remotely like this ever crossed my mind or my pen.'[84]

It is clear, then, that we are to understand Raz's ascriptions of function as descriptive in nature. From these ascriptions Raz attempts to derive support for exclusive positivism. The argument is complicated, but runs essentially as follows:

1. Legal directives (e.g. laws and judicial decisions) are necessarily capable of being authoritative.

2. For any directive, d, which is capable of being authoritative, it must be possible to identify d without relying on reasons or considerations on which d purports to adjudicate, i.e., without relying on any of the dependent reasons upon which the authority based his or her decision to issue d.

3. Therefore, for any law, l, it must be possible to identify l without relying on any of the reasons or considerations on which it purports to adjudicate.

[83] Lyons, 'Moral Aspects of Legal Theory', 245.
[84] 'Authority, Law and Morality', 324.

4. According to inclusive positivism (as well as the theories of Dworkin and natural lawyers) it is not always possible to identify a law, l, without relying on reasons or considerations which l purports to adjudicate upon and settle.

5. Therefore, inclusive positivism (as well as the theories of Dworkin and natural lawyers) must be rejected as inconsistent with the authoritative nature of law.

6. However, it is possible to identify 'the three common sources of law, legislation, judicial decisions, and custom' without relying on any reasons or considerations which these sources purport to adjudicate upon and settle.[85]

7. Exclusive positivism is alone in identifying the law exclusively with such sources.

8. Therefore, exclusive positivism is alone in being consistent with the authoritative nature of law.

We have already noted Raz's reasons for premise 1. It is in the very nature of law necessarily to claim authority, and therefore to be capable, conceptually, of possessing it. Thus legal directives must be capable of being authoritative, of being exclusionary reasons for action which do not compete with, but rather replace, citizens' dependent reasons for action. Premise 2 finds support in the arbitrator analogy. Raz asks us to consider our response to an arbitrator who, in identifying his decision to the disputants, says merely that he made the only correct, i.e. the most fair, decision. The phrase 'most fair decision' may in fact serve uniquely to identify the arbitrator's ruling, but as Raz rightly notes, it is a totally unhelpful description. If the disputants could agree on what is most fair, they would have had no need for the arbitrator in the first place. An arbitrator's decision serves its intended role only if it can be identified and understood independently of the disputed considerations it was meant to settle. The subjects of an authority 'can benefit by its decisions only if they can establish their existence and content in ways which do not depend on raising the very same issues which the authority is there to settle'.[86]

Premise 4 relies on the fact that inclusive positivism allows for the possibility that moral argument might sometimes be required to determine the existence, and perhaps even the content or meaning, of

[85] Ibid. 305.   [86] Ibid. 304.

valid laws. Suppose, for instance, that a tax law has been enacted partly for reasons of justice and equality. Perhaps the law establishes a progressive tax rate which is believed to further equality by requiring more from those more able to pay. Were it possible to challenge the validity of such legislation on the premise that it violates a constitutional right to equality, then in determining whether the legislation is valid law, we might be forced to entertain questions of justice and equality in taxation. But these are the very same considerations the statute was meant to settle. It could not effectively serve as an authoritative directive which settles, to a degree at least, the relevant issues of justice and equality.

Premises 6 and 7 are key elements in Raz's Authority Argument. Simple facts concerning its enactment, declaration, or existence as a customary social standard, in conjunction with a morally neutral understanding of the meaning of its terms, are sufficient, on this account, for determining the scope and effect of any legal directive. In explanation Raz notes that income tax laws are intended to settle 'what is the fair contribution of public funds to be borne out of income'. In order to determine the existence and content of such laws, all one need do is 'establish that the enactment took place, and what it says. To do this one needs little more than knowledge of English (including technical legal English), and of the events which took place in Parliament on a few occasions. One need not come to any view on the fair contribution to public funds.'[87]

This feature of legal directives allows them, in Raz's view, to serve their crucial mediating role. Unlike, e.g., Dworkinian legal principles, whose existence, content, and force cannot be established without the aid of a contestable Herculean theory of political morality, Raz's legal sources have the capacity to replace, pre-empt and exclude political morality altogether in the practical deliberations of citizens.[88] All one needs to know about a statute, for example, is 'what it says' and that it was duly enacted. Thus, exclusive positivism, which is alone in identifying the law exclusively with such directives, is alone in being fully compatible with law's authoritative, mediating role in our practical deliberations. It alone is fully compatible with what Raz's descriptive-explanatory theory of law identifies as 'the very point and purpose' of a social institution

---

[87] Ibid. 306.
[88] For Raz's critique of Dworkin on just this point, see ibid. 305–10.

which claims to provide authoritative guidance to all citizens within
its scope.

This is an ingenious argument which penetrates to the very heart of
philosophical controversies concerning the nature of law. It rests
upon simple observations concerning the claims of law together
with a sophisticated theory of practical reasoning as involving
reasons of different kinds: dependent and exclusionary. It therefore
deserves our careful consideration. As with all the arguments considered above, however, our final verdict will be that the Authority
Argument neither threatens inclusive positivism nor provides conclusive support for exclusive positivism. It is undeniable that law is
in some sense necessarily authoritative, but Raz's analysis of what
this involves seems to capture only one non-essential feature of
authoritative guidance. That the law is necessarily authoritative
does not imply that the existence and content of all legal directives
can and must be established independently of dependent moral
considerations, that moral considerations must be excluded entirely
from determinations of law. What may lead one to think it does is
the misleading analogy between law and Raz's arbitrator. The two
are significantly different in relevant respects.

11. THE AUTHORITY ARGUMENT: A CRITIQUE

Let us begin our examination of Raz's argument by noting that
authorities come in a variety of forms. For example, there are practical authorities, such as judges, legislators, and arbitrators, whose
decisions (not the threat of sanctions should those decisions be disregarded) seem capable of altering reasons for action. That the legislators of a reasonably just and established legal order enacted a law
seems to offer at least a reason for doing what that law requires.
Whether it provides an exclusionary reason is of course another
question entirely, but it seems undeniable that authoritative utterances can have significant effects on our reasons for action. No
positivist would wish to deny this.

Within the category of practical authority, there are a number of
distinctions to be drawn. Raz himself notes the difference between
legislative authorities, such as Members of Parliament or Congress,
and adjudicative authorities, such as arbitrators and judges.[89] The

[89] See ibid. 298.

role of the latter, as we have seen, is supposed to be to render decisions which settle disputed questions, to issue authoritative directives which replace, as reasons for action, the contested dependent reasons of the disputants. Legislative authorities, on the other hand, might be thought to serve a slightly different role. Raz considers, but ultimately rejects, the idea that legislative authorities, unlike their adjudicative counterparts, introduce new, non-dependent reasons for action. Legislation is justified, he argues, only in so far as it is based upon (even though it pre-empts) some of the existing dependent reasons for action of citizens. Consider an Act of Parliament imposing a parental duty to maintain children. As Raz notes, parents have such a (moral) duty independently of any such Act. And, as he argues convincingly later,[90] legislative acts are justified only to the extent that they reflect, and help to enforce, reinforce, and perhaps clarify, define and co-ordinate, the pre-existing, dependent reasons for action of citizens.

There are also, of course, theoretical authorities whose pronouncements can affect our reasons for belief. That Albert Einstein believed a certain claim in theoretical physics is a reason for me to believe that claim too, even though I am virtually ignorant of his grounds for the claim. As Hart says in his discussion of the peremptory nature of authoritative utterances, the statements of theoretical authorities do not create obligations to believe, but the reasons for belief constituted by those statements are in a sense peremptory because they are 'accepted as . . . reasons for belief without independent investigation or assessment of the truth of what is stated'.[91]

It should be noted that there is nothing in Hart's account, nor is there anything, I believe, in the view proposed by Raz, to suggest that authoritative reasons for belief are necessarily exclusionary. And surely this is as it should be. It is easy to imagine cases where an established authority's belief that p is true provides me with what Hart calls a 'content-independent' reason for belief which is nevertheless not exclusionary. If I am a reasonably competent physicist, there is nothing to prevent me from counting Albert Einstein's belief as a content-independent reason, b, for believing some proposition of theoretical physics, p. Yet I can accept b without thereby rejecting q, r, and s, which bear directly on the truth of p, as additional good reasons for believing p. Einstein's authority counts, in such a case,

90 See ibid 308 ff.
91 'Commands and Authoritative Legal Reasons' in *Essays on Bentham*, 261.

but not exclusively. Of course if (a) I have some of my own grounds for thinking that *p* might be true; (b) those grounds are highly suspect because I really know almost nothing about physics; but (c) I am, for some reason, required to decide between *p* and not-*p*, then I might be warranted in treating Einstein's belief in *p* as exclusionary, as not merely outweighing but rendering irrelevant whatever feeble grounds I myself might have for believing (or disbelieving) *p*. But this seems to be a special case, and one which, if I am lucky, will not often arise. More often than not, a theoretical authority's belief will provide me with some reason to believe *p* which I can add to the reasons which I have for thinking that *p* is true, where these latter reasons are not merely content-independent reasons for believing *p* but reasons for *p* itself. The greater the authority's expertise within the area the greater is the weight I am justified in attributing to the reason his belief provides. And the greater the degree of my incompetence, the more justified I am in relying on that weighted reason for belief. But accepting the authority of an expert's belief does not mean that I must treat myself as completely incompetent. As we shall see shortly, an analogous point needs to be made within the sphere of practical authority. There is, as we shall see, no reason to think that accepting the practical authority of law entails, necessarily, that we exclude all other dependent reasons, moral or otherwise. It might mean merely that we should ascribe weights to these reasons that are different from the weights they would have independently of the authority's existence.

In any case, it is plausible to say that all practical authorities are alike in so far as they both should and normally do issue authoritative directives based on the pre-existing, dependent reasons applying to their subjects. Likewise, it is reasonable to say that, sometimes, the directives of practical authorities must be accepted as pre-empting (at least some) dependent reasons. As we shall see in a moment, it is also highly plausible to say that the directives of practical authorities sometimes do not exclude dependent reasons but rather provide grounds for assigning those reasons greater or lesser weight than they would ordinarily carry in our practical deliberations. What is not plausible, however, is to infer from any of this that the directives of practical authorities must always be identifiable independently of all dependent reasons, moral or otherwise. More to the point, it is unacceptable to infer from the fact that valid legal directives are like arbitrators' rulings in being

[handwritten margin note: [slightly inaccurate applic y dear f dependent reasons + exclusionary reasons.]]

authoritative that it must be possible to identify their existence and content independently of all moral arguments. It is here that Raz's analysis may be led astray by his arbitrator analogy. There are some important features of arbitration which may not be shared by law.

particular features of arbitration

First, the necessity of being able to identify and understand an arbitrator's ruling without recourse to the relevant dependent reasons is a feature of arbitration only because the principal function of this practice is usually to settle a dispute which cannot otherwise be resolved. It is not merely a desirable feature of arbitration that it result in the settling of a dispute. This seems to be one of its defining features. Arbitration is a social practice which cannot be understood independently of recognizing that this is what it is primarily for. Of course, one can understand what arbitration is for, and thereby ascribe a function or purpose to it, without approving of it or thinking it morally worthy. This is because we are not forced to agree with Dworkin that understanding a social practice requires the search for, and normally the discovery of, morally worthy purposes.

So the normal function of arbitration is to settle disputes. But it is not clear that this is necessarily the only point of the exercise. Suppose that the purpose to be served by resorting to arbitration were different, or more plausibly, that it were accompanied by other purposes or goals. There might then not be the necessity that a decision be identifiable without recourse to any dependent reasons. I can imagine an arbitrator who wishes his decision partly to serve an educative function as well. He may wish the parties to see that they really do have the ability and means to discover fair solutions themselves, thereby encouraging them to try harder in future rounds of negotiation. Or perhaps he thinks that agreements originating from the parties themselves tend to be more stable and long-lasting, being based on collegiality rather than the imposition of a thoroughly authoritative solution. It is not uncommon for arbitrators to think this way: they are often prepared to suspend proceedings temporarily thereby providing the disputants with an additional opportunity to settle the issues themselves. But in so doing the arbitration, and thus the power to issue an authoritative ruling, is itself suspended. Of more interest and relevance would be a case where the arbitrator did exercise his power by issuing a decision, but it was a decision whose interpretation required partial appeal to some of the contested dependent reasons. In such a case the arbitrator would provide only partial guidance, still leaving the disputants with a bit of a puzzle concerning the disputed dependent reasons. But the puzzle would be one whose pieces were fewer in number and, it would be hoped, easier to deal with and resolve amicably. In describing his (perhaps only temporary) decision in such a case, the arbitrator would presumably have to say more than that his decision was the fair one, but his description might nevertheless require limited appeal to dependent reasons. He could narrow the range of acceptable options and the reasons upon the basis of which one of these options is to be selected by the parties.[92]

A second important point about arbitration is that the reasons further recourse to which would normally defeat its purpose (i.e. to settle the dispute) are the contested reasons the arbitrator's directive is meant to replace if he is forced to issue an authoritative directive. Should other possible reasons for action enter into the identification or interpretation of the directive, then it is not so clear that the normal purpose would necessarily be thwarted. There could, for instance, be agreement among all parties on some moral principle necessary for interpreting the arbitrator's directive. Perhaps the dispute was not over what this principle requires but concerned whether that principle is the only relevant one. In such a case, the necessity to appeal to the moral reason articulated by the principle in order to understand the directive would be of no hindrance whatsoever.

So how do these two points bear on the soundness of Raz's Authority Argument? First, it should now be clear that inclusive positivism is falsified by the analogy between law and arbitration only if the sole or overriding function of law is to settle practical controversies about dependent reasons, or if this is a function non-satisfaction of which to a significant degree results in something other than law.[93] Only if (a) the very, or at least an essential, point of law is

---

[92] It might be objected that what I have described is not really arbitration as we currently understand that practice. As it is now understood, the whole point of arbitration is to settle issues conclusively by the issuing of exclusionary rulings. To this I would make the following reply. Call it what you will, arbitration or something else, say 'rationation', the practice described in the text seems possible and workable in some contexts. More importantly, it allows for authoritative guidance which is not exclusionary in nature. My point would then be that law is not necessarily like arbitration, as opposed to rationation, owing to its authoritative nature. It is consistent with the authoritative nature of law that it be like rationation in which partial, though not exclusionary, authoritative guidance is the norm.

[93] We should understand the phrase 'practical controversies' in a very broad sense, as including such things as social co-ordination problems like traffic management.

that it should conclusively and authoritatively settle disputes about dependent reasons; and (b) this point would be completely frustrated were it ever necessary to consider dependent moral reasons for action in identifying and interpreting valid laws; do we get (c) any reason at all for preferring exclusive to inclusive positivism. But why should we accept (a) and (b)?

Take (a) first. Why should we believe that the authoritative settling of disputes about dependent reasons by way of exclusionary directives is the law's only defining function, or a function of essential importance? As we saw earlier in our discussion of the Argument From Function, there is little reason to accept this claim, and certainly no reason to saddle all defenders of positivism with it. Consider once again charter societies which have incorporated into their rules of recognition, or the conditions for validity recognized within their rules of recognition, certain rights of political morality which serve as criteria for valid laws and valid interpretations of laws. Such societies seem obviously to accept, as values which sometimes compete with the resolving or settling of practical disputes about dependent reasons, the non-violation of important moral rights by public institutions and authorities. It is accepted that directives purporting to be authoritative, i.e., purporting to be valid law, may none the less be non-authoritative, non-binding, invalid, all because they violate constitutionally sanctioned rights of political morality. Rules deriving from duly enacted legislation, as well as decisions made by judges in legal cases, may in fact be 'no law at all' if they violate certain dependent moral reasons for action recognized in a charter or rule of recognition. Within such societies, some degree of 'unsettledness' is wisely accepted as a reasonable price to pay for the sake of other values considered to be of at least comparable importance. Of course it is not always possible within charter societies to determine the existence and content of valid legal directives by establishing only their social sources and 'what they say'. It is sometimes necessary for lawyers and judges to engage in substantive moral argument. Indeed, in at least some charter societies it is true that, for any purportedly valid legal directive whatsoever, dependent moral reasons will bear on its validity, even if these reasons never figure explicitly in a case involving that directive. This is because in such societies a directive is legally valid only if it violates none of the rights of political morality included within the charter. And to establish that fact would require one to consider dependent moral reasons and arguments concerning such reasons.[94]

But now an important question arises. Do the above considerations mean that 'legal' directives within charter societies are not really law at all because they lack the capacity to be authoritative, a capacity which Raz correctly identifies as a defining feature of law? Not in the slightest. It is tempting simply to say at this point that it would be wildly implausible to charge members of charter societies with conceptual confusion about the nature of their so-called legal systems, to claim that they foolishly believe that moral rights serve as conditions for legal validity within their systems of law when it is impossible for this to be so, or that they confusedly believe that their charter systems are legal systems when in fact they cannot be. But we needn't rest content with this simple reply. A more forceful response is to establish the possibility of explaining legal authority without accepting the requirement that legal directives be authoritative in Raz's very strong, exclusionary sense of that term. It is to this task that we now turn.

Consider the wide variety of things which can be meant in referring to the law as authoritative. What is normally meant is that legal officials have certain institutionally defined rights, liberties, immunities, and powers not enjoyed by those who lack their authority. This, among other things, is what we mean in calling them legal officials. Judges and policemen, for example, may forcibly confine people, coerce them into paying compensation to others, and so on. These same actions, were they undertaken by people lacking the proper authority, would clearly be wrong. To call the law authoritative also means, as Raz correctly observes, that the decisions and directives of people we call legal officials have a certain status not shared by similar, non-authoritative decisions of private

---

[94] Canada seems to be a society in which the validity of all laws is subject to moral conditions. Part VII, section 52, subsection 1 of the *Canada Act*, of which the *Charter* is a principal component, specifies that 'The Constitution of Canada is the supreme law of Canada, and any law that is inconsistent with the provisions of the Constitution is, to the extent of the inconsistency, of no force or effect.' Any Canadian legislation, or judicial or administrative decision, which violates the rights of political morality to which legal recognition is given in the *Charter* is legally invalid. In other words, a condition of validity for any and all Canadian Acts, or judicial or administrative decisions, seems to be that they do not violate certain rights of political morality. It would appear that it is never possible in Canada to establish the validity of a law (or decision) by ascertaining simply that it was enacted (or made) and 'what it says'.

citizens. Regardless of what he might have thought, Richard
Nixon's opinion concerning the state of American law governing
executive privilege lacked the status of a Supreme Court judgment.
The latter is always binding, legally, whereas Nixon's judgment,
regardless of its competence, was a non-authoritative opinion with
no legal-adjudicative consequences. Lower courts in the United
States must always somehow reconcile their judgments with those of
the Supreme Court even if they disagree with them. Lower courts
have always been entitled to ignore Richard Nixon's opinions even
if they think them right. His opinions lack the authority of Supreme
Court judgments.

To say that lower courts are required to reconcile their decisions
with the authoritative judgments of higher courts is not, of course, to
suggest that they must always follow those judgments slavishly. As
we saw in Chapter 3, the degree and type of deference required may
depend on factors like the level of court(s) in question and the
institutional force that a higher court's judgment has in the particular type of case with which the lower court is faced. But whatever the
force of the precedent, the court's judgment must always in some
way be reconciled with it. At the very least the court will have to
distinguish the authoritative judgment by citing some relevant
difference between it and the instant case. The mere fact that the
court must distinguish the earlier judgment, and not ignore it
entirely, means that that judgment has some degree of authority.

There is no reason to think that authority is an all or nothing
exclusionary matter. As Dworkin observes, 'Raz thinks law cannot
be authoritative unless those who accept it never use their own con-
victions to decide what it requires, even in [a] partial way. But why
must law be blind authority rather than authoritative in the more
relaxed way other conceptions [of law] assume?'[95] One such conception is sketched by Stephen Perry who offers an extensive critique of
Raz's claim that law provides exclusionary reasons for action.
According to Perry, Raz's account is 'clearly too narrow'.[96] On his
alternative account of authority, an authoritative utterance provides
a 'second-order reason [which is] a reason for treating a first-order
reason as having a greater or lesser weight than it would ordinarily
receive, so that an exclusionary reason is simply the special case
where one or more first-order reasons are treated as having zero

---

[95] Law's Empire, 429.
[96] 'Judicial Obligation, Precedent and the Common Law', 223.

weight.'[97] Perry applies this alternative view of second-order reasons to the practices of common-law legal systems and concludes that neither precedents nor statutes are treated as providing exclusionary reasons. Rather they express second-order reasons to weigh certain first-order reasons, described in the relevant case reports and statute books, more heavily than normal, i.e. more heavily than in other contexts in which authority is not present and reasons compete equally on their respective merits alone. Regarding precedents, for instance, Perry notes that common-law courts do not look upon a previous decision as precluding all consideration of the reasons for it. Rather, a court will consider itself bound by the authority of the precedent unless it is 'satisfied that the collective weight of the reasons supporting the opposite result is of greater strength, to some specified degree, than the weight which would otherwise be required to reach that result on the ordinary balance of reasons'.[98] A court considers itself bound by authority to the extent that it will follow the precedent 'unless it is convinced that there is a strong reason for holding otherwise'.[99] Perry calls this 'the strong Burkean conception' of precedent and argues convincingly that it accords better than Raz's exclusionary account with the actual practices of Anglo-American judges. It also accords better with our earlier observations concerning the variety of institutional forces to which judges may be subject when confronting 'binding' decisions and laws. In our terminology, Raz is wrong to identify the institutional force of law with one particular kind of force: exclusionary. As Perry observes, this is but a 'special case where one or more first-order [dependent] reasons are treated as having zero weight'.[100] The institutional force properly ascribed to an earlier decision will generally be a function of several factors, including its age, the position within the judicial hierarchy of the courts which set and have followed the precedent, the position of the court contemplating departure, and the number of times the precedent has been cited and relied upon to decide earlier cases. Where the threshold of force is set will also vary from one area of the law to the next. '[B]eing able to predict and rely upon what a court is likely to decide is undoubtedly more important in contract law than in negligence law.'[101]

So recognizing the authority of judicial decisions does not require

---

[97] Ibid.   [98] Ibid. 222.   [99] Ibid.
[100] Ibid. 223.   [101] Ibid. 241–2.

Summary conceiving of them as providing exclusionary reasons for action. It is enough that they be thought of as affecting the weight of other reasons for action, unlike non-authoritative decisions which lack this normative property. Similar things can be said about legislative directives. The judgments of Congress or Parliament possess a special status not enjoyed by private decisions or the decisions of public figures with no legislative authority. What this means, in part, is that judicial decisions must somehow be reconciled with legislation. But once again one must be careful in interpreting this claim. To recognize the authority of Parliament is not necessarily to accept that its decisions completely pre-empt and replace all of the reasons upon which they are based and upon which a judge might base her decision. As Raz himself notes, 'On many issues statutes represent but the first step towards [this] stage.'[102] An example: legislation may require that employers provide laid-off workers with fair severance pay but leave it to the parties concerned, or the courts should the issue ever come before them, to determine what in a particular case is in fact fair. It is sometimes 'better to settle for ... laws ... that fix the framework only and leave the courts room to apply deliberative [i.e. dependent] reasons within that frame-work'.[103] The statute is authoritative, then, even though it fails to pre-empt and replace all dependent reasons.

So even Raz himself seems to agree that the authority of legal officials and their directives can intelligibly be acknowledged with-out supposing that this bars all appeal to dependent reasons. And this is because, among other things, legal officials often issue authoritative directives which fail in advance to settle all disputes on a certain range of issues, like fair severance pay. Raz would no doubt insist, however, that by not settling such disputes completely and in advance by way of fully exclusionary, authoritative direct-ives, legislators fail to settle them fully by law. In fixing only a legally binding framework which must be filled out by appeal to dependent moral reasons, legislators grant judges discretion to step beyond the law and create new legal directives within the frame-work provided, by appealing directly to dependent moral reasons. But unless we accept that a law, for reasons dismissed earlier, can extend only so far as it can be identified and applied independently of all moral reasons, we have no reason to accept this picture. We have no reason to suppose, for example, that in a case where it is

[102] Raz, 'The Problem About the Nature of Law', 216.   [103] Ibid.

beyond dispute that a certain rate of severance pay is unfair, the law, partly via our moral understanding of fairness, and partly by 'what it says' explicitly, does determine that the rate of pay is illegal-because-unfair. All this despite the fact that dependent reasons of fairness must be appealed to, or are presupposed, in reaching this legal conclusion.

Let us now turn to the second point noted above concerning the nature and usefulness of arbitration. We agreed that if the sole or an essential purpose of arbitration is to settle a dispute conclusively, then a decision whose identification or interpretation requires appeal to disputed dependent reasons will not be particularly useful. But we also noted that it fails to follow that it must always be possible to identify and interpret an arbitrator's decision without recourse to any moral arguments or principles. The set of all moral reasons is not identical with the set of dependent reasons under dispute in an arbitration case. It might, for example, be clear to all concerned what the just solution is, and only unclear whether the agreed facts of justice are sufficient to outweigh, say, reasons of inefficiency, loyalty or perhaps even compassion. A decision which makes reference to justice, and whose interpretation therefore requires appeal to agreed moral reasons of justice, can therefore be quite serviceable.

This last point is crucial for our investigation of the respective merits of inclusive and exclusive positivism. Consider again a charter system with constitutionally entrenched moral rights serving as criteria for valid law. These moral rights need have no relation whatsoever to the disputed dependent reasons which a law attempts (partly) to settle. The validity of a piece of legislation, for example, might be challenged on moral grounds which are unrelated to the dependent reasons the statute sets out to settle. *Andrews* v. *Law Society of BC*[104] concerned a regulation of the British Columbia Law Society requiring Canadian citizenship for the practice of law. Whatever the dependent reasons for this statute might have been, they were not the reasons of moral equality upon which the Court's declaration of invalidity was based. It follows that inclusive positivism, which allows such moral criteria for valid law, cannot be refuted on the simple ground that it would make the identification of a valid legal directive dependent on 'the considerations the weight and outcome of which it was meant to settle'.[105]

[104] [1986] 4 WWR 242 (BCCA).   [105] 'Authority, Law and Morality', 304.

I conclude, then, that there is nothing in the authoritative nature of law which is inconsistent with inclusive positivism. Raz's arbitrator analogy and the Authority Argument of which it is a crucial part provide us with no good reason to reject that thesis in favour of exclusive positivism.

12. TAKING STOCK

In the course of this chapter we have examined a number of arguments which either have been or could be offered in support of exclusive positivism against its rival, inclusive positivism. In each case the argument was found to be wanting. Some, such as the Arguments From Intellectual Clarity and Bias, beg the very issues in question while others, such as the Argument From Function and the Institutional Connection Argument, are consistent with inclusive positivism. Of course we cannot dismiss the possibility of discovering further arguments which would succeed in demonstrating the superior status of exclusive positivism. But until such time as this possibility is realized we seem entitled to conclude that inclusive positivism is at the very least a viable theory of law.

It would be a mistake, however, to think that our results have been purely negative and that we have failed to uncover positive support for inclusive positivism. In fact several virtues have come to light. One virtue is that the theory, unlike Raz's exclusive alternative, seems better able to explain what appears to be an obvious fact: that moral tests for the validity and content of laws have been explicitly recognized within some legal systems. As Hart notes, 'In some systems [of law] as in the United States [and we may now add Canada with its new *Charter of Rights and Freedoms*], the ultimate criteria of legal validity explicitly incorporate principles of justice or substantive moral values.'[106] As will be argued in greater detail in the next chapter, inclusive positivism would seem to permit us to view these accepted tests in the natural, and I believe generally accepted, way: as explicitly moral tests for law which require judges and lawyers to engage in substantive moral argument when deciding questions of legal validity. Our conclusion will be that inclusive positivism allows us to escape a distorted picture of the way in which

[106] *The Concept of Law*, 199.

charters are understood, interpreted, and applied. We will also see that inclusive positivism allows us to recognize the possible role of moral considerations in determinations of law without denying that laws and criteria for laws must have the appropriate institutional connections. Unlike traditional natural-law theory which denies the necessity of such connections, inclusive positivism places them front and centre by insisting that moral reasons are sometimes relevant but only to the extent that the legal system recognizes them as such. In this way inclusive positivism combines the virtues of exclusive positivism with those of rival views like Dworkin's integrity theory. Unlike Dworkin, who appears to insist that the law, because of what it is, necessarily includes pedigreed sources of law together with moral factors of various kinds, inclusive positivism accepts this as one possibility among others. In this breadth of scope we perhaps find its greatest virtue.

5

CHARTER CHALLENGES

1. INTRODUCTION

In the preceding chapter I argued that inclusive positivism, which acknowledges the conceptual possibility of legally recognized or pedigreed moral tests for the validity and content of law is at the very least on a par theoretically with exclusive positivism which denies this possibility. At various stages in the argument reference was made to challenges to legal validity made under documents like the Canadian *Charter of Rights and Freedoms*. It was suggested that these charter challenges seem typically to involve substantive moral arguments purporting to undermine legal validity. I suggested that it is mistaken to view such challenges as anything but attempts to demonstrate either that pedigreed criteria for legal validity have not been satisfied, and that what seems to be valid law is in fact no law at all, or that a law must be understood or interpreted in such a way that it does not infringe upon a pedigreed moral right protected by the Charter. In the former instance, morality figures in arguments purporting to challenge the existence of valid law. In the latter case, it figures in arguments intended to establish the content of valid law, the law contained within the instruments (for example, the statutes or precedents) employed for its expression. If this view of charter challenges is correct, then it follows that the existence and content of law does sometimes depend on moral factors. It further follows that any version of positivism which accepts this as a theoretical possibility is, on that account alone, superior to any version which does not.

The primary objective of the present chapter is to develop further the suggestion that inclusive positivism is a better theory of law than exclusive positivism because it offers a better theoretical account of charter challenges. In pursuing this objective, I shall be discharging a debt incurred earlier when the reader was asked simply to assume that moral arguments do figure sometimes in charter challenges, and that such arguments do sometimes seek, successfully, to challenge (or establish) the existence or content of valid laws. It is now time to argue for these two assumptions. I shall do so by considering the Canadian Charter and how it functions within the Canadian legal system. Although I shall offer no direct support for this claim, it is clear that other charters or bills of rights, e.g. the American *Bill of Rights*, function in similar ways within their respective legal systems.

2. MORAL ARGUMENTS?

The conclusion we wish to establish is that inclusive positivism is preferable to Raz's exclusive version because it provides a better account of the moral argument which takes place in charter challenges. Our first order of business, then, must be to substantiate the premise that moral argument does indeed sometimes take place in such cases. Without this premise, the argument cannot even begin to get off the ground.

It might seem abundantly obvious that charter challenges in Canada often rely on moral arguments. After all, in listing its fundamental rights and freedoms, the authors of the Canadian Charter used terminology which figures prominently in virtually all modern moral theories. The right to equality (section 15), for instance, is a paradigm moral right. So too is the right not to be deprived of liberty, except in accordance with fundamental justice (section 7). Liberty and fundamental justice quite clearly bear moral meanings. But the mere use of terms which admit of moral meanings is, in itself, clearly insufficient to establish our premise. From the fact that two normative systems share a certain common vocabulary it fails to follow that their common terms have identical referents or that they have identical or even similar meanings. This is clearly true in the case of law and morals. The interpretation given to a legal term is often quite different from the corresponding moral term. One who plea bargains a murder charge down to manslaughter may yet be morally condemned as a murderer. In the moral sense he remains a murderer, even though, legally, that label cannot be ascribed to him. What is legally judged to be fair business practice may quite properly be assessed as morally unfair, and so on. So in and of itself the mere use of terminology which bears moral meanings in some contexts is of little argumentative force.

Yet perhaps it is not the terminology which is of importance, but rather the way that the judiciary has come to approach and understand it. It is fairly clear that most Canadian judges have been willing to adopt a non-legalistic, broad, purposive, or liberal approach to the Charter. In *Big M Drug Mart*, for instance, then Chief Justice of the Canadian Supreme Court, Brian Dickson, declared that the proper approach to interpreting the rights and freedoms listed in the Charter is a 'purposive' one. The meaning of a right or freedom, he noted, is to be determined by 'an analysis of the purpose of such a guarantee; it [is] to be understood . . . in the light of the interest it was meant to protect'. In explaining himself further, Dickson said that the interpretation of a Charter provision must be 'a generous rather than a legalistic one'. At the same time, he noted, it is crucial that courts do not 'overshoot the actual purpose of the right or freedom in question' but respect the fact that the Charter was 'not enacted in a vacuum . . . and must therefore . . . be placed in its proper linguistic, philosophic and historical contexts'.[1]

According to Dickson, interpretation of the Canadian Charter should be generous rather than legalistic, aimed at fulfilling the interests that document was meant to protect. These interests are to play a far more central role in its application than is typically the case with many other types of legal standards and instruments, for example, tax law or administrative regulations. It is this fact, no doubt, which led one legal commentator to remark that the 'Charter imposes substantive new responsibilities on the courts. It requires not only that they deal with new issues but that they reconsider traditional methods of reasoning.'[2] They must eschew a narrow, legalistic approach to Charter adjudication in favour of a much broader one which more firmly focuses on the interests or objects the Charter sets out to protect. Of course, these objects are often none other than those fundamental rights and freedoms of political morality to which the Canadian Charter gives legal recognition and protection.

It is reasonably clear, then, that the Supreme Court of Canada believes that the interpretation of the Charter should be governed by

[1] *R* v. *Big M Drug Mart* [1985] 1 SCR 295 at 344.

[2] W. W. Black, 'Canadian Charter of Rights and Freedoms', in J. E. Magnet (ed.), *Constitutional Law of Canada*, 2.

[handwritten margin note at top: objects? rights + freedoms? or purposes + interests?]

the objects or interests it was meant to protect. If so, then it is also reasonably clear that moral argument will often figure in charter challenges. If one must interpret the Charter in light of its objects, and those objects are often rights and freedoms of political morality, then it follows that one cannot determine what the Charter means, and thus the conditions upon legal validity which it imposes, without determining the nature and extent of the rights of political morality it seeks to guarantee. Yet one cannot do this without engaging, to some degree at least, in substantive moral argument. This argument will of course be, as Dickson said, sensitive to the linguistic, philosophic, and historical context in which the Charter and its rights and freedoms are to be placed. This however is not an objection to the point being urged here, since such sensitivity is precisely what one would expect of responsible reflection concerning moral rights and freedoms, including those enjoying legal recognition. It would be a serious mistake to think that reasoning about moral rights and freedoms, whether private or public, can take place independently of contextual considerations. What one is entitled to expect from government, other public institutions, and indeed from other private citizens, depends in large part on shared understandings, expectations, historical circumstances, and so on—in short, on the linguistic, philosophic, and historical context in which all moral arguments must take place. It seems to have been some such point as this to which La Forest J, was alluding when he noted that 'what is important is that the Charter provisions seem ... to be deeply anchored in previous Canadian experience. By this, I do not mean that we must remain prisoners of the past. I do mean, however, that in continuing to grope for the best balance in specific contexts, we must begin with our own experience.'[3]

[handwritten margin note: Why does not this recast the enterprise somewhat as history of Cdn values?]

There is a current trend within modern moral philosophy which stresses the essential role of local custom, history, and practice in actually defining the standards of moral deliberation appropriate for use within a community. On this view, 'rationalistic' attempts to discover universal, moral principles valid for all times and places, much as one finds in classical natural-law theory, are thoroughly misguided. Moral standards are in part 'local' and conventionally based. Writers who fall within this movement include Bernard Wil-

---

[3] *Thompson Newspapers Ltd.* v. *Canada (Director of Investigation and Research Restrictive Trade Practices Commission)*, [1990] 1. SCR 425 at 539.

liams, Stuart Hampshire, and Annette Baier.[4] Although Dickson's view of charter deliberation is consistent with this particular conception of morality, it does not entail or presuppose it. Recognizing the importance of context and local circumstance in moral reasoning is perfectly consistent with the belief in universal moral principles, valid for all times and places, principles establishing rights such as those recognized in the Canadian Charter. As we saw earlier, even Aquinas was fully cognizant of the role of local custom and circumstance in 'determining' the natural law. Given different expectations, mutual understandings, and historical circumstances, principles like 'Wrong-doers should be punished' or 'Act so as to maximize the balance of happiness over unhappiness caused by one's actions' will license very different actions, laws, and institutional arrangements. The utilitarian, for instance, will only insist that the validity, as opposed to the application, of his ultimate principle is not itself determined by local understanding or conventional agreement. Likewise for Aquinas, who insists that the fundamental principles of the natural law are the same for all persons at all times and in all circumstances. Particular determinations of these universal principles may vary with historical circumstances and local custom (and possibly the decisions by fiat of human sovereigns and judges), but the principles themselves remain always and everywhere the same. So we need not take a stand either way on these controversial issues of moral theory in order to appreciate the Canadian Supreme Court's view that interpretation of Charter rights must be sensitive to linguistic, philosophic and historical contexts. Whether contextualist considerations determine what the principles of equality (section 15) actually are within Canada, or whether they determine only what the universally valid principles of equality require within the local circumstances prevailing within late twentieth-century Canada, the following point remains: the fact that a charter challenge must be placed in its proper linguistic, philosophic and historical contexts is consistent with the proposition that charter challenges often hinge on moral arguments.

In any event, the manner in which Canadian judges approach their task of interpreting and applying their Charter seems to offer some basis for the premise that moral argument is often involved in

---

[4] For a representative sample of the thoughts of such writers, see S. Clarke and E. Simpson (eds.), *Anti-Theory in Ethics and Moral Conservatism*. See also E. Simpson, *Good Lives and Moral Education*.

Charter adjudication. But more support is needed here, if only because the evidential value of judicial testimony in these matters might be questioned. Consider a parallel with the philosophy of science. Some philosophers of science adopt the methodological principle that it is better to look at what scientists actually do, rather than at what they say about what they do, when one is attempting to support or question a theory about the nature of science or about scientific reasoning and methodology. One obvious reason for this principle is the simple fact that being a good scientist in no way guarantees that one is a good philosopher, any more than being a good philosopher means that one can do elementary-particle physics. Richard Feynman, the celebrated physicist and Nobel prize winner, had the following to say concerning the suggestion that scientists should give more consideration to social problems, in particular, that they should be more responsible in considering the impact of science on society: 'I believe that a scientist looking at non-scientific problems is just as dumb as the next guy—and when he talks about a non-scientific matter, he sounds as naive as anyone untrained in the matter.'[5]

Perhaps Feynman's point, made only partly in jest, can be generalized to other non-scientific questions, such as the proper philosophical characterization of science and scientific reasoning. It is quite natural to think that the best people to consult in determining the nature of a practice like science or law are the actual participants, especially those whose views carry significant weight, like Supreme Court judges. Who knows a game better than those who play it? But perhaps this isn't so and we must accept the proposition that many scientists could very well harbour misconceptions of what it is they are up to when they set out to construct scientific hypotheses and theories. They may know how to do what they do, but be unable to offer a philosophically accurate account of what it is that they do. They may think, for example, that they are discovering objective, theory-independent facts, when in reality their so-called objective facts are thoroughly theory laden and influenced by all sorts of extraneous elements. As noted in Chapter 2, it is plausible to hold that moral and social biases determine not only what a scientist will choose to examine, but what he will think of as a viable theory and as data which his theory must accommodate. Most sci-

[*margin note: Appeals to experts about native practice*]

[5] R. P. Feynman, 'What Do You Care What Other People Think?'—Further Adventures of a Curious Character, 240.

entists also think that they are ascertaining the nature of a material reality which, in the words of David Hume, 'would exist even though we and every sensible creature were absent or annihilated'.[6] But maybe they are wrong and there is no material reality existing independently of human minds. Perhaps, as Berkeley put it, 'esse est percipi'.[7]

Now, if such instances of widespread misconception are possible within science, then why not in law? Is it not possible that Canadian judges simply misconceive the fundamental nature of the enterprise in which they are all engaged? Perhaps judges are victims of some sort of 'false consciousness', or of a myth which seeks to legitimize what they do, as a Marxist philosopher of law might say. If so, then they may all think that they are sometimes engaged in substantive moral argument in charter challenges when in fact they are not, just as they may think that in hard cases, their decisions are discretionary, when in fact (if this is a fact) they are all attempts to determine and enforce pre-existing legal rights.[8]

In answer to this radically sceptical objection to reliance on judicial testimony, we might begin with the following observation. While we must acknowledge the theoretical possibility that Canadian courts are generally confused about what it is they are about in Charter cases, the burden of proof is surely on one who wishes seriously to urge this possibility as a sufficient reason to dismiss judicial characterizations of judicial practice. If those who participate in legal adjudication believe and speak and write as if their common practice requires X, then barring any good reason to the contrary, we philosophers who seek to provide descriptive/explanatory accounts of the law, are surely justified in accepting that the practice really does require X. Yet the purely theoretical possibility of widespread misconception is clearly not such a good reason. We should not be Cartesian sceptics in such cases, sceptics for whom the mere logical possibility of error precludes acceptance of the obvious. The point being made here is further reinforced by the fact that it is the judges themselves who seem mainly to be responsible for the existence and content of the rules and standards govern-

---

[6] D. Hume, as quoted in M. Calkins (ed.), *Berkeley Selections*, p. xxii.

[7] G. Berkeley, *A Treatise Concerning the Principles of Human Knowledge*, 24, s. 3.

[8] According to Dworkin, judicial decisions attempt typically to enforce pre-existing rights, despite judicial rhetoric about the need for judicial legislation within the 'gaps' or 'interstices' of law. See *Law's Empire*, 359–63. Dworkin's critique of the positivist's theory of judicial discretion will be discussed later in Chapter 7.

ing adjudication. It is not as if those rules and standards are created and enforced by external bodies who might, for that reason alone, be thought to grasp them better than those who only follow them. Unlike games such as tennis and chess, where rules and standards originate from sources other than the participants themselves, standards of adjudication arise from the beliefs, decisions, and actions of judge-participants. Rules of recognition, change, and adjudication, are social rules or customs originating mainly in the beliefs, attitudes, and activities of judges. It seems very unlikely that these individuals are terribly confused about the nature of what they have created. It is possible, but only just.

Assume, however, that I am wrong about all this, and that the way the judges view what they do has absolutely no probative force whatsoever because, after all, they could be wrong—just as nearly everyone was at one time wrong in thinking that the Earth was flat. If we make this assumption, then our only avenue for determining whether Canadian judges are right in thinking that moral argument does sometimes figure prominently in Charter cases is to look ourselves at what they actually do, how they actually decide such cases. Fortunately this task poses little difficulty. A careful reading of virtually any charter challenge reveals that moral argument does play a vital role. I shall conclude my defence of the premise that moral argument often plays a role in charter adjudication by briefly examining one such case, *Andrews* v. *Law Society of BC.*[9]

The appeal was heard before the BC Court of Appeal and raised the issue whether a requirement of Canadian citizenship as a prerequisite to the practice of law violated section 15 of the Charter. Section 15 falls under the title 'Equality Rights' and reads as follows:

15(1) Every individual is equal before and under the law and has the right to the equal protection and equal benefit of the law without discrimination and, in particular, without discrimination based on race, national or ethnic origin, colour, religion, sex, age or mental or physical disability.

Section 15 makes it unconstitutional for any law or other legal instrument to discriminate against persons, unless such discrimination can be justified under section 1 of the Charter. Section 1 states that:

---

[9] 4 WWR 242 (BCCA) The Court of Appeal's decision was later upheld (3 to 2) by the Supreme Court of Canada. See *Law Society of BC* v. *Andrews*, [1989] 56 DLR (4th) 1. Although there are some important differences between the reasoning of the two Courts, they do not affect the argument of this book and will be ignored. We will concentrate exclusively on the judgment of MacLachlin JA (as she then was).

1. The Canadian Charter of Rights and Freedoms guarantees the rights and freedoms set out in it subject only to such reasonable limits prescribed by law as can be demonstrably justified in a free and democratic society.

The question whether section 1 could be used to override the effect of section 15 was crucial to the case. For reasons of simplicity, and because it in no way affects the present argument, we shall ignore the possibility of a section 33 override. The latter empowers Parliament or the legislature of a province to 'expressly declare in an Act of Parliament or of the legislature, as the case may be, that the Act or a provision thereof shall operate notwithstanding a provision included within section 2 or sections 7 to 15 of [the Charter]'. Section 33 also provides that a declaration made under its terms 'shall cease to have effect five years after it comes into force or on such earlier date as may be specified in the declaration' and that re-enactment is possible.

The major issue before the Court in *Andrews* was whether the citizenship requirement imposed by the Law Society of British Columbia amounted to discrimination. This question led to another more basic issue of both moral and philosophical importance: How does one define 'discrimination' for purposes of interpreting section 15? It is in answering this latter question that we see the first signs of substantive moral argument. Three basic answers were proposed. First, there was the definition proposed by the Law Society which had been accepted by the trial judge.

> D1: L is discriminatory if and only if 'it draws an irrational or irrelevant distinction between people based on some irrelevant personal characteristic for the purpose, or having the effect of imposing on certain of them, a penalty, disadvantage or indignity, or denying them an advantage.'[10]

The key here is the notion of rationality. A law is discriminatory only if there is no rational basis for it. It might be objectionable in many other ways, but so long as any distinction it draws is sensible in light of what the law sets out to do, then the law is not discriminatory. This is a very weak definition in the sense that it employs means-end rationality as its criterion for discrimination. Regardless of the ends sought, or the effect upon people of the means used in realizing those ends, a law is not discriminatory so long as it really

[10] *Andrews*, at 246.

does work effectively towards its goal(s). The result, as the BC Court well realized, is that many laws which ruthlessly but effectively help to realize morally objectionable ends, or which serve to victimize innocent parties, will be judged non-discriminatory. Laws licensing genocide might be non-discriminatory on D1 if the elimination of a particular race was the desired end and the laws adopted did help to bring that about.

As a result of the above considerations, the BC Court rejected D1. This is surely not what 'equality' and 'freedom from discrimination' mean in general, let alone within the philosophical and historical context of late twentieth-century Canada. A second definition was proposed by the appellant, Andrews:

D2: L is discriminatory if it draws any adverse distinction on the basis of a personal characteristic or category.

The Court was equally unhappy with this definition. Were it to be adopted, a vast number of existing laws, which necessarily draw adverse distinctions among people based on their personal characteristics, would be deemed discriminatory and thus in violation of section 15. Laws governing such things as maternity and disability leave, for example, would be discriminatory. Most people welcome time off work, but only those who are disabled or pregnant are allowed this privilege under these laws. Thus, according to D2, these provisions are discriminatory since those who are neither pregnant nor disabled are adversely treated on the basis of personal characteristics. This kind of consequence was in itself sufficient reason, in the Court's mind, for thinking that D2 is unacceptable, though it did go on to list several other reasons why the definition had to be rejected.[11]

A third definition was accepted by the judges and used as their basis for finding in favour of the appellant, Andrews:

D3: L is discriminatory if it draws any unreasonable or unfair distinctions, distinctions which are unduly prejudicial.[12]

There are some important observations to be made regarding D3. In the Court's view, the test under D3 must be objective, that is, based on whether the law is in fact discriminatory, not on whether the lawmakers, or those who might have acted under its authority, sincerely believed that it was discriminatory. Were the test subjective, then perhaps one would be required to establish only non-

[11] Ibid. at 249.   [12] Ibid. at 250–2.

moral, empirical facts about what people's moral beliefs actually are or were. But an objective test clearly means that the Court must itself determine whether L, in actual fact, does draw unreasonable or unfair distinctions, and this determination cannot be made independently of moral deliberation:

> [T]he question to be answered under s. 15 should be whether the impugned distinction is reasonable or fair, having regard to the purposes and aims and its effect on persons adversely affected. I include the word 'fair' as well as 'reasonable' to emphasize that the test is not one of pure rationality [as with D1] but one connoting the treatment of persons in ways which are not unduly prejudicial to them. This test must be objective, and the discrimination must be proved on the balance of probabilities. ... The ultimate question is whether a fair-minded person, weighting the purposes of legislation against its effects on the individuals adversely affected, and giving due weight to the right of the Legislature to pass laws for the good of all, would conclude that the legislative means adopted are unreasonable or unfair.[13]

Plainly this test for discrimination requires some measure of moral deliberation. The parallel between the test proposed, what a fair-minded person would conclude, and what is required by 'ideal observer theories' of morality is in fact quite striking. Ideal observer theories vary, but generally they make a claim along the following lines. 'If we want to know whether something is morally right, the question is: "Would it be permitted by the moral code which an omnipercipient, disinterested, dispassionate [or benevolent] but otherwise normal person would most strongly tend to support as the moral code for a society in which he expected to live?"'[14] Neither this, nor the test proposed by the BC Court, is subjective or based on means-end rationality. On the contrary, they are both objective, and purport to answer the relevant questions by determining what is fair and reasonable, by asking what a 'fair-minded person' would think about the matter in question.

Upon adopting D3 as their criterion for discrimination, the judges went on to apply it to the Andrews situation. They ruled that the Law Society's citizenship requirement was indeed discriminatory, and thus in violation of section 15, because it was neither fair nor reasonable for someone in Andrews' position to be denied a licence to practise law. Of course the violation of a Charter right does not in

[13] Ibid. at 252–3.
[14] R. B. Brandt, *A Theory of the Good and the Right*. The theory seems to have originated in Adam Smith's *The Theory of the Moral Sentiments*.

[handwritten margin note: Very carefully + conveying illustration of need for normative moral judgment in determining constitutional validity of Code laws]

itself entail that the offending measure is unconstitutional and therefore invalid. It may yet be justified under section 1, which validates infringements under certain conditions. The question therefore arose whether a citizenship requirement, acknowledged to be unfair and therefore discriminatory, could none the less be justified in a free and democratic society. A second question arose too, which had to be answered first: How does one go about answering the first question? What standards, if any, apply? Fortunately an answer to this second question had already been provided in *Regina* v. *Oakes*, where the Supreme Court of Canada had enunciated several principles to govern the application of section 1.[15] These may be summarized as follows:

1. The onus of proving that a limitation on any Charter right is reasonable and demonstrably justified in a free and democratic society rests upon the party seeking to uphold the limitation [in this instance, the Law Society].

2. The presumption is that Charter rights are guaranteed unless the party invoking section 1 can bring itself within the exceptional criteria justifying their being limited.

3. The standard of proof under section 1 is [as it is under section 15] the preponderance of probabilities.

4. It must be proven that the objectives to be served by the measures limiting a Charter right are sufficiently important to warrant overriding a constitutionally protected right or freedom. At a minimum, the objectives must be shown to relate to societal concerns which are pressing and substantial in a free and democratic society.

5. It must be shown that the means chosen—the offending provisions—are reasonable and demonstrably justified. This, the BC Court noted, involves three components:

   i. The measures must be fair and not arbitrary—they must be carefully designed to achieve the objective in question and rationally connected to it.

   ii. The means should impair the right as little as possible.

   iii. There must be proportionality between the effects of the limiting measure and the objective—the more severe the prejudicial effects of a measure, the more important the objective must be [the 'proportionality test'].

[15] *R.* v. *Oakes*, [1986] 1 SCR 103, 50 CR (3d) 1.

Having set out the appropriate standards to be applied, the Court went on to argue that section 1 could not be utilized to justify the Law Society's discriminatory citizenship requirement. The apparent objectives of the requirement could not be said to relate, in any reasonably clear way, to societal concerns which are pressing and substantial. The effects of the means chosen were not proportional to the importance of the objectives sought, and were not in fact rationally related to them: citizenship is in no way a necessary condition of being a good lawyer, as is evidenced, the Court thought, by the absence of any such requirement in other common-law jurisdictions.[16] The appeal was therefore granted. The citizenship requirement was invalid owing to its unconstitutionality.

Judging from the above analysis, it is apparent that answering the questions posed by section 1 will often require appeal to pure means-end rationality of the sort discussed above in relation to D1. In addition, it will invariably require a certain amount of historical investigation into the law and political morality of other democratic jurisdictions. But as with section 15, it is also clear that section 1 sometimes demands a degree of moral deliberation. One simply cannot determine whether a measure is fair without contemplating moral premises. One cannot determine proportionality without considering the moral and political importance of the various objectives and concerns which find support in the Charter and in the offending measures. One cannot determine whether a limit can be demonstrably justified in a free and democratic society without engaging in substantive arguments of political morality. As constitutional lawyer Peter Hogg notes, 'the phrase "demonstrably justified" calls for normative judgment by the court as to the legitimacy and necessity in a free and democratic society of the impugned restriction on liberty'.[17]

So what is required by section 1 of the Canadian Charter is not the kind of reasoning which strives to be neutral with respect to, or totally detached from, concerns of political morality. The issues are not purely factual in nature, nor are they purely technical legal matters. What is required by section 1 is some measure of normative, moral judgment which tackles the tricky issues involved whenever one is called upon to strike a reasonable balance between competing moral and political interests. Section 1, then, requires a significant measure of moral reasoning. In determining the

---

[16] *Andrews*, at 257.　　　[17] Peter Hogg, *Constitutional Law of Canada*, 689.

constitutional status of laws in Canada, courts must often consider
their 'moral merits'. For good or ill, in Canada the existence of law *(But still ,*
is not one thing, its merit or demerit another thing entirely. The two *+less are*
have been joined by Canada's rule of recognition and the charter it *judicial*
validates.   *judgements g its*
                                                         moral merit,)
                                                    hots its moral merit

3. DOES IT FIGURE IN THE RIGHT WAY?

If the arguments of the preceding section are sound, we are entitled
to accept the premise that Charter cases sometimes involve moral
argument. Even if one were totally to discount the evidential value
of the judges' own reflections about their reasoning with respect to
the Canadian Charter, we have ample evidence in how they actually
carry out that task—in what they do as opposed to what they say
they do. Our examination of *Andrews* serves to illustrate that moral
reasoning does occur, as it does in many other cases as well, cases
like *Morgentaler* and *Oakes*. Indeed, if the analysis of *Andrews* is
correct, it follows that application of sections 15 and 1 will almost
invariably be guided, in part, by moral considerations. And section
1, at least, is involved in virtually all cases arising under the
Canadian Charter.

So moral deliberation does figure in some Charter cases. Whether
it figures in all or even most charter cases in all charter systems is an
interesting question, but one with which we need not be concerned.
Our aim is only to show that sometimes in some jurisdictions the
existence and content of valid laws depend on moral considerations,
and, for this purpose, providing only a few instances serves to establish our premise.

Moral deliberation does figure then. Our next step must be to
show that it figures in the right way. That is, if our findings are to
provide support for choosing inclusive positivism instead of Raz's
exclusive theory, it must be shown that the moral standards
employed in charter cases sometimes function as tests for the existence or content of valid laws. Without this additional premise we
have no reason to prefer inclusive positivism.

Offhand it would seem that moral considerations do serve the
role which inclusive positivism warrants as possible but exclusive
positivism rejects as inconceivable. In *Morgentaler*, for instance, we
appear to have what functioned for over twenty years as valid law

being declared to have been unconstitutional and thus of no force or effect. The ground for this declaration was violation of section 7 of the Charter which recognizes a right to life, liberty, and security of the person—a right which cannot be denied except in accordance with the principles of fundamental justice. As the courts made plain, 'fundamental justice' is to be understood as including substantive, not merely procedural justice. And whatever one's view about the need for moral reflection in determining the nature of procedural justice, it seems clear that that need is present when substantive justice is at issue. To determine the requirements of substantive justice (one of the interests or objects of section 7, in terms of which that section is to be understood), one must engage in moral deliberation. If so, we seem, again, to have legal rights, whose content depends on moral considerations, being used to demonstrate the invalidity of a statutory instrument (section 251 of the *Criminal Code of Canada*[18]). This, of course, is a possibility well recognized by inclusive positivism.

But it is not a possibility recognized by exclusive positivism. If we accept that theory, the above account, which we will call the inclusive account, just has to be wrong. If the existence and content of a law, and the legal right or obligation it purports to establish, can never, under any circumstances and to any degree, be a function of moral considerations, then we seem inevitably led to the following conclusions. Appearances to the contrary, when the Canadian Supreme Court considered whether section 7 of the Charter was violated by section 251 of the *Criminal Code*, they could not conceivably have been trying to determine the existence or content of valid law by seeing whether subordinate legislation (section 251) violated superior law (section 7). They had to have been doing something else entirely. Similarly, when the BC Court of Appeal considered whether section 15 must be understood in such a way that it was unjustifiably infringed by the Law Society's citizenship requirement, they could not conceivably have been trying to determine the existence or content of valid law by seeing whether the citizenship requirement was in conflict with superior law. They could not have been attempting to understand and apply legal tests for legal validity because, for example, the crucial test of discrimination, and hence violation of section 15, is whether people are being treated unreasonably or unfairly—and this test, as we have

18 RSC 1985, c. C–46, hereinafter the *Criminal Code*.

seen, is at least sometimes partly a moral one. So they too must have been doing something entirely different.

Yet if the courts were not attempting in these cases to determine the existence or content of valid law by asking whether a suspect provision unreasonably infringes superior law, what exactly were they doing? Let us focus on *Andrews* once again. What could the BC Court of Appeal have been doing when it addressed the question whether the citizenship requirement was invalid because it violated section 15, and whether section 15 was violated because the citizenship requirement was unfair to Andrews?

There is only one obvious possibility according to exclusive positivism. If the Court was not attempting to determine the content of a valid law (section 15) containing a legal criterion for the validity of subordinate law, then it must have been attempting to determine the content of something other than law, and applying that something else, in some way or other, to make the citizenship requirement invalid. In applying its fairness test, the Court must have been relying on non-legal, moral standards, presumably not to determine that the citizenship requirement was invalid owing to its conflict with superior law, but to make it invalid by declaring it to be so.[19]

It is important to be clear how exactly the Charter is to be conceived on this alternative, which we will call the exclusive account. According to this interpretation, section 15 does not itself constitute or contain a legal criterion for validity. Rather it only makes reference to an extra-legal, moral criterion to which judges are required or at liberty to appeal in charter challenges. Section 15 directs them to step outside of law and to seek guidance from an external source of non-pedigreed norms, namely, the norms of political morality. A useful parallel is perhaps to be found in foreign law which we considered earlier in noting that the law is only a subset of the norms which have institutional force for judges. Courts are sometimes required by law to make reference to, and indeed sometimes to apply, the law of a foreign legal system in deciding cases. According to the exclusive account, the Charter requires much the same. It

[handwritten margin notes: "Construction of Charter, on exclusive posm's view."]

[handwritten margin note, left: symbol]

---

[19] Later we will consider another alternative which might seem open to exclusive positivism. On this option, the Court did not make the citizenship requirement invalid by its decision. Rather, the Court determined that the requirement already was invalid, owing to its conflict with extra-legal moral standards. As we shall see, however, this option is one that is not really open to the defender of exclusive positivism. He pursues it at the risk of surrendering to the inclusive positivist.

[handwritten margin note, bottom left: "But isn't that true, to at least a degree?"]

When are argts/factors essential to a prior/judicial argt pats of laws, & when not part/ so? When are they generally accepted tests of legal validity?

158   CHARTER CHALLENGES

requires Canadian judges to apply the standards of what amounts to a different kind of foreign system. And just as we would not accept that foreign law becomes part of our legal system just because our judges must sometimes apply it in their decisions, we should not think that standards of political morality are thereby incorporated into Canadian law as legal tests for legal validity, just because our judges must sometimes make reference to them when they decide Charter cases. We should no more think this than we should think that the rules of grammar are part of Canadian law because Canadian judges must sometimes make reference to these rules when deciding cases in which the interpretation of a legal norm is at issue.

On the exclusive account, then, the Court in *Andrews* did not, when it based its decision on the unfairness of the citizenship requirement, enforce an existing legal right (to equality) against an already invalid measure (the citizenship requirement) which would have been valid were it not for the conflict with section 15. On the contrary, it exercised its power, sanctioned by sections 15 (equality) and 52 (supremacy of the Constitution) to make unconstitutional what otherwise would have and had been perfectly valid law. The Court did not discover a legal conflict. It discovered a conflict between law and political morality, and by its decision settled the conflict in favour of the latter. Of course, it is consistent with the exclusive account to claim that the Court's decision, though it was based on the enforcement of a non-legal, moral right, created a new legal right. The effect of the decision in *Andrews* would have been to grant a new legal right to lawyers not to be subject to a citizenship requirement. The Court's decision, as an authoritative act with the appropriate pedigree and institutional force, was quite capable of creating such a legal right, just as decisions of Parliament, which are themselves often based on reasons of political morality, are obviously capable of creating new legal rights.

This, then, is the alternative account of Charter adjudication to which exclusive positivism seems most obviously to lead. Our next step is to consider whether the account provides an adequate descriptive-explanatory account of Charter cases. There are several reasons for thinking that it does not.   ①

First, the exclusive account is simply counter-intuitive. It seems quite at odds with our ordinary understanding of a constitutional document like the Canadian Charter. The latter is commonly conceived as a measure which creates and entrenches fundamental legal rights Canadians possess against governments and government agencies. It flouts that understanding to suggest that the Charter does not in fact serve this role at all, but instead only makes reference to non-legal, moral rights upon the basis of which judges are legally empowered to create new legal rights and invalidate what would otherwise be valid legal measures. In so far as it is part of the fundamental law of Canada, the Canadian Charter is quite naturally viewed as itself creating basic legal rights enforceable in Canadian courts. Pointing out that moral reflection is sometimes required for determining the content of these superior legal rights does not in any way disturb that natural understanding.

Of course it is also part of our common understanding that standards of political morality such as one finds recognized in the Charter are sometimes subject to various kinds of indeterminacy. In cases where indeterminacy figures, judges are thought to play a leading role in shaping the contours of the political morality legally recognized in the Charter. They do so, as they do in any other area of law where indeterminacy is encountered, by exercising their discretion and creating new legal rights. The exercise of this discretion should be, and normally is, sensitive to the linguistic, philosophic, and historical contexts within which rights of political morality are rooted. But this still leaves room for a measure of authoritative, judicial creativity, for Thomistic 'determination'. In cases where such creativity is present, judges will do as the exclusive account claims they always do when Charter rights, whose interpretation requires appeal to political morality, are in play. They will create new legal rights and use these to invalidate existing legal rights. The Charter's regions of indeterminacy are perhaps greater than in many other areas of law where more closely textured terms are used, terms like 'vehicle', 'radio telegraph', and 'assault'. But terms like 'equality', 'discrimination', and 'liberty' are not so open-textured as to admit of no determinate meaning whatsoever. If so, then to the extent that Charter provisions employing such terms do admit of determinate meaning, they do create fundamental legal rights Canadians possess against government and governmental agencies.

To view Charter rights as analogous to foreign law, then, flouts our understanding of them. Another factor weighting against the exclusive account is the language Parliament chose to characterize the Charter. Unlike its predecessor, the Canadian *Bill of Rights*, the Charter is a constitutional document. As such it has a special institutional force, clearly described in section 52 (1) of the *Constitution Act*, 1982, which claims that the Constitution is the supreme law of Canada and that any law that is inconsistent with the Charter is, to the extent of the inconsistency, of no force or effect. Taken literally, section 52 (1) flatly contradicts the exclusive account, and we have yet to see any good reason not to construe it literally. Section 52 (1) does not say that upon judicial declaration that a legal measure is inconsistent with a (foreign) right referred to, but not granted by, the Charter, the measure shall from that moment on be of no force and effect. Rather, it says that any measure which is in conflict with a Charter provision is, to the extent of the inconsistency, of no force or effect. Of course inconsistencies do not begin to exist only when judges declare that they exist. On the contrary, a judge will rule that there is an inconsistency only because he believes that a legal conflict already exists by virtue of the Charter and its various provisions. As Peter Hogg notes, 'the Constitution operates of its own force, and not by virtue of its application by the courts'.[20] And as Field J said with respect to the American Constitution, 'An unconstitutional act is not a law; it confers no rights; it imposes no duties; it affords no protection; it creates no office; it is, in legal contemplation, as inoperative as though it had never been passed.'[21]

So any legal measure, such as section 251 or the Law Society's citizenship requirement, which is inconsistent with sections 7 or 15 of the Charter is, independently of a judge's decision in a Charter challenge, of no force and effect. Yet as we have seen, the contents of sections 15 and 7 are partly determined by considerations of political morality. It seems to follow from the plain language of the Charter, then, that standards requiring some measure of moral reflection for their very understanding are a part of Canada's accepted conditions for legal validity. This is something Canadian judges seem to recognize in their decisions.

There are further reasons for rejecting the exclusive account. For instance, it does not easily explain certain features of Canadian Charter challenges. At the very least, any explanation it suggests is less consonant with these features than the inclusive account, according to which judges are indeed attempting to determine the existence or content of valid law when they hear Charter challenges,

---

[20] Hogg, *Constitutional Law of Canada*, 345.
[21] *Norton* v. *Shelby County* (1886) 118 US 425 at 442; quoted in Hogg, *Constitutional Law of Canada*, 344.

despite their partial reliance on moral considerations. One such feature is that the legal system treats a measure declared invalid as though it were invalid at the time that the actions giving rise to litigation occurred.

Consider *Morgentaler*. When section 251 was finally struck down, the obvious fact that Morgentaler had violated section 251 was no longer an acceptable basis for prosecution. All legal action against Morgentaler consequently ceased. The main reason, of course, is that in declaring section 251 unconstitutional, the Court ruled that section 251 had been of no force or effect when the acknowledged violations occurred. The effect of the Court's decision was the recognition that Morgentaler had been within his legal rights. He had not in fact performed actions which were illegal at the time. Were the exclusive account accepted, on the other hand, illegal acts would indeed have occurred. It was, by this reasoning, only upon declaration of invalidity by the Court that section 251 became invalid. Prior to that time the legislation had force and effect, and actions in violation of it would indeed have been illegal, criminal acts. But if so, would not prosecution still have been in order? And if not, what is the explanation?

With the inclusive account we have a ready and obvious explanation. The Court discovered a conflict in law between section 251 and a more authoritative legal provision. It discovered that section 7 was in conflict with section 251 and that the latter therefore had been of no force and effect at the time Morgentaler and his colleagues were procuring abortions. In short, the Court discovered that Morgentaler had at all times been acting within his legal rights. The legal obligations purportedly imposed by section 251 did not in fact exist when they acted. 'An unconstitutional act is not a law; it confers no rights; it imposes no duties.'[22]

The exclusive account, by contrast, offers no ready explanation for why prosecution was so clearly out of order. There was no recognition by the Court that its declaration had retroactive effect, that it was declaring to have been invalid what was in fact valid at the time. Nor was there any acknowledgement that this highly unusual step, for which a very special type of justification would surely have been in order, was the reason why prosecution would have to cease. Furthermore, there was no sense that the legal system was granting Morgentaler and his colleagues a favour by no longer

---

[22] Ibid.

prosecuting them for their previous crimes. On the contrary, it was clear that prosecution was, and always had been (subsequent to the enactment of the Charter) ruled out legally, owing to the fact that the criminal law of abortion had been of no force and effect; it imposed no legal duties.

A second, related source of difficulty for the exclusive account lies in section 24 (1) which reads as follows:

Anyone whose rights or freedoms, as guaranteed by this Charter, have been infringed or denied may apply to a court of competent jurisdiction to obtain such remedy as the court considers appropriate and just in the circumstances.

Charter infringement is recognized as a viable ground for legal remedy. If the exclusive account is accurate, however, it is not at all obvious why such a remedy should be forthcoming following a successful Charter challenge. And the reason is simple: no legal rights would have been violated. Any legal rights as might exist would come into being only with the Court's decision. Barring retroactivity, which again seems not to have been contemplated, activities pursued under the authority of a law later rendered invalid by a court [e.g. the arrest and prosecution of Morgentaler or the denial of Andrews' licence to practise law] would have been quite legal prior to that decision. But if so, then why should a remedy be forthcoming? The offending party violated no one's legal rights! He may have violated a moral right, but surely it is not the task of the judiciary to enforce non-legal, moral rights against perfectly valid legal rights.

On the other hand, if, as the inclusive account insists, the Charter does establish legal rights which exist antecedently to, and independently of, judicial decisions in cases like *Andrews*, then remedies seem quite appropriate. If the BC Court was correct in its (morally guided) interpretation of section 15, Andrews' legal rights had been violated by the Law Society. He should, therefore, have been entitled to an appropriate legal remedy.

Putting all these points together, we seem to have a fairly persuasive case for rejecting the exclusive account and opting instead for the inclusive account. The latter provides a much more coherent account of Charter cases. On this view, the Canadian Charter creates legal rights whose content is partly dependent on moral considerations, and judges in cases like *Andrews* and

Morgentaler are required to determine what these rights are and to apply them against less authoritative, offending measures.

4. AN ALTERNATIVE EXCLUSIVE ACCOUNT?

It might be objected that I have been uncharitable in characterizing the account to which exclusive positivism seems committed. Perhaps the defender of that theory would wish to offer a modified account, according to which the moral standards to which the courts appeal in cases like *Andrews* and *Morgentaler* are indeed foreign to the legal system, but nevertheless serve, in virtue of their recognition within a charter, as criteria for legal validity which have force independently of judges' decisions to invoke them. If so, then to the extent that legal measures—for example, section 251 of the Canadian *Criminal Code*, or the Law Society's citizenship requirement—are in conflict with these 'foreign' standards, they are, for that reason alone, legally invalid. And this is so even before a court declares that there is a conflict in a Charter case.

Were this modified exclusive account adopted, the defender of exclusive positivism would face fewer of the difficulties discussed above. Indeed, his account would be virtually identical to the inclusive account, except for the fact that the latter does not view the standards to which appeal must be made in determining the content of Charter provisions as equivalent to foreign law. According to the inclusive account, the standards of fairness to which appeal must be made in determining violations of section 15 are part of the content of that section, and therefore part of the law. Fairness, the moral standard, has, on this account, been incorporated into the law and functions as a legal standard of validity. But not so on the modified exclusive account. The defender of this view would still want to insist that invalidity is based on conflicts between legal and 'foreign', moral standards. But his account would share all the other desirable features of the inclusive account. It would be consonant with the language used in section 52(1) of the Charter, and with the various other features of Charter challenges examined above. For instance, it too would have a ready explanation for why legal remedies seem an appropriate response in some successful Charter challenges.

Attractive as it may be, the modified exclusive account is clearly a position to which the defender of exclusive positivism cannot subscribe. And the reason should now be fairly obvious. It is true, on this account, that the content of a Charter provision is not a function of moral factors. All such a provision ever does is instruct judges to consult certain moral standards lying outside the law, and understanding this instruction requires no moral deliberation. Carrying out the instruction does, but understanding it, i.e. understanding the law, requires 'little more than knowledge of English (including technical legal English), and of the events which took place in Parliament on a few occasions'.[23] But the same cannot be said for the validity of measures such as the Law Society's citizenship requirement, or section 251 of the *Criminal Code*. Whether the standards in terms of which the validity of these measures is partly to be established are foreign or not, the fact remains that, on the modified exclusive account, the legal validity of these measures is determined in part by moral considerations whose understanding requires moral deliberation. If this view is advanced by the defender of exclusive positivism, he will be forced to admit that the conditions for legal validity accepted within the Canadian legal system include moral conditions. That such moral conditions count as conditions of validity can be determined independently of moral reflection. But the conditions themselves require moral reflection for their understanding, interpretation, and application. The defender of the modified exclusive account will be forced to concede, for example, that a condition for the validity of any legal measure within Canada is that it does not unfairly discriminate against individuals in a way which cannot be justified in a free and democratic society. But if this is so, then the existing conditions for valid Canadian laws include moral conditions, a possibility the defender of exclusive positivism is most anxious to deny. Whether those conditions are foreign or not seems really beside the point.

5. CONCLUSION

The defender of exclusive positivism seems truly committed to the original exclusive account. But we have seen ample reason to reject it in favour of the inclusive account. If so, then we are entitled to conclude that inclusive positivism provides a much better descrip-

---

[23] 'Authority, Law and Morality', 306.

tive-explanatory account of Charter adjudication than exclusive positivism. On that account, then, it is a much better theory of law.

The aim of the present chapter has been to show that moral argument does sometimes figure in determinations of law and that exclusive positivism, which rules this out as impossible, is therefore deficient. Charter challenges serve, in this context, as counter-examples to the exclusive positivist's universal claim about the kinds of factors which necessarily figure in determinations of law. Owing to the logic of our argument we are not required to consider to what extent legal systems provide further counter-examples to the exclusive positivist's claim. One counter-example is all we need. Nevertheless, it may be instructive to note that moral factors appear to serve analogous roles in many other areas of law as well. It seems a widespread feature of law that arguments which appeal to the authority of constitutions, statutes, precedents, or customs can often be challenged by counter-arguments which assert that the constitution, statute, judicial decision, or custom does not apply in the case at hand because if it were to apply this would result in a manifest injustice, absurdity, or moral repugnance. Sometimes these arguments are made by way of interpretation and sometimes by way of an invitation to set aside the authority invoked. Owing to the institutional force of the pertinent authority it is not always possible for the court or official to give effect to an argument of this sort, but such arguments are often encountered and sometimes accepted. In many instances, for example, courts willingly follow the 'golden rule' according to which a legal rule's content and effect are determined by its 'plain meaning' unless this 'leads to manifest absurdity or [moral] repugnance'.[24] In such cases, standards of morality and rationality serve to determine the very content of valid legal norms, something again which the exclusive positivist must deny. So Charter challenges, in which an explicit authority is conferred on courts to set aside or suspend or confine the scope of an apparent law on (among other things) moral grounds, is only one instance of a phenomenon which seems to pervade many legal systems and areas of law. Further counter-examples, should we wish to provide them, could be found in other places.

---

[24] B. Parke in *Becke* v. *Smith* (1836). In Chapter 8 I shall defend the normative thesis that courts should not be reluctant to follow the golden rule in attempting to determine the very meaning or content of valid legal rules.

6

HERCULES

1. INTRODUCTION

For our purposes, the distinguishing feature of inclusive positivism is the claim that moral considerations can, but need not, figure properly in determinations of law, i.e., attempts to determine the existence or content of valid laws. Since moral considerations do seem to figure in this way, we have good reason to think that inclusive positivism is a better descriptive-explanatory theory of law than exclusive positivism.

But an important question arises at this point. Perhaps the appropriate conclusion to be drawn from our previous discoveries is not that inclusive positivism is the better theory, but that legal positivism is obviously inadequate because that theory is identical with exclusive positivism and the latter necessarily precludes political morality from the possible grounds of law. In other words, the appropriate conclusion may not be that we have reason to adopt a version of positivism, i.e. inclusive positivism, which provides conceptual space for morality in determinations of law, but that positivism must be abandoned altogether because it necessarily excludes morality from the possible grounds for valid law, and morality does sometimes seem to figure in this way. To put the point in a slightly different way, perhaps inclusive positivism is not really a version of positivism at all, but rather a theory which is not significantly different from Dworkin's integrity theory, or the natural-law theories of Aquinas and Augustine. As with inclusive positivism, each of these gives pride of place to moral factors in determinations of law. So perhaps we haven't discovered reasons for preferring a particular kind of positivism but reasons for rejecting positivism altogether in favour of a non-positivistic theory of law like Dworkin's integrity theory.

We have already seen one respect in which inclusive positivism differs from the integrity theory. The former is a general, descriptive-

explanatory theory of law, whereas the latter is a 'constructive interpretation' of 'our law', by which Dworkin presumably means the
legal practices of western liberal democracies.[1] But that aside, the
question still remains: Just how far can one go in admitting a
determining role for morality while maintaining one's claim to be
offering a version of positivism? In admitting that legal validity can
be a function of controversial matters of political morality, is it
possible that one thereby abandons all right to be called a legal
positivist? As should be obvious at this stage, I wish to answer this
last question with a resounding No. Inclusive positivism is, I believe, a conceptually possible version of positivism. Moreover it is
clearly distinguishable from and preferable to its rivals. We have
already seen why this is so with respect to exclusive positivism, and
to a lesser extent natural-law theory. The time is now at hand to
tackle Dworkin's integrity theory, the most powerful contemporary
rival to legal positivism.

One way of addressing our present concerns is to consider the
extent to which inclusive positivism can accommodate Dworkin's
insights into the role of moral factors in determinations of law and
remain, in any meaningful sense, a version of legal positivism. This
is the specific question upon which we shall focus in the present
chapter. Our strategy will be as follows. We shall assume what our
earlier arguments reveal, that Dworkin is to some degree right about
the considerations which judges within Anglo-American legal systems sometimes take into account in establishing the pre-existing
legal rights and obligations of litigants. These considerations sometimes include principles of political morality, of the sort which
figure in landmark cases like *Riggs* v. *Palmer* and *Henningsen* v.
Bloomfield Motors,[2] and Charter cases like *Morgentaler* and
Andrews. We shall also take as given, that these considerations of
political morality are not, as exclusive positivism maintains, necessarily analogous to foreign law. They are not all extra-legal considerations to which judges may or must or characteristically do
repair when exercising their strong discretion. Rather, at least some
of these principles are part of the law and judges are bound to
respect whatever institutional forces they possess.

What reasons might there be for thinking that these features of

---

[1] If this is not what Dworkin means by 'our law', then it is far from clear what he
does mean.

[2] *Henningsen* v. *Bloomfield Motors* 32 NJ 358, 161 A. 2d (1960).

Anglo-American legal practice are necessarily inconsistent with positivism, which is thereby shown to be inadequate? In other words, what reasons are there for thinking that inclusive positivism is not a version of positivism at all? In what follows we shall consider five arguments originating in Dworkin's work, each of which purports to show a basic inconsistency. In showing why and how these arguments misfire as attacks on inclusive positivism, we will discover further reasons for thinking that that theory really is a viable version of legal positivism. We will also have shown that Dworkin is wrong in his claim that positivism is fundamentally flawed because it is unable satisfactorily to accommodate the role sometimes played by political morality in determinations of law. That political morality figures in determinations of law provides no reason at all to prefer the integrity theory to positivism, because inclusive positivism is a coherent, plausible version of positivism and it too recognizes this possibility.

2. THE VALIDITY ARGUMENT

The first argument purporting to show a basic inconsistency between positivism and a determining role for political morality will be called the Validity Argument. It is found in Dworkin's early attack on positivism and runs as follows:

1. According to positivism, a law is a special sort of standard, distinguishable from all other sorts of non-legal standards in virtue of its meeting certain tests of legal validity.

2. In Hart's view the tests for legal validity are outlined or displayed in the rule of recognition, the master social rule which validates all the other legal standards of the system.[3]

3. So, for the positivist Hart, all law is valid law.

4. 'Validity', however, 'is an all-or-nothing concept, appropriate for rules but inconsistent with a principle's dimension of weight.'[4]

---

[3] Positivists differ, of course, on the nature of the fundamental test for validity. John Austin argues that valid laws are the general commands of the sovereign—the individual or group of individuals who enjoys the habitual obedience of the bulk of a population and who habitually obeys no one else. In the following discussion we shall follow Dworkin in taking Hart's theory as our primary example of positivism, with the understanding that what is said of Hart, *qua* positivist, is also true of other positivists like Austin, Bentham, Kelsen, and Raz. It is also true of defenders of inclusive positivism.

[4] *Taking Rights Seriously*, 41.

5. Therefore rules can be valid.

6. But principles of political morality, of the sort which figure in cases like *Riggs*, *Henningsen*, *Morgentaler*, and *Andrews* cannot, because they have weight, be valid.

7. Therefore, principles of political morality cannot satisfy the criteria of legal validity outlined or displayed in the rule of recognition.

8. More specifically, principles cannot count as valid law.

9. Rather, principles must, for the legal positivist, stand outside the law, as extra-legal standards to which judges may or characteristically do resort when exercising their quasi-legislative, discretionary powers. That is, principles of political morality must serve as grounds for creating new laws, not factors which help establish the pre-existence and content of valid laws.

10. Conclusion: Positivism is inconsistent with the roles played by principles of political morality in establishing the existence and content of pre-existing law and the legal rights and obligations it establishes. Positivism must be rejected.

In his early assault upon 'the model of rules', Dworkin emphasized principles and how they figure in legal argument. Till Dworkin pointed out their important role and how they often differ from less flexible and more concrete legal rules, the tendency in legal theory had been to conceive of laws as a special set of rules which were (usually) applied to determine the right result in legal cases. The important jurisprudential questions were: What is a rule? How does it differ from predictions about how courts will act in legal cases (Holmes) or commands addressed to judges and directing them to apply sanctions under certain defined conditions (Kelsen) and so on? How do we distinguish those rules which are law from the vast array of other standards by which we judge people's behaviour but which are not enforceable, as law, in courts? These were the questions upon which, following Hart and Kelsen, legal philosophers tended to focus.

But all that changed with Dworkin. As Dworkin noted, once we notice that principles do sometimes figure in legal cases, we see that they do so quite often. Yet if, as Dworkin suggests, such standards are incapable, because they have weight, of satisfying the validity tests contained within the rule of recognition, then we seem to have very good reason to reject positivism. It fails to capture a good deal of what counts as law because a good deal of law is expressed in principles.

As we shall now see, however, there is no reason at all to suppose that a valid law cannot also have weight. More specifically, there is no reason to think that those principles which do possess weight cannot also satisfy validity tests found in a rule of recognition. Indeed, weight is but one kind of 'institutional force' possessed by valid legal standards and, just as with other types of institutional force, its variability is perfectly consistent with the 'all-or-nothing' quality of validity.

The Validity Argument is sound only if the following three propositions are true:

(a) Principles necessarily have weight.
(b) Rules necessarily do not have weight.
(c) Legal validity and weight are logically inconsistent properties.

It would take us too far afield to discuss (a) and (b), which can be safely ignored for two reasons. First, they have been seriously challenged elsewhere.[5] Second, since the Validity Argument is sound only if (c) is true, then if we can show that (c) is in fact false, the question whether (a) and (b) are true becomes moot. So we will concentrate on (c). Why should we suppose that legal validity and weight are logically incompatible properties, that a standard which necessarily has weight necessarily lacks validity? The following brief examination of these properties reveals that we have no reason at all to suppose this.

Let us begin with the notion of legal validity. To call a standard or norm, S, legally valid in a legal system L is to say (i) that S satisfies certain criteria for membership within L, criteria which are outlined in a rule of recognition or standards, like the Canadian Charter, which are validated by a rule of recognition—and (ii) that S must therefore be given due consideration in any case arising in L to which S applies. The sort of consideration to which S is entitled will depend largely on the secondary rules of adjudication accepted within L. As we saw earlier in our discussion of the varying institutional forces of precedents, sometimes a standard must be followed regardless of the judge's views concerning its appropriateness; at other times the standard can be overridden, outweighed, or indeed

---

[5] See for instance J. Raz, 'Legal Principles and the Limits of Law'; S. Munzer, 'Validity and Legal Conflicts'; C. Tapper, 'A Note on Principles', and R. Tur, 'Positivism, Principles and Rules'.

changed if the right reasons exist. Factors like the level of court at which the standard was introduced and the time-span between the precedent and the instant case often figure in the adjudication rules which determine whether a particular judge is able to escape the precedent's institutional force. Sometimes, as with the English Court of Appeal and decisions emanating from the House of Lords, the standard must be followed in any case to which it applies. According to Dworkin, all valid rules are of this sort, not as a matter of legal practice but as a matter of sheer logic. 'Rules are applicable in an all-or-nothing fashion. If the facts a rule stipulates are given, then either the rule is valid, in which case the answer it supplies must be accepted, or it is not, in which case it contributes nothing to the decision.'[6] But as will now be shown, a rule which contributes nothing at all to a particular decision can none the less be legally valid, and remain so, despite its failure to contribute. The same is true of principles.

There is no reason to think that L's adjudication rules cannot specify conditions under which standards like S need not be followed. For instance, an adjudication rule can specify that any rule R1 from source T1 must give way to any conflicting rule R2 from source T2 in any case to which both apply. Examples of this are the priority of statute law over case law in common-law systems and *e.g.* the paramountcy of federal law over provincial law in Canada. Of course, on Dworkin's view of rules, a rule R1 which gave way because it conflicted with a rule R2 could not conceivably be, or at least remain, valid. If 'the rule is valid the answer it supplies must be accepted'. Since R2's answer is not accepted, it follows, on Dworkin's account, that it cannot be valid. But it is just this that I wish to deny. R1's giving way to R2 does not logically preclude its remaining legally valid.

Consider the Canadian doctrine of federal paramountcy which has been developed to deal with conflicts between federal and provincial laws. If it has been determined that some such conflict exists, then the provincial law must, in the case in which the conflict occurs, yield to the federal law. It is considered inoperative to the extent, but only the extent, of the inconsistency. In other words, it remains a valid rule of the legal system and maintains its institutional force and resultant power to determine decisions in cases where it does not conflict with federal law. In addition, the doctrine imposes a

---

[6] *Taking Rights Seriously*, 24.

temporal limitation. If and when the federal law is repealed, the scope of the provincial law's power automatically widens to cover those areas where previously there had been a conflict.[7]

It is clear, then, that 'S is legally valid in L' does not necessarily entail that S must be followed in any case in L to which it applies. Its institutional force is logically independent of its validity. Factors in addition to S's validity must be considered in determining its contribution, if any, to a particular legal decision. One such factor is often the standard's source within the system. Another such factor is sometimes its weight, which is a variable as opposed to an all-or-nothing property like source. American courts, for instance, have had occasion to weigh the principle of freedom of speech, P1, against principles establishing rights to security of person and property, P2.[8] They are thought to do so by, among other things, assessing and weighing the consequences for the community of adhering, in a certain set of circumstances, C1, to P1 as opposed to P2. It is thought that weight is a matter of degree. It is also thought that P1 may have more weight than P2 in C1 and yet have less weight in C2. It may be permissible to make inflammatory political speeches—P1 outweighs P2 in C1. It is not permissible falsely to shout fire in a crowded theatre—P2 outweighs P1 in C2.[9] The standards which here compete are conceived as being actually or potentially less or more weighty than one another in a given context. This is why weight is the appropriate notion to use in describing the institutional forces possessed by these standards and the competition between them. Weight is a matter of degree.

This notion of weight seems to apply in areas other than law. Consider morals. The principle of beneficence is usually outweighed by the principle that one ought to keep one's promises, when the harm which can be prevented only by breaking the promise is very slight. But as the potential harm increases, or the promise decreases in importance, the relative weight of the prin-

[7] On the paramountcy doctrine, see P. Hogg, *Constitutional Law of Canada*, 113–14. For cases in which the paramountcy doctrine figured prominently, see *Tennant* v. *Union Bank of Canada* [1894] AC 31; *A.-G. BC* v. *A.-G. Ca* (employment of Japanese) [1924] AC 203; *Royal Bank of Canada* v. *Larue* (1928) AC 187; *Re Bozanich* [1942] SCR 130; *Reference re s 92(4) of the Vehicles Act 1957* (Saskatchewan) [1958] SCR 608; *A-G Ontario* v. *Policy-holders of Wentworth Insurance Co* [1969] SCR 779.
[8] See e.g. *Terminiello* v. *Chicago*, 337 US 1 (1949).
[9] See *Schenck* v. *United States*, 249 US 47 (1919).

ciple of beneficence increases. And this increase may reach the point
where the principle outweighs its competitor in the given context.

Compare now the situation in law where it is accepted that any
standard from inferior source T1 must yield in any case to any
conflicting standard from superior source T2. Say, as in Canada, any
statute from a provincial source must yield to any conflicting federal
statute. The notion of being outweighed is here inappropriate to
describe the fate of the provincial statute. The two standards are not _overridden_
weighed or balanced with the understanding that the provincial _vs_
statute just might in a given case prevail over its federal counterpart. _outweighed_
The institutional force is logically quite different. In the absence of
even a chance to compete the statutes are not weighed at all. Given
their respective sources, the defeated statute is simply ignored for the
purpose of decision. It is not outweighed; it is in this case of conflict,
simply overridden.[10]

We can usefully compare here how the notion of being overridden
is sometimes thought to operate in morals. R. M. Hare has noted
that moral judgments override aesthetic judgments. What this is
taken to mean is that a moral judgment always, and regardless of
circumstances, wins out over a competing aesthetic judgment. The
latter is totally overridden (or pre-empted), not outweighed. The
same might be thought to be true of judgments of etiquette, 'good
taste', and possibly prudence.[11]

Returning now to the case of the Canadian paramountcy doctrine,
it is important to stress again that a provincial law's being overridden does not entail, as a matter of logic or legal practice, that it
therefore ceases to have legal validity and institutional force. To be
sure, a legal system's secondary rules could specify that an overridden statute is thereby invalidated, but clearly this is not necessary.
The same seems true of standards whose institutional force can be
outweighed. When courts weigh competing principles enshrined in a
charter or bill of rights, they are quite obviously weighing principles ✓
which have, and may continue to have, validity within their system.
This is most certainly true in Canada where the outweighing of a
Charter principle (or, if one likes, the right or freedom it articulates)
is explicitly recognized and provided for in section 1.

---

[10] We might, if we wish, follow Raz's lead here, and say that the defeated statute is ✓
pre-empted or excluded. The federal statute provides an exclusionary reason which
does not compete with but eliminates the reason provided by the provincial statute. In
what follows we will continue to speak of a standard's being overridden.

[11] See Hare, _Freedom and Reason_, 168 ff.

There are three main outcomes of the preceding discussion. First, with validity and weight, as with what can be legally overridden and yet be valid, we do not find any pair of logically inconsistent properties. In terms of distinctions drawn earlier in this book, validity and institutional force are different properties. A standard which lacks validity presumably has no institutional force; but it is quite possible for a valid standard to lack institutional force or to have its institutional force overcome in some way by a competing standard. It might, e.g., be overridden or outweighed in a particular context. Second, a principle, or any other sort of standard for that matter, can have weight or be overridden without it thereby following that it logically could not satisfy tests for validity contained within a rule of recognition. In both cases we simply find no conflict. Third, it is fallacious to argue that moral criteria for legal validity are excluded by positivism because such criteria—e.g. moral principles of equality which no legislation may unreasonably infringe—must be weighed before their effect on a decision is determined, and weight is logically inconsistent with the all-or-nothing quality of (legal) validity, a property which, according to defenders of positivism, all legal standards possess, and which serves to distinguish them from all other kinds of non-legal norms. In short, the Validity Argument gives us no reason at all to disqualify inclusive positivism as a possible form of legal positivism.

3. THE PEDIGREE ARGUMENT

Clearly there is nothing in the positivist's notion of legal validity which logically precludes weighted standards of political morality from satisfying the validity tests of the rule of recognition. Dworkin has argued, however, that principles of political morality could not conceivably satisfy the *kind* of validity test which must, on the theory of legal positivism, be contained within a rule of recognition. The kind of test to which positivism is limited, according to Dworkin, is the sort of test one finds in exclusive positivism, content-neutral, source-based, pedigree tests whose satisfaction is independent of any and all moral considerations. As I shall now attempt to show, however, this Pedigree Argument rests upon a serious misunderstanding of positivism and thus provides no grounds for rejecting inclusive positivism as a viable form of that theory.

The following is essentially what I take to be Dworkin's argument. Again, we will follow Dworkin in supposing that Hart's descriptive-explanatory theory of law serves as the obvious paradigm of positivism.

1. Hart, in so far as he espouses legal positivism, is committed to the view that law is a set of special rules which can be 'identified and distinguished by specific criteria, by tests having to do not with their content but with their pedigree or the manner in which they were adopted or developed. These tests of pedigree can be used to distinguish valid legal rules from spurious legal rules ... and also from other sorts of social rules ... that the community follows but does not enforce through public power.'[12]

2. A principle, however, is a principle of law to be applied in any case to which it has relevance only if it is a principle of political morality which figures in the best constructive, Herculean interpretive theory of the settled law.

3. The attempt to determine what that best theory is, and therefore what principles it renders legal, 'must carry the lawyer very deep into political and moral theory, and well past the point where it would be accurate to say that any "test" of "pedigree" exists for deciding which of two different justifications ... is superior [and thus which principles are principles of law]'.[13]

4. So legal principles could not possibly satisfy the content-neutral, source-based, pedigree tests contained within the positivist's rule of recognition.

5. Thus legal principles could not, according to legal positivism, count as valid legal standards.

6. Positivism is therefore incompatible with the existence and (moral) nature of legal principles.

7. And inclusive positivism, which claims to be a version of legal positivism which allows for the existence and (moral) nature of legal principles is incoherent.

Before proceeding to the most obvious question raised by the Pedigree Argument—Why is positivism necessarily wedded to pure pedigree criteria for validity?—a few preliminary comments are in order. First, Dworkin clearly understands positivism to be identical with exclusive positivism. Where Raz speaks of source-based criteria which are such that determining whether they have been satisfied requires no appeal to moral considerations, Dworkin talks of con-

[12] *Taking Rights Seriously*, 17.   [13] Ibid. 67.

tent-neutral, pedigree criteria of validity. All one needs, on both the account sketched by Dworkin and the one defended by Raz, is 'little more than knowledge of English (including technical legal English), and of the events which took place in Parliament [or Congress] on a few occasions'.[14] Second, one need not accept Dworkin's account of how legal principles become law—i.e. by figuring in the best constructive interpretation of the legal system—in order to appreciate the force of the Pedigree Argument against inclusive positivism. As we saw in the preceding chapter, courts must often grapple with difficult questions concerning the demands of equality, liberty, fundamental justice, and due process if they are to determine legal validity. It is true that charters are usually enacted, and that their principles of political morality are not therefore part of the law because they figure in a constructive interpretation of settled law. On the contrary they quite clearly have the pedigree Dworkin and Raz seem to require. It remains true nevertheless that understanding these provisions requires moral reflection because their content is moral in nature, and such content cannot be ascertained independently of moral deliberation. More importantly, in so far as the validity of legislation and judicial decisions depends on the satisfaction of these legally recognized standards of political morality, it is true that more than pedigree is often relevant in determining legal validity. If a charter specifies moral criteria, and if, as the Canadian Charter says, 'any [putative] law that is inconsistent with the provisions of the [Charter] is, to the extent of the inconsistency, of no force or effect', it follows that more than pedigree counts in determining the existence and content of valid law. So if positivists are indeed restricted by their theory to pedigree tests for validity, it follows that positivism is indeed unsatisfactory and inclusive positivism is internally incoherent. It is incoherent because it claims to be a form of positivism according to which more than pedigree can count in determining validity.

This now brings us to our main question concerning the Pedigree Argument. Why must a defender of positivism restrict himself to content-neutral, pedigree tests for validity? The first thing to note is that there are plenty of theorists generally thought to be positivists who do not so restrict themselves. Consider the following passages from Hart. 'In some systems [of law], as in the United States, the ultimate criteria of legal validity explicitly incorporate principles

[14] 'Authority, Law and Morality', 306.

of justice or substantive moral values.'[15] 'Bentham ... recognized ... that even the supreme legislative power might be subjected to legal constraints by a constitution and would not have denied that moral principles, like those of the Fifth Amendment, might form the content of such legal constitutional restraints.'[16] As Hart goes on to note, Austin's view was that any such constraints on supreme legislative power could not conceivably be legal but only moral or political in nature. Yet even Austin recognized 'that a statute, for example, might confer a legislative power and restrict the area of its exercise by reference to moral principles'.[17]

Finally, consider the following remarks made by Hart in his review of Lon Fuller's *The Morality of Law.*

There is, for me, no logical restriction on the content of the rule of recognition: so far as 'logic' goes it could provide explicitly or implicitly that the criteria determining validity of subordinate laws should cease to be regarded as such if the laws identified in accordance with them proved to be morally objectionable. So a constitution could include in its restrictions on the legislative power even of its supreme legislature not only conformity with due process but a completely general provision that its legal power should lapse if its enactments ever conflicted with principles of morality and justice. The objection to this extraordinary arrangement would not be 'logic' but the gross indeterminacy of such criteria of legal validity. Constitutions do not invite trouble by taking this form.[18]

Unless we are to bar Hart, Bentham, and Austin from the positivist's camp, it would seem we must reject the claim that positivists restrict themselves to content-neutral, pedigree criteria for legal validity. Some espouse inclusive positivism. If moral principles can be explicitly incorporated into the rule of recognition of a legal system, L, as constraints upon the validity of subordinate law—if, that is, 'moral principles, like those of the Fifth Amendment, might form the content of ... legal constitutional restraints'—then the following is clearly true.

---

[15] *The Concept of Law*, 199.

[16] 'Positivism and the Separation of Law and Morals', 51. In the quoted passage Hart cites Bentham, *A Fragment On Government, 1 Works* 221, 289–90 (Bowring edn., 1859) ch. IV, paras 33–4.

[17] Ibid. In the quoted passage Hart cites Austin, *The Province of Jurisprudence Determined* (Library of Ideas edn., 1954), 184–5.

[18] 'Lon L. Fuller: The Morality of Law', in *Essays in Jurisprudence and Philosophy*, 361.

(i) Whether a putative law, X, is legally valid in a system L can indeed be, in part at least, a function of X's content, not merely its pedigree or source.

(ii) The Pedigree Argument is unsound owing to the falsity of its first premise.

The reason why (i) and (ii) follow should by now be clear. To determine the validity of X in L one may be required to consider whether X violates an incorporated moral principle, to determine, for instance, whether X unreasonably violates the principles of fundamental justice in a way that cannot be justified in a free and democratic society. But to determine this, as we have seen, one must be concerned with much more than X's source or pedigree. One must consider its content, whether it is unjust. To be sure, both X and any moral principle, P, in terms of which X's validity may have to be assessed will, for the defender of positivism, each have its pedigree. As we saw earlier in our discussion of the Institutional Connection Argument, moral principles count for the positivist, but only to the extent that the legal system provides for this possibility via a rule of recognition, or a legal standard validated by it. When morality counts it is only because legal practice makes it count. Unlike natural-law theory, positivism in all its forms denies that law, by its very nature, includes moral tests for validity which exist independently of legal practice.

If I am right about (i) and (ii), the question naturally arises: What are we to make of the positivist's dictum that the existence of law is one thing, its merit or demerit another? In accepting the possibility that legal validity might depend on moral validity does one not admit that there is some sort of 'fused identity between law as it is and as it ought to be'?[19] Is this not to abandon positivism altogether and to play directly into the hands of the defender of natural-law theory, or Dworkin's integrity theory which can, for present purposes, be considered a variety of natural-law theory? Of course not.

As with positivism, it is very difficult to find a description of natural-law theory which captures what is more or less common to all or even most of its varieties.[20] But at the risk of oversimplification, perhaps the following will do. '[B]y and large it would seem to

[19] 'Positivism and the Separation of Law and Morals', 58.

[20] For an attempt to provide such a description, see W. K. Frankena, 'On Defining and Defending Natural Law' in S. Hook (ed.), *Law and Philosophy*. See also A. P. d'Entreves, *Natural Law*, *passim*.

be intrinsic to the theory to hold that conformity to natural law is the criterion not merely of a just law but of law itself.'[21]

So for the defender of natural-law theory, law is, in some sense, and to some extent at any rate, essentially moral in nature. The content of what truly counts as a legal system and the manner in which law is administered are not totally within the discretion of human beings; the natural law (or political morality if the version of natural law in question is Dworkin's integrity theory) sets limits to legal validity, limits which exist independently of any criteria for validity a legal system happens to adopt as a matter of variable legal practice. Morality counts to some extent whether or not a legal system recognizes this fact. I shall call this claim the 'first tenet of natural-law theory'.

Now it is clear that those who espouse inclusive positivism have not embraced anything like the first tenet of natural-law theory. The moral requirements in terms of which legal validity can be established or challenged are those, and only those, which have as a matter of contingent social fact, i.e. legal practice, been incorporated into a rule of recognition or subordinate standards validated by that rule. And, of course, as Hart makes plain in the passage quoted above, a rule of recognition need not contain any such criteria at all; hence the distinct possibility of a totally wicked, or morally quite vacuous, and yet perfectly legal or lawful system of social regulation. This, as we saw earlier, is the very possibility which defenders of positivism wish, for various reasons, to stress. Of course, if a theorist claiming to be a legal positivist had for some reason claimed it to be conceptually necessary that a system of law contain a rule of recognition incorporating moral requirements for legal validity, then he would have accepted the first tenet of natural-law theory and repudiated his positivism. Yet all Hart and other defenders of inclusive positivism want to say is that it is possible that there be systems of law in which, as a matter of contingent legal practice, the accepted tests for validity require that a subordinate standard or decision not violate certain moral principles recognized as tests for validity. This is perfectly consistent with the rejection of natural-law theory and the acceptance of inclusive positivism, the

[21] Richard Wollheim, 'Natural Law', in P. Edwards (ed.), *The Encyclopedia of Philosophy* Vol. 4, 452. But again, see J. Finnis, *Natural Law and Natural Rights*, 351, where Finnis claims that 'a theory of natural law need not have as its principal concern, either theoretical or pedagogical, the affirmation that "unjust laws are not law"'.

view which insists that if legal validity is in some way, in some particular system a function of moral validity, it is only because a rule of recognition makes it so.[22]

In order to be perfectly clear on what is being asserted by both the defenders and detractors of inclusive positivism, one might usefully consider their responses to the following three propositions:

P1: *Necessarily*, what counts as a valid law, X, of a legal system, L, is determined by tests which deal solely with X's pedigree or source, and which totally ignore X's content (moral or otherwise).

P2: *Possibly*, what counts as a valid law, X, of a legal system, L, is (or is not) determined by tests which deal solely with X's pedigree, and which totally ignore X's content (moral or otherwise).

P3: *Necessarily*, what counts as a test or criterion for the validity of a law, X, in a legal system, L, is determined solely by pure pedigree—by what is in fact accepted within the particular legal community in question as the ultimate tests for law.

Dworkin's Pedigree Argument assumes that the positivist is committed to P1, and that he cannot, therefore, find room within the law for principles of political morality and the ways in which they sometimes function in determining the existence and content of valid law. But this assumption is false. Defenders of exclusive positivism are committed to P1, but not those positivists, like Austin, Bentham, and Hart who espouse inclusive positivism. All positivists are, in virtue of their thesis concerning the conceptual separation of law and morality, and their view that a legal system is, fundamentally, a social institution which sets its own limits and criteria for membership, committed to P2 and P3. But these are quite different from P1 and do not entail P1. The defender of natural-law theory, of course, denies P2 because he denies P3, and agrees with defenders of inclusive positivism who reject P1. Exclusive positivism, on the other hand, affirms all three propositions.

In accepting P3, all defenders of positivism reject the notion of criteria of lawfulness or legal validity inherent in something outside of particular legal systems and their accepted tests for validity. They reject the notion of a 'natural law' containing another, transcen-

---

[22] See Hart, 'Legal Positivism', in P. Edwards (ed.), *The Encyclopedia of Philosophy*, Vol. 4, 418–20 and Wollheim, 'Natural Law', 452.

dental set of criteria which the laws of human legal systems must satisfy. On the contrary, law is a human, social invention and particular communities of persons set the criteria for validity by which the laws of their legal systems are governed. These criteria have a social origin. Contrary to P1, but in agreement with P2, they may or may not include reference to moral principles.[23]

So we may conclude that the Pedigree Argument fails to undermine inclusive positivism as a version of legal positivism. But if, as now seems clear, not all defenders of positivism are committed to P1, the defining feature of exclusive positivism, the question naturally arises as to why a philosopher of Dworkin's calibre might have supposed that they are. There are several possible explanations. First, as examples of criteria for validity, some positivists do tend to use content-neutral pedigree tests. Hart, for instance, normally uses, for purposes of illustration, 'Whatever Rex I enacts is law' and 'Whatever the Queen in Parliament enacts is law'.[24] But as should now be obvious, Hart does not intend his list of examples to be exhaustive of the kinds of tests for legal validity a system might adopt.

A second possible explanation hinges on confusions about the ambiguity of the term 'validity', which is sometimes used, as is in deductive logic, to denote a formal, or in some sense content-neutral, property. A distinction is normally made between an argument's formal validity, which is a matter of its logical form or syntactical structure, and its soundness, which can be determined only if one also examines the content of the argument, to determine whether its premises are true. If one were to assume that 'validity' always refers to a purely formal notion, then one could be led quite easily to the false conclusion that defenders of positivism, in so far as they assert that all laws are valid according to recognized tests of validity, are logically committed to the proposition that all laws must satisfy purely formal, content-neutral tests for validity; and from this one could be led quite naturally to the equally false conclusion that all positivists accept P1 and reject content-dependent tests of the sort recognized as possible by inclusive positivism.

It is clear, however, that 'validity' is not always used to denote a

---

[23] For similar objections to the Pedigree Argument, see D. Lyons, 'Principles, Positivism and Legal Theory'; E. P. Soper. 'Legal Theory and the Obligation of a Judge: The Hart/Dworkin Dispute'; and Jules Coleman, 'Negative and Positive Positivism'.

[24] *The Concept of Law*, 93, 108.

purely formal property. A morally valid principle is often thought to be one which not only passes certain formal tests, such as universality of form, but which is true or justified, something which, Kant notwithstanding, cannot be determined independently of examining the principle's non-formal content. The notion of a valid contract is similar in this respect. Courts sometimes deny legal validity to bargains in which one party has 'unconscionably taken advantage of the necessities of the other' and whether a bargain is of this sort is surely a question which cannot be answered without examining its content.

A third possible reason for Dworkin's error may have to do with the undeniable fact that some writers within the tradition of legal positivism do in fact subscribe to P1. As we have seen, the foremost contemporary example is Raz, who explicitly restricts possible tests for legal validity to non-moral tests. Raz distinguishes what he calls the 'strong social thesis' that the identification of no law in any legal system ever turns on moral argument, from the 'weak social thesis', that 'sometimes [in some systems] the identification of some laws turns on moral arguments'.[25] For reasons which we considered above and ultimately rejected, Raz accepts the strong social thesis, which we renamed exclusive positivism. But as our discussion of the Pedigree Argument reveals, positivists like Hart, Bentham, and Austin clearly accept the weak social thesis, i.e. inclusive positivism. Dworkin's argument misfires as an attack on positivism because he fails to recognize inclusive positivism as a distinct, viable version of that theory.

4. THE ARGUMENT FROM FUNCTION

A fourth possible explanation for Dworkin's error in holding all positivists committed to P1, and therefore exclusive positivism, stems from his views regarding the positivist's 'picture of law's function'.[26] We have already encountered a form of this argument in our discussion of Raz. We now turn to a slightly different version put forward by Dworkin for exactly the same reasons which motivated Raz: the undermining of inclusive positivism as a coherent version of legal positivism. In defending his assumption that positivists are indeed committed to P1, Dworkin makes the following claims.

[25] *The Authority of Law*, 47.   [26] *Taking Rights Seriously*, 347.

1. Positivists conceive of law as a public institution one of whose primary functions is to provide a 'settled, public, dependable set of standards for private and official conduct'.[27]

2. Hart claims that this function is fulfilled largely by the introduction of a rule of recognition which stipulates 'public features whose presence or absence will be decisive in identifying other rules as legal rules. [Hart] says that the acceptance of this sort of secondary rule marks the transition from a pre-legal society to a society with law, because the public features made decisive by the secondary rule will cure the defect of uncertainty latent in pre-legal practice.'[28]

3. But if this primary function of law, perhaps its *raison d'être*, is to be fulfilled, at least three things must be the case.

4. The public tests for legal validity must be such that it can be easily determined whether a particular standard satisfies them and is therefore valid law.

5. The question of which valid standards apply to a particular legal case must be fairly easy to determine; and

6. The question of what the applicable valid standards require in a particular legal case must likewise be fairly easy to answer.

7. In the light of proposition 4, the positivist must dismiss the possibility of moral criteria for legal validity. That is, given proposition 4, judicial appeals to controversial moral principles like fundamental justice and equality must amount to the creation not the discovery of valid law.[29] If the status of a standard as valid law were to depend on inherently controversial and contestable questions of political morality, then, according to the positivist, the whole point of law is lost.

8. In the light of propositions 5 and 6, the positivist must exclude principles of political morality as possible candidates for valid laws. Principles of political morality, unlike valid legal rules, do not stipulate clear answers which must be accepted, even when it is clear that they do apply.[30] Rather they provide very general reasons which incline or argue in a particular direction. They must be weighed before their effects on a decision can be determined, and

---

[27] Ibid.   [28] Ibid.

[29] This is the view we earlier called the exclusive account.

[30] Of course, if our earlier discussion of the Validity Argument is sound, then this is not necessarily true of rules either. Rules, like principles, can have varying institutional forces.

weight is often a matter of considerable controversy, as evidenced by cases like *Riggs* and *Henningsen* where there was agreement about the applicable principles but disagreement about how they should be weighed against each other.

9. Thus, a secondary rule of recognition which incorporated moral tests for legal validity in the ways sanctioned by inclusive positivism would 'introduce no further determinacy and could not mark a transition to anything'.[31] To quote Hart himself, 'Constitutions do not invite trouble by taking this form.'[32]

10. Thus, the positivist's views concerning (one of) the law's defining functions excludes inclusive positivism as a possible form of legal positivism.

This argument is very similar to Raz's Argument From Function and many of the replies we made to it apply equally well here. First, the argument clearly exaggerates the extent to which defenders of positivism are concerned to stress the law's capacity to resolve social issues in a clear, determinate manner. As noted earlier, Hart and other positivists explicitly argue that we should deliberately frame laws in flexible, open-textured terms so as to avoid absurd or repugnant results in unanticipated cases.

Now if the avoidance of absurd results serves in the minds of a positivist like Hart as a sufficient reason to recommend the deliberate framing of indeterminate rules, then it is clear that not all defenders of positivism view certainty, predictability, and the related values as of total or overriding importance in law. That laws should not commit us to absurd or repugnant results, or that they should not (unintentionally or otherwise) violate fundamental rights and freedoms of political morality, are aims which positivists can recognize and endorse. A positivist is not barred from recognizing such ends for law in his descriptive-explanatory ascriptions of function. The same is true of his moral-evaluative ascriptions of function, should he wish to make any when departing from his usual business of offering a descriptive-explanatory theory of law. He could, if he chose to do so, offer a normative theory about what a legal system should be like, and include within that theory a recommendation concerning the adoption of moral criteria for validity.

A second objection to Dworkin's Argument From Function is that it seems to rest on an exaggerated contrast between the certainty

---

[31] *Taking Rights Seriously*, 347.
[32] *Essays in Jurisprudence and Philosophy*, 361.

obtainable from rules whose validity is solely a function of pure pedigree or social source, and the supposed instability introduced if, e.g., the validity or content of a law is sometimes partly based on its conformity with standards of political morality. As previously observed, it is a commonplace that pedigreed rules are often subject to considerable controversy over their proper interpretation, and the procedures to be used in trying to understand them and what they imply for legal cases. Pedigreed rules sometimes conflict with one another and have 'gaps'. It is also beyond dispute that questions of political morality sometimes, though obviously not always, admit of easy answers upon which all reasonable members of a community would agree. It follows that allowing some questions concerning the validity and content of laws to depend on factors in political morality need in no way conflict with the assertion that an important function or point of law is to serve as a dependable public standard.

A third, related, objection to Dworkin's Argument From Function is that it overstates the degree of uncertainty that is introduced if moral criteria for validity are included in a rule of recognition. If legal validity were always to depend on controversial questions of political morality, then of course great uncertainty, instability, and perhaps even social chaos would be the result. Thus if a society were to stipulate, as its rule of recognition simply that 'All disputes are to be settled as justice requires',[33] then the set of standards for public and private use within that society would undoubtedly be no more dependable and stable than it would be were there no rule of recognition at all. One might well agree with Dworkin that the adoption of such a 'rule of recognition' would introduce no further determinacy and could not mark a transition to anything of much significance, least of all anything remotely like a modern legal system.

But it is clear that inclusive positivism is in no way committed to a rule of recognition of such a deeply indeterminate sort. It is true in Canada, for example, that all laws have, as a condition of their validity, that they do not violate the principles of political morality recognized in the Charter. So in theory, political morality always counts. But normally it is clear that no Charter right is unrea-

---

[33] Soper, 'Legal Theory and the Obligation of a Judge: The Hart/Dworkin Dispute', 512. Cf. Raz, *Practical Reason and Norms*, ch. 4 on 'systems of absolute discretion' and R. Tur, 'Positivism, Principles and Rules', 63.

sonably infringed, and so the validity and content of Canadian law is seldom challenged on these grounds. Everyone knows that almost all Canadian law satisfies the Charter and acts accordingly. It operates effectively without unsettling influences from political morality which, again, is not always as indeterminate as some might have us believe. Principles of political morality do have their penumbras of uncertainty and are sometimes indeterminate, i.e. they sometimes fail actually to determine an answer. In such cases, 'determinations' may, as Aquinas recognized, be required by judges. But such cases are the exception. Most of the time, most people know that sections 7 and 15 of the Canadian Charter are satisfied by Canadian legislation. There is nothing in the Charter which unsettles Canadian law to the point where a positivist (or anyone else for that matter) must question whether Canadians, in adopting their Charter, have abandoned their legal system entirely in favour of something else altogether.

We have been supposing thus far that moral principles figure in law only to the extent that the law recognizes their role in some fairly determinate way, either through enactment, as with the Canadian Charter, or through judicial recognition in a long line of decisions. As Dworkin himself has noted, certain fundamental maxims of the common law, like the principle that the courts will not allow themselves to be the vehicles of injustice, acquire their status as law not through enactment but through judicial recognition.[34] In both instances, however, principles of political morality acquire their status as law by acquiring the appropriate pedigree, a pedigree which can figure easily in the positivist's rule of recognition.

But Dworkin is also of the view that some principles of political morality count as law even though they have no recognizable pedigree, indeed have never before been enunciated in a legislature or court of law. They count as law because they figure in the best interpretive theory of the settled law. It will be instructive at this stage to ask whether a positivist could go so far as to agree with Dworkin on this matter. Could he accept something like Dworkin's account of how (some) principles of political morality acquire their status as law, without thereby running afoul of the thesis that an important function of legal systems is to introduce a degree of certainty and stability into questions of proper conduct? In other

[34] See *Taking Rights Seriously*, ch. 3, *passim*.

W thinks a pos. could admit possibly a R of R which prescribes that rules of system include a ~~rule~~ principles which provide the best interp theory of the settled law. H looks as though W adopts sthg like such a rule in his chap 8, so he should in consistency allow this possib.

words, could he accept a rule of recognition which prescribes that the system's legal principles include those principles which provide the best interpretive theory of the settled law? Or would allowing such a 'Herculean criterion for law' necessarily lead to the denial that law marks a transition to a system of social regulation in which 'the public features made decisive by the secondary rule [of recognition] will cure the defect of uncertainty latent in pre-legal practice'? The answer to this last question is Certainly not. *NB*

A rule of recognition containing Herculean tests for law need not be anywhere as indeterminate and useless as might initially be thought. For one thing, the Herculean test for legal principles is logically dependent on other criteria for validity, a point to which Dworkin fails to give proper recognition.[35] According to that test, principles of political morality which figure in the best interpretive theory of the settled, i.e., pre-interpretive, law count as binding law. This test, then, logically requires that there be a vast body of (more or less) settled legal standards to be interpreted; and the existence of such a body requires, presumably, that there be other criteria of validity in terms of which it can be identified. There must be some way to tell what counts as settled law, even if at the post-interpretive stage of deliberation some of this settled law might be discounted as corrigible mistake, i.e. not valid after all. Let us suppose that these tests exist as accepted standards of validity, and that they identify a wide range of settled standards, like those contained within the Canadian *Criminal Code*, that are sufficient to guide conduct in the vast majority of cases. Let us suppose next that the accepted rule(s) of recognition also contain Herculean, interpretive criteria for legal principles, to which appeal is made 'when the standard materials provide uncertain guidance'.[36] The adoption of such a secondary rule might well mark a transition to something of very great significance, to a 'kind of human institution which is of decisive importance to the regulation of social life'.[37]

impt point (one demonstrated by MacC. ix LRTLT

Of course the degree of stability and determinacy introduced would depend to a rather large extent on what the more fundamental criteria of validity were and how well standards were framed in accordance with them by legislators and judges. Dworkin seems himself to acknowledge this in a reply to John Mackie's charge that

---

[35] For a similar criticism, see S. Burton, 'Ronald Dworkin and Legal Positivism', 117–25.

[36] *Taking Rights Seriously*, 326.   [37] *The Authority of Law*, 52.

a Herculean test for law 'designates more cases as hard cases—allows more room to challenge what is taken to be settled law—than positivism does'.[38] Dworkin writes: 'It is in fact a difficult question whether my theory allows more "settled" law to be challenged. Much depends upon details of doctrine and practice in particular jurisdictions—for example whether these allow over-ruling of undesirable precedents.'[39] Here we get recognition that the methods by which hard cases are handled depend on practice, a point stressed by positivists who wish to insist that criteria for validity, and the methods by which the institutional forces of laws satisfying those criteria are determined, depend on accepted practice. There is nothing in the nature of law itself which determines, e.g., that moral criteria must be accepted, or that precedents must be overruled or changed when seriously in conflict with rights of political morality. But it is not clear that Dworkin really does wish to acknowledge this fact. As noted earlier in Chapters 2 and 3, Dworkin seems to present his conception of law as one according to which legal rights are necessarily moral rights. As with defenders of traditional natural-law theory, his view seems to be that the nature of law itself determines the role morality must play in legal practice. It is here more than anywhere else perhaps that Dworkin's integrity theory is distinguishable from inclusive positivism. The former asserts that morality necessarily figures in law and legal judgments, the latter only that this is possible. Any connections there might be between law and morality are contingent, not necessary.

The fourth and perhaps most telling objection to Dworkin's Argument From Function is that it fails adequately to distinguish between what might be thought desirable in a legal system and what might be thought essential to its very existence. This distinction is related to our earlier contrast between moral-evaluative and descriptive ascriptions of function, though it is not identical with it. The reason for this is that 'desirable' does not necessarily mean morally desirable. Things can be desirable for all sorts of reasons, only some of which are moral. I might find a certain kind of costly food desirable but perhaps not morally desirable if my having it deprives someone else of the basic nourishment he needs and which he would have were we both to eat something a bit cheaper and less

---

[38] *Taking Rights Seriously*, 361. In 'The Third Theory of Law', Mackie argues that Dworkin's theory allows judges to play fast and loose with the settled law.
[39] *Taking Rights Seriously*, 362.

tasty. The latter would, in a sense, be morally desirable though not desirable as delicious food. The same could be true of a legal system. A ruthless dictator bent on establishing overwhelming power over a population might find a certain morally pernicious legal arrangement desirable for his own purposes. In one sense the arrangement would be desirable, in another quite the opposite.

These complications aside, we can still ask the following question. Assume that positivists view the relative determinacy and stability which law is capable of bringing to social life as important. Can their view be that this is an essential feature of law? Or must their position be that this feature serves as a criterion in terms of which a legal system, (whose status as a legal system is established on other grounds—e.g. by seeing whether it has rules of recognition, change and adjudication, and claims supremacy over a population) can be evaluated or judged? In other words, is their view that the provision of these valued social commodities, to some significant degree, is a defining feature of law, or alternatively one important criterion in terms of which systems of law can be evaluated via a normative theory of some kind?

I am strongly inclined to think that defenders of positivism would choose the latter option. Imagine that a system of social regulation possesses all the hallmarks of a municipal legal system. It has judges, lawyers, courts, litigants, secondary rules of recognition, change and adjudication, and so on. Imagine further that its fundamental secondary rules allow for less determinacy and stability than is possible, say because they allow Herculean criteria for legal principles, or because they stipulate rights of political morality like due process, liberty, and equality as criteria of validity applicable to all subordinate laws. Is it not obvious that positivists would refuse to view such a system as a failed attempt at law, a perversion of law? Would they not instead view it as a system of law deficient in certain respects, but perhaps desirable in others? If not, they would clearly be in danger of promoting a fused identity between what law is and what it ought to be,[40] and forgoing the many advantages which, in the view of positivists, one reaps from a wide concept of law which separates the existence of a legal system from its moral

[40] Coleman makes a similar point in 'Negative and Positive Positivism', 147. Cf. R. Tur, 'Positivism, Principles and Rules', 50, where it is suggested that to define law in functionalist terms 'would be to flirt with Natural Law Doctrine or to embrace ethnocentrism, both of which positivism seeks to avoid'.

and political evaluation—a concept which allows for the possibility of immoral, wicked, or otherwise highly unsatisfactory legal systems. Whether one agrees with positivists that a wider concept is indeed theoretically preferable, it is indisputable that this is their view, and that Dworkin's Argument From Function would be rejected on the familiar ground that the existence of law is one thing and its merit or demerit quite another. The positivist's descriptive-explanatory theory of law should not be transformed, against his will, into a normative theory about what it is desirable to have in legal systems.

7

DISCRETION AND LEGAL THEORY

1. THE DISCRETION ARGUMENT

In the last chapter we examined three arguments, each purporting to show that positivism is inconsistent with a rule of recognition containing moral tests for valid law, and that inclusive positivism is therefore incoherent. The Validity Argument was shown to be unsound on the ground that weight and validity are logically compatible properties. The Pedigree Argument was seen to fail because the moral tests for law sanctioned by inclusive positivism are only contingent features of some possible legal systems. The Argument From Function was discredited on a number of grounds, the primary one being that it seriously exaggerates the positivist's concern for certainty and finality in the law, casting his views concerning how law sometimes serves these values into a form he would reject, namely, a normative theory of law.

In this chapter we consider two further arguments which might be offered to show that positivism is inconsistent with moral tests for law, and that inclusive positivism is therefore internally inconsistent. Both arguments appeal to the idea of discretion, a notion which was extremely important in Dworkin's early assault upon positivism.[1] The first argument runs as follows.

According to inclusive positivism, the fact that judges and lawyers appeal to principles of political morality as grounds for determinations of law is consistent with legal positivism. But this is wrong. It is an implication of the positivist's theory of legal reasoning that any appeal to moral principles must always be *discretionary*. It must involve the creation of new law, not the discovery of pre-existing, valid law. So inclusive positivism is internally incoherent after all,

[1] See 'Judicial Discretion' and *Taking Rights Seriously*, ch. 3, formerly called 'The Model of Rules'.

because it flatly contradicts the positivist's theory of judicial discretion.

This Discretion Argument raises a number of questions. First, what exactly is meant by 'discretion'? As we shall see shortly, it is not at all clear what this term means, even to Dworkin whose early assault upon Hart's positivism depended crucially on the notion. Second, why should we suppose that a positivist must say that any judicial reference to principles of political morality is necessarily discretionary, must amount to the creation of new law not a determination of existing law? We will begin with the first question which will involve us in an extensive discussion of Dworkin's theory of strong discretion. Only by investigating this notion thoroughly will we gain a full appreciation of the Discretion Argument and why it cannot validly be used to attack inclusive positivism, or any other positivistic theory of law.

2. STRONG AND WEAK DISCRETION

Questions about judicial discretion held centre stage in legal philosophy during the 1970s and early 1980s. This was due in large measure to Dworkin's provocative attempt to discredit positivism by undermining what he took to be its commitment to judicial discretion as the only possible explanation for reasoning in hard cases. These are cases where for some reason the law provides uncertain guidance and reasonable lawyers and judges continue to disagree about what it requires even after all the facts have been presented and agreed upon, and the settled law brought to bear on them. Many legal philosophers accept that discretion is the mode of reasoning employed in hard cases. They follow Hart's lead in suggesting that judicial discretion is an unavoidable feature of legal systems, that hard cases do and must arise in which the law runs out and the judge must appeal to, e.g., his own or the community's sense of justice to decide issues left unresolved by the law. As observed earlier, Hart went so far as to argue that recourse to this kind of discretion is not a necessary evil, but something we should welcome as a means of achieving flexibility and rationality in the law. Hart believes that we are wise sometimes to adopt loose, open-textured rules in situations where it seems reasonable not to pin ourselves down in advance. There is often too much we cannot anticipate and so it is better to use significantly open-textured terms like 'reasonable' and 'fair' in drafting rules than to try to settle the future blindly and in advance with more closely-textured terms. If we can't tell in advance what might be reasonable in a case we cannot anticipate, it is better to allow judges, and people who will be called upon to apply the rules to their own conduct, to decide those matters themselves when the concrete cases arise. In other words, it is preferable to allow them considerable discretion in applying the rules.

Of course it is possible to try to eliminate discretion entirely by creating highly specific, concrete rules which attempt to settle all questions in advance. Instead of specifying that people may use reasonable force in defending themselves against aggressors, one might try foolishly to specify in minute detail all the possible kinds of aggression that there are, all the conceivable circumstances in which these might arise, and how victims are entitled to respond to those kinds of aggression in those particular circumstances. Such an attempt would be sheer lunacy: but according to Hart it could not possibly succeed anyway. Open texture would still be encountered and cases in which discretion is necessary would still arise. '[U]ncertainty at the borderline is the price to be paid for the use of general classifying terms in any form of communication.'[2]

Judicial (and law-subject) discretion is viewed by Hart as a necessary feature of law because law necessarily involves the communication of standards of behaviour and these necessarily have open texture. Judicial (and law-subject) discretion is also thought of as a desirable feature of law: it permits us to achieve flexibility and rationality in the application of legal standards.[3]

Dworkin disagrees. In his view, judicial discretion, as it appears to be conceived by philosophers like Hart, does not exist in Anglo-American legal systems, need not exist in modern systems of law, and is not by any stretch of the imagination something we should welcome even if it did exist. On the contrary, any theory which relies upon judicial discretion to explain decisions in hard cases not only mis-characterizes the adjudicative processes found in Anglo-American legal systems (i.e. it offers an interpretation which fails to fit the data) but is also morally and politically intolerable (i.e. it fails to put those practices in their best moral light). If, instead of

[2] *The Concept of Law*, 124–5.
[3] Hart's theory of judicial discretion will be investigated more fully in the next chapter. For present purposes the above account will do.

applying pre-existing laws to the case before him, a judge himself decides the issue which has, inadvertently or not, been left open for later settlement, then the result is gross unfairness. If in this way the judge 'makes new law and applies it retroactively in the case before him, then the losing party will be punished, not because he violated some duty he had, but rather a new duty created after the event'.[4] Democratic theory loses in the process as well. If judges decide these legally open issues by employing their own, or even the community's, sense of justice, then they assume the role of legislator, a role which ought to be reserved for elected officials who, unlike the majority of judges, are accountable to the electorate over whom they exercise authority. The judge should apply law, not make it.

doesn buy this argument in chap. 8? and this?

So Dworkin is concerned to undermine theories, like Hart's, which rely on judicial discretion. He claims that many of the arguments in favour of such theories rest upon a simple confusion concerning three different senses of the term 'discretion'. There is, he argues, discretion in a weak sense where the standards an official 'must apply cannot be applied mechanically but demand the use of judgment'.[5] No one, of course, disputes that hard cases which require this kind of judgment exist in law, though some might, for the sake of certainty and predictability, wish to minimize their number and the degree to which they require individual judgment. But law is not composed of algorithms, and so 'judgment calls' are inevitable.

Dworkin also distinguishes a second, weak sense of discretion: here the term is used to suggest that the official's decision is final and cannot be overruled by some other official.[6] Once again there are no disputes surrounding discretion in this sense. Supreme courts make final decisions, and it is natural, though perhaps misleading, to express this by saying that decisions in difficult supreme court cases are left to the judges' discretion. Where Dworkin sees the battle-lines being drawn is over the existence, necessity, and desirability of judicial discretion in a third, strong sense of the term. Unfortunately, and somewhat surprisingly, Dworkin has never been entirely clear about what he means by his key term 'strong discretion'. As I shall illustrate below, his attempts to explain the notion reveal two crucially different ways in which it might be understood. I shall argue that one of these two understandings of the notion leads to serious difficulties, and that Dworkin's attempt to overcome them both fails and suggests that he does understand strong discre-

[4] *Taking Rights Seriously*, 84.   [5] Ibid. 31.   [6] Ibid. 32.

tion in that troublesome way. Getting clear on these matters will help us later in our attempt to understand the Discretion Argument and its claim that inclusive positivism must view appeals to moral principles as discretionary, and that the theory is therefore not a coherent form of positivism after all. We will also be helped in this endeavour by drawing an important distinction between exercising and having strong discretion. There are, I shall argue, important differences between saying of judges that they have strong discretion and saying that they exercise strong discretion. These differences lead to different interpretations of the Discretion Argument, and different lines of defence in showing where it goes wrong in its critique of inclusive positivism. The initial plausibility of the Discretion Argument vanishes once these important differences are noted and brought to bear on the argument.

3. TWO INTERPRETATIONS

Dworkin suggests at one point in *Taking Rights Seriously* that the notion of discretion in the strong sense is used to claim that on some issue the decision of an official (e.g. a judge, a baseball umpire or a military sergeant) 'is *not controlled* by a standard furnished by the particular authority we have in mind when we raise the question of discretion'[7] or that on that issue the official is 'simply *not bound* by standards set by the authority in question'.[8] Thus, he suggests, a sergeant has discretion in the strong sense when he is told to pick any five men for patrol he chooses and we 'use this sense not to comment on the vagueness or difficulty of the standards, or on who has final word in applying them, but on their range and the decisions they purport to control'.[9] Dworkin adds that if 'the sergeant is told to take the five most experienced men, he does not have discretion in this strong sense because that order purports to govern his decision'.[10]

A crucial question emerges from these attempts to explain the notion of strong discretion. In order to facilitate discussion we will put our question in the negative by asking for the conditions under which a person does not have strong discretion. If an individual is not to have strong discretion on some issue is it necessary (a) that the

---

[7] Ibid. 33, emphasis added.   [8] Ibid. 32, emphasis added.
[9] Ibid.   [10] Ibid.

standards he is bound to apply *control* or *govern* the decision he must make, or (b) that those standards merely *purport* to control or govern the decision? As we have seen, Dworkin suggests that the sergeant who is ordered to pick his five most experienced men does not have strong discretion 'because that order *purports to govern his decision*'. This suggests that (a) is unnecessary and that (b) is sufficient. But of course Dworkin also states that an official's strong discretion 'means ... that his decision is not controlled by a standard furnished by the particular authority we have in mind when we raise the question of discretion'. This clearly suggests that (b) is insufficient and that it is necessary that there be standards which not only purport to control the decision but actually do so. Thus it is unclear which of the following two propositions Dworkin means to affirm:

P: An individual, S, lacks strong discretion on some issue if and only if S is bound by standards set by an authority and those standards purport to control (or govern) his decision.

C: An individual, S, lacks strong discretion on some issue if and only if S is bound by standards set by an authority and those standards do succeed in controlling (or governing) his decision.

Prima facie P and C are not equivalent. It is one thing to purport to do something, quite another actually to succeed in doing it. Whether the two propositions are indeed equivalent will depend on how one is to understand the phrases 'controls' and 'purports to control'. Presumably, a standard controls a decision if and only if (a) the standard is one which the decision-maker is duty-bound or required to apply in the circumstances, whenever it is applicable and not outweighed, overridden or pre-empted by another standard of more normative force;[11] and (b) the standard applies to the facts of the case and determines or dictates one and only one answer or decision. Thus if the sergeant is ordered by a superior to pick his tallest man for a certain specified military exercise, and it is undeniable both that Private Smith is the tallest man under the sergeant's

---

[11] This force could be what we earlier called 'institutional force', if the standard in question has an institutional source or is in some other way connected with institutional sources in the appropriate ways. For example, it might be a foreign standard which binding rules of adjudication require one to apply to one's own conduct or the conduct of others. But the force need not be institutional. For example, the standards of prudence may have normative force over our decisions in most contexts despite the fact that they do not derive from an institutional source.

command and that the superior's command has overwhelming normative force over the sergeant's decision, then the order determines
one and only one result: Private Smith must be chosen.

As for what it means to say that a standard purports to control or
govern a decision, the answer would appear to be this. If our
sergeant is ordered to pick his tallest man, then he is issued an order
which, by its very form, purports to control his choice. The order
purports to govern the decision because (a) it presupposes that there
is a tallest man, in much the same way as the proposition 'The tallest ?
Swede lives in Stockholm' presupposes that there is one and only
one Swede who is taller than every other Swede; and (b) it, in conjunction with institutional rules requiring military personnel
(normally) to follow all orders issuing from superior sources,
charges the sergeant with the responsibility of choosing that particular individual. On this interpretation, the order purports to control
the decision because it purports to single out a unique decision which
must be accepted, given the relevant institutional rules and the
inescapable force with which they provide the order. On the other
hand, an order requiring the sergeant simply to pick a tall man does
not even purport to control the decision because it does not presuppose that there is only one tall man, and it does not charge the
sergeant with the responsibility of choosing any one individual in
particular, of coming to any one decision concerning who is to be
chosen. It allows him to choose from among whatever tall men
happen to be under his command. If, as a matter of fact, there
happens to be only one man under the sergeant's command who
could, with any plausibility, be described as tall, then in these
special circumstances the order would effectively control the decision, even though it does not purport to do so.

It should be noted that when the sergeant is given a certain lati-
tude concerning his choice, say he is told only to pick a reasonably
tall man, not necessarily the tallest man, the order might be said
both to control and to purport to control the sergeant's decision. partially
'Control' need not mean fully control; it can mean partially con- Control
trol. Even though the order neither singles out nor purports to
single out one and only one choice, it does restrict, and is intended to
restrict, the range of acceptable choices to some degree. It rules out,
as possible choices, all the sergeant's men who are not tall. Even the
sergeant's order to pick 'any five men for patrol he chooses' requires
that the sergeant make a choice, that he choose five individuals, and

that those individuals be men. It would seem that virtually all authoritative standards exert, and are intended to exert, some degree of control over decisions, including those whose normative force can be overridden or outweighed. As we saw earlier, that a standard has normative force does not mean that it must be followed in all cases to which it applies. For reasons of simplicity and because it does not affect the arguments of this section, 'controls' will hereafter be understood to mean fully controls. In saying that a standard controls a decision we will mean (a) that whatever normative force the standard has is not defeated in the circumstances by competing considerations; and (b) that the standard singles out a uniquely correct decision which must be accepted if the decision-maker is to comply with the standard. It purports to control if it has such force and also presupposes that there is a uniquely correct answer.

If these interpretations of 'controls' and 'purports to control' are accepted, then the two phrases are obviously not equivalent. As noted, an order can control a decision even though it does not purport to do so. Even more important is the possibility that an order might purport to control a decision and yet fail to do so. Suppose that there is no tallest man under the sergeant's command, that Privates Smith and Jones are of precisely equal height and taller than all the rest. Or suppose that the sergeant is ordered to pick his five most experienced men for a certain dangerous patrol exercise. The sergeant's men might all be of precisely equal experience, or some might be more experienced at patrol exercises while others are more experienced at dangerous exercises and there is no reason whatsoever to think that one kind of experience is, in the circumstances, preferable or more relevant. In the first instance, the order makes reference to a single scale but in relation to that scale it fails to single out only one individual: there is a tie. In the second instance, the order makes reference to two relevant scales, but fails to single out only one individual because each individual excels on one of the two scales and the scales are not weighted, or it is indeterminate which of the two, if either, is of more weight. In both cases, it is clear that, despite the relevant order, and despite the institutional rule requiring the sergeant to follow the relevant order in the circumstances,[12] his decision is not fully controlled. The order fails in

---

[12] In this respect the sergeant is like the judge in the English Court of Appeal who knows that he must follow the precedent regardless of whether he thinks that the precedent is a good one. Military orders have differing institutional forces just like

what it sets out or purports to do. It presupposes what is not the case and makes an impossible demand.

If P and C are therefore not equivalent, one must ask which Dworkin means to affirm. How we assess theories concerning the existence, necessity, and desirability of strong discretion will differ depending on which is intended. The same can presumably be said of the Discretion Argument and our assessment of it. I shall now try to show that Dworkin in fact intends interpretation P. My main ground for supposing this lies in his apparent attempt to overcome certain serious difficulties which accompany the proposition.

Along with interpretation P comes the following obvious question. What if binding standards which purport to control a decision in fact fail to do so? Does it not follow that in such cases the decision-maker has strong discretion to choose from among the alternatives which the standards leave open? Dworkin apparently thinks not. The question whether a decision-maker, e.g. our sergeant, has strong discretion seems, for him, to be logically independent of whether authoritative standards actually succeed in singling out a uniquely correct answer. The crucial question is whether the decision-maker is *entitled to suppose* that the relevant authoritative standards fail to control the decision fully and that he may therefore step beyond them to make a choice among alternatives left open, a choice based upon standards which the decision-maker, not the authority, sees fit to be applied. In Dworkin's view the sergeant in the above cases is not so entitled, but rather is 'bound to reach an understanding, controversial or not, of what his orders ... require and to act on that understanding'.[13] He must attempt to determine, e.g., who are the five most experienced men, even if there is no unique set of five men to whom the definite description 'the five most experienced men' might properly be assigned.

Applying this understanding of 'strong discretion' to judicial contexts leads to some interesting results, and may lend an unwarranted air of plausibility to the Discretion Argument. The law's failure to provide a unique solution to a legal question is not, as might have been supposed, a sufficient condition for a judge's having strong

precedents do, and as with precedents, this institutional force is different from whatever moral force a military order might have. A judge faced with an immoral precedent with institutional force is in a position analogous to a subordinate military officer ordered to perform an immoral action.

[13] *Taking Rights Seriously*, 36.

discretion on that question.[14] If true, this has important implications for questions concerning the place, if any, for strong discretion in legal cases, particularly those involving Charters and
bills of rights where it is natural to think that the significantly
open-textured nature of the moral concepts used in such documents inevitably means a good deal of judicial discretion. But if
Dworkin is right, this picture is totally inaccurate, so long as the
law always purports to control legal decisions, including Charter
decisions. Even if, as Hart argues, the open-textured nature of all
modes of communicating standards of behaviour logically entails
that at some point those standards must prove indeterminate, and
even if, as John Mackie and many others have argued, it will
inevitably prove indeterminate which of two or more competing
interpretive theories of the law, or some portion of it, is the
strongest, it does not, surprisingly enough, follow that judges
have, or must have, a quasi-legislative strong discretion.[15] So
long as a judge, like the sergeant, is bound by the institutional
force of standards, however indeterminate, which merely purport
to control his decision fully, he does not have strong discretion.
Rather he has the duty to find the uniquely correct answer which
the law purports to provide. And Dworkin's view has always been
that the judge's position is in this respect identical to that of the
sergeant who is ordered to pick his five most experienced men.
The judge is required by what Dworkin terms 'the ground rules of
the enterprise' (by which he means, presumably, what we have
been calling secondary rules of adjudication) always to search for

[14] Cf. Dworkin's comment on *MacPherson*: 'The law may not be a seamless web;
but the plaintiff [Mrs. MacPherson] is entitled to ask Hercules to treat it as if it were.'
(Ibid. 116.)

[15] A good deal of discussion arose from Dworkin's early claims concerning the
existence of right answers to all legal questions, even those upon which there is deep
division of opinion. Dworkin seems now to be less concerned to defend the
uniqueness thesis and so discussion of this issue has tailed off somewhat. But whether
the thesis is true still seems to be a crucial question for Dworkin given his project of
showing that legal decisions enforce existing legal rights and are not discretionary, a
view which, so far as I can tell, he has never relinquished. Places where the uniqueness
thesis has been questioned include: John Mackie, 'The Third Theory of Law'; H. L.
A. Hart, 'American Jurisprudence Through English Eyes: The Nightmare and the
Noble Dream', 123–144; David Lyons, 'Principles, Positivism and Legal Theory'; R.
Shiner, 'The Metaphysics of Taking Rights Seriously'; E. P. Soper, 'Legal Theory and
the Obligation of a Judge: The Hart/Dworkin Dispute'; C. L. Ten, 'The Soundest
Theory of Law'.

the answer determined or dictated by the standards of law.[16] These ground rules presuppose that there always is a uniquely correct answer, and they charge the judge with the legal-adjudicative responsibility of finding it. In this respect the rules are like the order requiring the sergeant to pick his five most experienced men, which presupposes that there is a unique set of five who are most experienced.

If this is how Dworkin would have us understand the notion of (strong) discretion, then his view is open to some rather serious objections. If P is true, then to say that an individual lacks strong discretion is to say that he must never suppose or assume that his decision is not fully controlled; he must always proceed on the assumption that the standards he is to apply succeed in controlling his decision. But what if he has reason to suppose that those authoritative standards in fact fail to control his decision fully? The sergeant might know that the order to pick his five most experienced men fails to control his decision when his men are of precisely equal experience, or that an order to pick his tallest man fails in this respect when Privates Smith and Jones are of precisely equal height but taller than all the rest. It is clear that such cases are possible. Yet if the sergeant knows fully well in these cases that his decision is not completely controlled, does he not also know that if he is to make a decision on the basis of his orders, he must choose from among alternatives which those orders leave open? It would seem so. What are the options? But then is it not also true that in such cases the sergeant has, and knows that he has, strong discretion to choose from among those open alternatives?[17]

Not if interpretation P is accepted. The sergeant's orders do purport to control the decision and therefore he does not have strong discretion. But now the denial that he has strong discretion takes on

---

[16] In *Taking Rights Seriously*, 100, Dworkin restricts the thesis to 'standard civil cases', thus omitting from its scope criminal cases. In order to facilitate discussion, we will follow Dworkin's lead and characterize him as suggesting that the law purports to control *all* judicial decisions fully, with the understanding that he does recognize exceptions to this blanket statement. For a defence of the claim that, *contra* Dworkin, the ground rules of civil adjudication in the Anglo-American legal systems explicitly allow for considerable strong discretion, see Barbara Baum-Levenbrook's 'Discretion and Dispositive Concepts'.

[17] I am assuming here that the sergeant is unable to ask for further instructions or clarification of the order and that there are no other standards which serve in conjunction with the order to identify a unique solution. Even if there are other standards these too might fail to determine a uniquely correct answer.

a rather hollow ring. What significance is there in this denial when the decision-maker knows that the standards set by the authority fail to eliminate all but one possible choice? He cannot discover and accept a uniquely correct decision when he knows that none exists. And if he cannot do so, then he cannot be 'bound to reach an understanding, controversial or not, of what his orders ... require, and to act on that understanding'.[18]

Dworkin appears to realize that these objections can be raised against interpretation P when it is applied to judicial contexts, and it is his apparent attempt to meet these objections which gives us the strongest grounds for supposing that it is indeed P, not interpretation C, which he means to affirm.

As we have seen above, Dworkin's controversial theory of adjudication includes the claim that the correct answer in a hard case is that answer which is provided by the best interpretive theory of the settled law. Yet this account fails to exclude the logical possibility that there might sometimes be a set of equally good constructive interpretations each better than all other interpretations which have been or might be offered. If these equally good interpretations sometimes provide incompatible answers to the question posed by a hard case, then the law will sometimes fail to control the judge's decision fully, and the judge might well know that it fails in this respect.

Having admitted this possibility, Dworkin attempts to soften the blow by suggesting that one can speak about the probability that a legal system 'will produce many or few cases that are in fact ties'.[19] If the system is a 'primitive' one, in which the pre-interpretive data to be interpreted are thin, then it is

probable ... both that the judges will judge that several cases ... are ties, and that in fact several cases will be ties. Since there is very little settled law, more than one theory of law, critically different for the result in a hard case, will often offer equally good [interpretations of] the settled law, and will seem to offer equally good [interpretations] to many judges.[20]

Later Dworkin suggests that under such conditions it would be 'silly', 'unreasonable', and indeed 'irrational' for 'the enterprise', i.e. the legal system, to 'instruct judges to ignore [the] possibility of a tie'.[21] In other words, it would be irrational for the accepted rules of adjudication to require judges to proceed as if the law always did

---

[18] *Taking Rights Seriously*, 36.   [19] Ibid. 286.   [20] Ibid.
[21] Ibid. 287.

succeed in controlling their decisions fully. It would, in these circumstances, be unreasonable for those rules to deny judges strong discretion. But now, Dworkin continues, suppose

that the legal system these judges administer is very advanced, and is thick with constitutional rules and practices, and dense with precedents and statutes. The antecedent probability of a tie is very much lower; indeed it might well be so low as to justify a further ground rule of the enterprise which instructs judges to eliminate ties from the range of answers they might give. That instruction does not deny the theoretical possibility of a tie, but it does suppose that, given the complexity of the legal materials at hand, judges will, if they think long and hard enough, come to think that one side has, all things considered and marginally, the better of the case. This further instruction will be rational if the antecedent probability of error in a judicial decision seems greater than the antecedent probability that some case will indeed be, in fact, a tie, and if there are advantages of finality or other political advantages to be gained by denying the possibility of tie cases at law. Of course, the instruction will be not rational but silly if the legal system is not sufficiently complex to justify that calculation of antecedent probabilities.[22]

So Dworkin's response to the objection raised above is to claim that hard cases arising in mature legal systems are never in fact like the simple case of the sergeant who knows that Privates Smith and Jones are of precisely equal height or that his men are all of equal experience. The standards binding within such systems are so numerous and complex that it is virtually certain that a judge will never be in a position to know, or even to entertain seriously the possibility, that in some particular case those standards fail to control his decision fully. Thus these legal systems are perfectly reasonable in adopting ground rules of adjudication which require judges always to proceed on the assumption that the law succeeds in controlling their decisions fully; and since these systems do, in Dworkin's view, adopt such ground rules, it follows that judges within these systems never have strong discretion.

There are serious problems with this response. First, it is not clear that we should deny, with virtual certainty, that a judge in a mature legal system could either know or reasonably believe that his decision is not fully controlled. At the very least this seems theoretically possible. Yet if it is possible that a judge should possess such

---

[22] Ibid. 286–7. C.F. Dworkin, 'No Right Answer?', 83–4; and R. Sartorius, 'Social Policy and Judicial Legislation', 158–9.

knowledge, this is enough to cast doubt on interpretation P as an analysis of the very concept of judicial discretion in the strong sense. Second, proposition P is presumably not intended to apply only to judges who function within 'mature' legal systems. Rather, it is intended to apply to sergeants, chess referees, baseball umpires, judges in primitive legal systems, and judges in mature legal systems who are required to deal with newly developed areas of law which are not dense with relevant precedents and statutes. (Some claim, for instance, that this is now true in Canada where there is little existing jurisprudence surrounding the newly introduced Charter.) In short, interpretation P is intended to apply to any situation in which there is an individual who 'is in general charged with making decisions subject to standards set by a particular authority'.[23] Yet if P is a general claim which is intended to be analytic of the concept of discretion in the strong sense, it is obviously fallacious to defend it by appeal to contingent features of certain special cases where, it is claimed, the complexity of the standards which must be applied ensures that one could never know, and would likely be wrong were one to assume, that a particular decision is not fully controlled. There are quite clearly other possible cases where the individual concerned can possess this knowledge, and here the acceptance of proposition P would force one to the absurdity of denying that he has discretion in the strong sense.

I conclude that interpretation P is seriously flawed as an explication of the concept of strong discretion, and that Dworkin's attempt to defend the thesis fails.

4. TWO OBJECTIONS

Before turning to defend interpretation C and the analysis of strong discretion it suggests, I should first like to answer two objections which could be made against the argument thus far.

First, it might be suggested that my interpretation of the term 'control' is not Dworkin's and that this vitiates my critique of his analysis of strong discretion.[24] The question whether a standard or set of standards controls a decision is, for Dworkin, independent of whether it singles out a uniquely correct answer. The crucial ques-

---

[23] *Taking Rights Seriously*, 31.
[24] I owe recognition of this objection to Barry Hoffmaster and Chris Gray.

tion is whether the decision-maker is *entitled* to step beyond the relevant authoritative standards and base his decision, in whole or in part, on non-authoritative standards. If the decision-maker is not so entitled, his decision is controlled (fully) and he has no strong discretion.

There is some plausibility in the claim that this is indeed what Dworkin means by 'controls', and consequently what he means by 'strong discretion'. For instance, if this interpretation is correct, then there is no significant difference between saying that a standard purports to control a decision and that it actually does so. This would explain the casual manner in which Dworkin interchanges the two notions in his attempts to define 'strong discretion'. In issuing an order which purports to control the sergeant's decision, the superior does control that decision, in the sense that the sergeant is bound to come to an understanding about what specific choice the order requires, regardless of whether there is in fact some one decision which it does require. Nevertheless, there is little of real substance to the objection. On the interpretation I have offered in section 3, one says that, for Dworkin, authoritative standards may purport, but fail, to control a decision, and yet the decision-maker still has no discretion in the strong sense. The reason for this, in Dworkin's view, is that the ground rules of adjudication may require the decision-maker to proceed as if the relevant standards do succeed in singling out a uniquely correct answer. On the alternative interpretation, which may indeed be more faithful to Dworkin's intent, authoritative standards may control the decision of a decision-maker, and thus deny him strong discretion, even when there is no uniquely correct answer. The reason is that the ground rules of the enterprise require the decision-maker to proceed as if the relevant standards do succeed in singling out a uniquely correct answer. Whichever interpretation is adopted, the point still remains that, in Dworkin's view, whether a decision-maker has strong discretion is independent of whether the standards he must apply single out a uniquely correct answer. It is rather a function of what the ground rules of the enterprise—e.g. military protocol or adjudication—entitle him to suppose in coming to his decision. Yet I find the interpretation offered in section 3 preferable largely because it brings into focus much more clearly the serious difficulty we have found in Dworkin's notion of strong discretion, namely, what we are to say about cases where authoritative standards purport to single out a uniquely correct decision, and yet the decision-maker is fully aware that they fail to do so? This failure, and the problems it brings, are too easily obscured by saying that in such cases the decision is none the less controlled. It seems far more honest to say that authoritative standards purport to control the decision but fail to do so, especially if one's aim is to claim that there is no need for discretion because the law always provides answers which judges are required to find and apply in legal cases. The question then becomes: Does the decision-maker, given this failure, have strong discretion? Dworkin apparently thinks not, whereas I have argued that he does.

A second criticism might arise over my ascription of interpretation P to Dworkin.[25] Is it fair to ascribe P to Dworkin in light of what he says about uniquely correct answers in law? As seen above, whether a decision-maker has discretion in the strong sense is, according to P, logically independent of whether there is a uniquely correct answer determined by the standards set by the relevant authority. Surely, it might be objected, Dworkin could not possibly have intended to embrace such a proposition. If he had, then why would he have been so concerned to show that 'for all practical purposes, there will always be a right answer in the seamless web of our law'?[26] And why would his early critics have been so concerned to show that not even Dworkin's super-judge, Hercules, would always be able to discover a uniquely correct answer in a uniquely best interpretive theory of the settled law?

This is a serious objection. There is, however, a way to understand Dworkin's concern for right answers which makes it quite compatible with his acceptance of proposition P. As we saw above, Dworkin seems to view the existence of strong discretion on some question, not as a function of whether there is a uniquely correct answer, but rather of what the ground rules of the enterprise entitle the decision-maker to suppose. Regardless of whether the relevant standards identify one and only one solution which is compatible with those standards, if the ground rules of the enterprise require him to ignore the possibility that the standards fail in this respect—the possibility that there is a tie—then he has no strong discretion. Dworkin is not, then, concerned to show that, in the case of modern legal systems, there always is a right answer in every hard case, so that he can then demonstrate that judges never have strong discretion and that 'the

---

[25] I owe recognition of this objection to H. L. A. Hart and Roger Shiner.
[26] 'No Right Answer?', 84.

positivist's theory of discretion' is therefore false. After all, the absence of strong discretion has nothing to do with whether there are always unique answers. Rather, Dworkin first argues that judges do not have strong discretion *because of what the ground rules of the enterprise presuppose*; he *then* sets out to demonstrate that, *contra* positivists like Hart, these ground rules are neither pointless, silly, nor irrational. He attempts to demonstrate the latter by arguing for a theory of interpretation according to which neither uncertainty nor disagreement concerning what is required by the authoritative standards of the enterprise, nor the inability to demonstrate in some logically rigorous fashion that these determine one answer as uniquely correct, entails that there is no right answer. It is just that an answer cannot be arrived at mechanically or easily, as one might arrive at a solution in logic or arithmetic, but requires the use of judgment, i.e. weak discretion. Once we realize these points about interpretation, and find room for controversial principles of political morality in the establishment of legal rights (something the positivist cannot allow in Dworkin's view, but which in fact he can),[27] it becomes clear that it is very likely, though by no means certain, that there is a right answer in any given legal case. It is also very likely that a judge will come to believe that there is such an answer, if only he thinks long and hard enough about the questions he must decide.

If the above represents the proper explanation of Dworkin's concern for right answers, then it is quite consistent with interpretation P. Dworkin's concern has been to show that the ground rules of the enterprise which (he thinks) require the judge to search for elusive right answers, and thus deny him any strong discretion, are neither silly nor irrational, as they would be if, as Hart seems to argue, *all* hard cases lack right answers because they involve uncertainty, and uncertainty entails open texture and indeterminacy.[28]

5. HAVING AND EXERCISING STRONG DISCRETION

I argued in section 4 above that proposition P is seriously flawed as an analysis of the concept of strong discretion, and that Dworkin's attempt to defend the thesis fails. An obvious way round these diffi-

---

[27] Establishing this point is of course the principal aim of this and the preceding chapters.

[28] We will consider Hart's argument for indeterminacy in the law more fully in the next chapter.

culties is to accept interpretation C instead, from which it follows
that an individual has strong discretion on some question if his
decision is not in fact fully controlled by authoritative standards, if
there is no uniquely correct answer to that question which is provided by those standards. It follows from C, unlike P, that whether
judges ever have strong discretion is logically dependent on whether
the law invariably succeeds in controlling judicial decisions fully.
Thus the arguments of philosophers like Hart and Mackie, which
attempt to show that right answers are not always possible become
directly relevant to the question whether judges have, or must have,
strong discretion.

But this interpretation of strong discretion has its own difficulties.
Some might object to the interpretation on grounds of practical
insignificance. They would point to typical hard cases, say Charter
cases like *Morgentaler* and *Andrews*, and argue that regardless of
whether, in theory, a right answer exists in such cases, it is nevertheless true that the judges who decide them have strong discretion.
They have strong discretion because the baffling nature of the issues
posed in these cases, and the fact that more than one answer can
reasonably be defended as legally correct, means that 'something in
the nature of a free choice between open alternatives must be
made'.[29] And as demonstrated by *Morgentaler* and *Andrews*, this
free choice often leads different courts, and indeed different judges
within one and the same court, to very different answers. Dworkin
would suggest that the complexity of the issues of political morality
often involved in charter adjudication entails a very low antecedent
probability of a tie from which the need for strong discretion arises.
But in fact it argues for the opposite conclusion: that in practice
there will be many ties because there will be many reasonable
answers from which different judges will extract different solutions
in exercising their unavoidable 'sovereign prerogative of choice'.[30]
Though there is something to objections like this, they are
fallacious as they stand, for reasons pointed out by Dworkin. First,
it does not follow from the mere fact that more than one decision
could reasonably be defended, and might be accepted, as the right
one, that 'something in the nature of a free choice between open
alternatives must be made'. Drawing on an analogy with history and

---

[29] *The Concept of Law*, 124. In using this quotation from Hart I do not mean to
suggest that he would necessarily take this line of argument.
[30] O. W. Holmes, *Collected Legal Papers*, 239.

science, Dworkin rightly points out that a judge in a hard case might be uncertain and in disagreement with others about how a hard case should be decided, and yet reasonably believe that there is one solution and that it is probably the one he has got. People often reasonably disagree about issues which they nevertheless believe admit of uniquely correct solutions. In a legal case in which this is so, the judge will not be forced into a free choice between open alternatives. Second, if (a) a judge in a mature legal system always would, if he thought long and hard enough about his decision, come to a reasoned belief that one decision is the right one; (b) there almost always are right answers in such systems because they are thick with precedents and statutes upon the basis of which one can always find what one takes to be a superior interpretation of the relevant law; and (c) any decision that the present case is one where there actually is no right answer would probably be wrong; then (d) it makes very good sense, and is of the utmost practical significance, to insist that judges do not have, and should never suppose that they have, strong discretion.

conditions under which "no strong discretion" would be supported.

This second reply raises some important questions. What if the law does not almost always control judicial decisions fully, but Dworkin is right that a judge would, if he thought long and hard enough about his decisions, always come to believe of one particular answer that it is determined by binding law? What if judges were in fact deluded in their optimism? It would follow from proposition C that judges might sometimes in fact have strong discretion, and yet be unaware of that fact and decide as if they did not. They would not believe that, nor would they decide as if, they have Holmes' sovereign prerogative of choice, even though in some cases, theoretically, they do, and would be convinced of this by a sharp philosopher if only they would listen. This seems unproblematic philosophically; judges, like the rest of us, sometimes make errors, despite what they would sometimes have us believe. Practically, of course, there might be a problem. If judges did sometimes have the discretion to decide in a reasonable manner undetermined by law, and knew or reasonably believed that they did, then they might be more inclined to respond rationally and fairly to the issues which the law left open, instead of always trying to find what would often turn out to be forced legal solutions. These would be solutions which allowed the judge to escape having to claim that the answer given was one he provided, and which allowed him to perpetuate the myth that he is only conforming his decision to standards set by other people. Instead of a reasonable decision we might be left with a 'technical' one which makes little sense in light of reasonable social aims and purposes, some of which might be the objects of the very rules in question.

But now consider another possibility which has important philosophical as well as practical implications. What if Dworkin is wrong in supposing that a judge inevitably will, if he thinks long and hard, always come to believe that one answer is right? What if judges would still believe, in some cases, that there is no right answer, even in theory? Alternatively, what if they were to believe, in some cases, that there is such an answer in theory but could see no compelling reason for supposing that any particular answer is the uniquely correct one? The judge's state of belief in this latter instance would be like that of the agnostic, who sees two possible answers to the question whether God exists, the theist's and the atheist's, but sees no good or compelling reason(s) to prefer one answer over the other, and therefore accepts neither. Proposition C entails that if there always are right answers in hard cases, as there presumably is in the hard case concerning God's existence despite considerable controversy and uncertainty over what that correct answer is, then judges never have strong discretion in those cases. Yet if the baffling and seemingly irresolvable nature of the typical hard case would result in a judge's sometimes not believing, even after all the hard thought he could muster, that one particular answer is the right one determined by law, then is it not true that a judge might sometimes be forced to choose in the way in which he is clearly entitled to choose if he has been explicitly granted strong discretion and his decision is not in fact fully controlled? A judge could no more accept an answer that he believes does not exist, than he could accept an answer that he knows does not exist. He could no more do this than an agnostic could choose to believe either the theist's or the atheist's claim about God's existence. And even if the judge believes that in theory a right answer exists, as the agnostic presumably does, but does not believe, of any of the reasonable answers he has entertained, that *it* is the right answer, then he will see no compelling reason to exclude any of those reasonable, and so far as he can tell, possibly-right answers. But if so, he cannot rationally and honestly judge one of them to be the right one. Any such judgment would be groundless and gratuitous. He must, therefore, choose on grounds other than those which argue that one of the possibly-right answers is actually right, and this seems to be precisely the sort of choice one is entitled to make when one has strong discretion.[31] Proposition C entails, however, that if, in theory, there always are right answers, these judges do not have strong discretion. Is it not more realistic, however, to reject C and to say that in such cases strong discretion *(This is a common air of Dworkin)* does exist despite the presence, in theory, of right answers—answers which could not, for all practical purposes, be discovered and which therefore carry little in the way of practical significance?

I shall now attempt to defend interpretation C by arguing that this last objection is the product of a common confusion arising from an ambiguity in sentences like 'Strong discretion exists in legal systems' and 'It is inevitable that there should be a place for strong discretion in legal systems.' The ambiguity can be brought to light by contrasting the following two propositions:

D1: S has strong discretion on issue X.

and

D2: S exercises strong discretion (or strong discretionary judgment) on issue X.

D1 and D2 mean very different things. D1 in conjunction with C entails that S's decision on X is not fully controlled by binding standards. The notion of strong discretion is used here to describe S's normative relationship to authoritative standards, to say that those standards fail to single out one particular answer on issue X which S is required to accept. Whether S has strong discretion is logically independent of S's beliefs regarding a right answer, but logically dependent on there being in fact such an answer.

The truth of D2, on the other hand, is logically independent of whether there is a right answer, and logically dependent on whether S believes that there is one and that it is one answer in particular. The notion of strong discretion is used here not to describe S's normative relationship to standards which have normative force over his decision-making, but rather to describe an actual decision or judgment that is made by S, to say that he made the sort of decision that he is entitled to make when he in fact has discretion.

---

[31] In the case of the question concerning God's existence, the choice might be made on grounds of not wanting to displease a theist who plays an important role in one's life. It could also be made on the basis of Pascal's wager.

It is crucial to note that D1 and D2 are logically independent of one another. D1 entails nothing about the sort of decision S will make, or about S's beliefs about issue X. D1 does, however, imply, in an extended sense of imply different from logical implication, the speaker's belief that S's decision is not fully controlled on issue X. But, of course, S may himself perceive the situation very differently. He might, for instance, believe that his decision is fully controlled in one particular way, that he has the right answer provided by the relevant authoritative standards.

Though D1 does not entail D2, it does, given C, entail the following:

D3: S's decision on issue X is not fully controlled.

Proposition D2 entails neither D3 nor D1. The exercise of strong discretionary judgment does not entail that the decision on X is uncontrolled. It entails only that S does not believe, of one of the possibly-right answers, that it is the actually-right answer. This might seem paradoxical. Is it not true, it might reasonably be asked, that S can exercise strong discretionary judgment only if he has the strong discretion to exercise? I see no reason why this must be so. Suppose a case in which S sincerely believes after much hard thought that his decision is not fully controlled and that he is therefore at liberty, because he has no other alternative, to choose between two answers neither of which is ruled out by the relevant authoritative standards. Suppose further that S's belief is incorrect, and that one of the two answers is in fact the right one which a Herculean effort would uncover. As argued above, S will, given his beliefs, be forced to make the sort of choice he is entitled to make when he has strong discretion. He cannot help but do otherwise, unless he declines to make a decision at all, which is hardly ever an option for judges. Is it not better to say that strong discretionary judgment was exercised unnecessarily, or perhaps even improperly, than to deny that such judgment was exercised, to deny that a choice, partially undetermined by law, was made? One might say that the judgment was improper if one's view is that S's belief that his decision was not fully controlled was arrived at far too hastily, that he gave up the search for a legally determined solution far too quickly and instead opted for his own solution. Yet whatever one's view about the way in which X was decided, or about S's perception of his normative relationship to authoritative standards, it cannot be denied that S made

This might mean: S is able to exercise a permitted liberty (range) choice only if he has that permitted liberty (if it is permissible) If it is not, because no strong discretion (normatively), then he is not able to exercise it.

the sort of choice he is entitled to make when he has strong discretion. And given this, it seems perfectly in order to insist that strong
discretionary judgment was exercised.

Before turning to consider very briefly the further significance of
these distinctions, we should perhaps note one additional proposition which needs to be carefully distinguished from D2.

D4: S exercises his strong discretion on issue X.

In saying that S exercises his strong discretion on X one seems to
imply that it is his to exercise, that he in fact has strong discretion.
Consequently, D4 seems to entail both D1 and D3, unlike D2 which
entails neither. Of course, D4 also entails D2.

6. A SIGNIFICANT DISTINCTION?

The distinctions drawn in the preceding section have not been sufficiently appreciated in the literature dealing with judicial discretion.
Discussions are often couched simply in terms of whether (strong)
discretion exists or must exist in legal systems, and in terms of the
moral and political implications of systems in which judicial discretion is a factor. Yet as should now be clear, to express the issues in
such loose terms is to invite serious confusion. On the other hand,
there are advantages to be drawn from clearly observing the distinctions defended herein.

For instance, sometimes the beliefs of judges about the extent to
which authoritative standards exert control over their decisions are
thought to be relevant in arguments about judicial discretion.
Dworkin adduces as evidence that Anglo-American judges do not
have strong discretion, the supposed fact that they never seem to
conceive of themselves as reaching a point where authoritative control ends. Judges do not, he writes, 'decide hard cases in two stages,
first checking to see where the institutional constraints end, and then
setting the books aside to stride off on their own. The institutional
constraints they sense are pervasive and endure to the decision itself.'[32] Now, if this is Dworkin's argument, it is open to objection on
at least two points. First, it is far from clear that Anglo-American
judges never conceive of themselves as reaching the limits of
authoritative control. The testimony of leading judges such as

[32] *Taking Rights Seriously*, 86–7.

Holmes, Radcliffe, Macmillan, and Cardozo bears witness to this fact.[33] It was Cardozo's view that 'every judge consulting his own experience must be conscious of times when a free exercise of will, directed of set purpose to the furtherance of the common good, determined the form and the tendency of a rule which at that moment took its origin in one creative act.'[34]

But there is another objection to Dworkin's argument, one which is easily seen once the distinction between having and exercising discretion is drawn. Even if it were true that judges believe that control never runs out, this would provide little in the way of support for the claim that they do not have strong discretion. The judges might simply be wrong about whether their decisions are always controlled. The truth of a proposition does not, as a rule, follow from the fact that it is widely accepted, and there is no reason to view this situation as providing an exception to that rule. It is important to stress that even if I am right, and judges do indeed believe that there are limits to authoritative control in some hard cases, this too has little bearing on whether they actually do have strong discretion. Once again, they might simply be wrong. It is at this point that the philosopher, not the judge, becomes useful. It is here that arguments about the inevitable open texture of language and other forms of communicating standards, about legal gaps, truth conditions for propositions of law, and the unavoidable underdetermination or incommensurability of interpretive theories of law, all philosophical issues with which the professional philosopher is particularly well suited to deal, become highly relevant. It is to the philosopher of law, and not necessarily the practitioner, that we should turn when asking whether judges have, or must have, strong discretion. Dworkin of course denies that there is any significant or meaningful distinction between philosopher and practitioner of law, but as we saw earlier in Chapters 2 and 3, there is every reason to think he is wrong about that and that it makes sense to say that the reflections of philosophers about these fundamentally philosophical issues are what we should be after. Recall what Richard Feynman had to say about scientists who delve into non-scientific questions. We can say the same thing about judges who tackle non-

---

[33] See Holmes, *Collected Legal Papers*, *passim*; B. Cardozo, *The Nature of the Judicial Process*, 103–4; Lord Macmillan, MJ, 'Law and Ethics'; and Lord Radcliffe, *The Law and Its Compass*, 11 and 14.

[34] Cardozo, ibid.

legal, philosophical issues: they are probably 'just as dumb as the
next guy'. Of course, if Dworkin were correct in thinking that the
question whether judges have strong discretion is a function solely
of what the 'ground rules of the enterprise' require them to assume,
then the testimony of judges would become relevant. Then the question would not be philosophical but factual. And one of the best
ways of determining what in fact are the ground rules of some enterprise is to ask its participants. This may explain why Dworkin incor-
rectly places considerable emphasis on judicial testimony in his
attempt to show that judges do not have strong discretion.

When we turn to the very different question whether
Anglo–American judges exercise strong discretionary judgment,
judicial testimony obviously becomes highly relevant. If there are,
as I have claimed, many cases in which the judge does not believe of
any one of the possibly-right answers that it is actually right, then it
follows that strong discretion is sometimes exercised. So even if
Dworkin could somehow show us that there are always uniquely
right solutions to the interpretive questions posed in hard legal
cases, the judges' belief that authoritative control sometimes comes
to an end ensures that, in one very important sense of the term,
strong discretion does indeed exist within modern Anglo-American
legal systems. It also shows that theories such as Dworkin's, which
seem to deny this fact, mischaracterize the practice of adjudication
within such systems.

On the other hand, when we turn to the question whether Anglo-
American judges *must* sometimes exercise strong discretion in deciding hard legal cases, it might seem that here judicial testimony is
again out of place. After all, even if the judges do exercise strong
discretion, it fails to follow that they must do so. As noted above,
Dworkin's view is that a judge in a mature legal system will, if only
he thinks long and hard enough, come to believe of one possibly-
right answer that it is actually right. The density and complexity of
the legal and moral materials in such a system ensure this. If Dworkin is right here, it follows that strong discretion need not be exercised even if it is in fact sometimes exercised. Perhaps the judges
should simply try harder.

Yet even here judicial testimony seems to be relevant, precisely
because that testimony suggests it is wrong to think that any Anglo-
American judge who thinks long and hard will not feel the need for
the exercise of strong discretion. Is it even remotely plausible to

suppose that judges of the calibre of a Holmes, a Cardozo, a Mac-millan, or a Radcliffe failed to think long and hard enough about the hard decisions they had to make, and did not attempt, to the best of their admittedly less than Herculean, but nevertheless quite sub-stantial, abilities to find the answers determined by existing law? Surely it is only reasonable to assume that they gave their decisions considerable thought, care, and attention, and attempted always to find a legally determined right answer, giving up the search only when all efforts to find it had failed.[35] Yet if we must make this assumption, then in the light of the judicial testimony cited above, we should not accept, as inevitable, that a judge will always find what he believes is a right answer, if only he thinks long and hard enough. Indeed we should accept the very opposite. We should accept that the exercise of strong discretionary judgment is virtually inevitable even if, as Dworkin argues, the mythical Hercules would never feel the need to resort to its exercise because there always are, in theory, right answers for him (and God) to discover.

It might be that Dworkin has a way round this last objection. It has always been Dworkin's position that his interpretive theory of law offers a more accurate descriptive account of Anglo-American adjudicative practices than the theories of the positivists. For example, he states at one point in *Taking Rights Seriously* that his theory that judicial decisions typically enforce existing legal rights 'has two aspects. Its descriptive aspect explains the present structure of the institution of adjudication. Its normative aspect offers a politi-cal justification for that structure.'[36] As we saw in Chapter 2 above, Dworkin has recast these claims in terms of 'interpretations' of legal practice which attempt both to describe legal practice—the pre-interpretive data—accurately, and to put that practice in its best moral light. We saw reason to criticize Dworkin's constructive interpretation as being either (a) a normative theory of adjudication, in which case it fails to meet the positivist's theory head-on because theirs is a descriptive-explanatory theory of law; or (b) a descriptive theory that is highly suspect owing to the distinct possibility that it is governed by wishful thinking, by the desire to find a moral justifica-tion for what is described. We questioned the philosophical pro-

[35] There is at least one famous judge of whom this assumption cannot perhaps be made: Lord Denning. On Denning's willingness to 'seek justice despite the law' see *Justice, Lord Denning and the Constitution*, P. Robson and P. Watchman (eds).
[36] *Taking Rights Seriously*, 123. See also 87, 96 and 101.

priety of constructing a theory such that the validity of its descriptive
component is governed by the requirement that what it describes is
justified morally. Suppose now that Dworkin were to abandon the
descriptive aspect of his legal theory, or at the very least acknowledge that it offers a less accurate 'fit' with the pre-interpretive data
than the positivists' theory does. He might, that is, loosen the 'fit'
requirement and allow the normative dimension more prominence.
The theory would then be not so much an interpretation of existing
practices as a recommendation about how those practices might
change so as to accord better with Dworkin's political vision of how
adjudication should be conducted. His claim then would not be that
judges neither have nor exercise strong discretion. The claim would
be (i) that they need not do so; and (ii) that they should not do so, for
the reasons of fairness and democracy discussed above. So if Dworkin were to loosen the requirement of fit and transform his account
into a fully normative recommendation, he might reply to my objections as follows.

Granted judges do presently feel the need to resort to strong
discretionary judgment in some hard cases. It remains, nevertheless,
that this need would not be felt if only judges (a) were to think long
and hard enough, and (b) were to reason, not like the positivist
Judge Herbert,[37] who too easily resorts to the exercise of strong
discretion because of his misguided theories of law and adjudication,
but like Hercules, who always tries to discover pre-determined right
answers in his constructive interpretations of the settled law, and
who always succeeds in finding an answer which he at the very least
believes is the correct one, even if in fact it is not.

Were Dworkin to adopt this line of reply, then my objection,
based on the simple observation that judges now seem to feel the
need to resort to strong discretionary judgment, would of course
fail. We would be left with the possibility that judges never would
feel this need if only they altered their jurisprudence and the
approach to hard cases it warrants. Appeals to judicial testimony
about past decisions would simply be out of place. But then a
different question would come to the fore. Instead of asking how
Dworkin's transformed theory stands in the face of judicial testimony and practice, we might raise the following important query.
Were judges to adopt Dworkin's recommendation, and now begin to

[37] See, ibid. 125, for the contrast between Dworkin's Hercules and the positivists'
Herbert.

[margin note: using Herculian model as a heuristic would not exclude cases of (careful) strong discretion in making new law.]

emulate Hercules instead of Herbert, would it really be true that they would never be led to the exercise of strong discretionary judgment? Would this be true even if Dworkin could convince us, and them, that Hercules (and God) would never be so led? Given that the Herculean task is just that, a task suitable for Hercules, this seems prima facie unlikely. That task, as we have seen, requires that the judge make highly complex judgments about political morality and about an institutional history that is often inconsistent and mistaken. In adjudicating the claims of litigants in hard cases, judges must weigh and interpret controversial standards of political morality and develop highly complex and difficult conceptions of contested concepts. All these and more must be dealt with satisfactorily if a right answer is to emerge for the judge. Is it not likely that an ordinary judge would sometimes find these issues so complex and baffling that he would, in the end, be forced to admit that he could not sincerely claim to believe that one of the possibly-right answers he has contemplated is the actually-right one? He need not, as we have seen, believe that there are ties, just that, so far as he can tell, he has no good reason for thinking that one of the possibly-right answers is the actually-right answer. He cannot choose one answer as best if he has not been able to discover good reasons for thinking it is one answer in particular, even if he has been persuaded by Dworkin that there always is such an answer awaiting Hercules' discovery. If so, then is it not more likely that our ordinary judge will be led sometimes to the exercise of strong discretionary judgment?

And would this not be the rational thing for him to do? Would it not be better if, in such cases, the judge gave up the rather fruitless attempt to discover an answer which might, in theory, exist within the mythical Hercules' interpretation, but which he has very little hope of ever discovering, and instead chose an answer which appeared to be reasonable in light of what appeared to the judge to be reasonable and relevant social aims and purposes? The judge probably would, in such instances, resort to the standards of political morality which figure so prominently in Dworkinian constructive interpretations. The difference would be that the search would not be for a pre-determined, uniquely right answer settled by authoritative standards, but for a reasonable answer which develops and adds to the law in a reasonable, defensible, but not necessarily uniquely correct, way. In short, the search would be for a defensible way to exercise one's strong discretionary judgment in the creation of new law.

7. A RETURN TO THE DISCRETION ARGUMENT

It is now time to return to the Discretion Argument and its claim that inclusive positivism cannot be a coherent version of legal positivism because on that theory all judicial appeals to standards of political morality must be discretionary. Political morality can never function for the positivist as a basis for determinations of (existing) law.

We should begin by asking the following obvious but important question. Precisely why must a positivist say that appeals to principles of political morality are always discretionary? There would appear to be two possible answers depending on whether what we have in mind is the judges' having or exercising strong discretion. Take the first alternative. Why would a positivist be committed to saying that an appeal to principles of political morality necessarily means that the judge has strong discretion? There are several possible reasons, none of which is valid.

First, anyone who accepts the Pedigree Argument and its premise that moral criteria for law are somehow incompatible with positivism will say that any attempt to discover an answer partly determined by moral criteria must, for the positivist, be a step beyond determinations of law. Appeals to moral principles will necessarily be appeals to considerations beyond the standards which have legal force for judges. In other words, they will necessarily be discretionary, despite any contrary beliefs on the part of misguided judges and legal theorists concerning the possibility of moral criteria for existing law. And even if the standards of political morality to which judges characteristically appeal in legal cases, say those to which reference is made in the Canadian Charter, serve in some case to single out one and only one answer which is consistent with them, this could not, according to the positivist, be a *legally correct* answer. The answer might be uniquely determined, but not by the authoritative standards of law; and so its discovery must be discretionary. As we saw above, however, the pedigree argument is unsound. We cannot therefore validly use it to saddle the positivist with any particular views about the need for discretion.

Second, anyone who conceives of positivism as necessarily

denying the objectivity of all moral values will hold that attempts to discover answers determined by standards of political morality are necessarily discretionary. They will result in the prescription of law not its discovery. Again he will add, in light of our earlier discussion of what it is to have strong discretion, that this will be so regardless of any misguided beliefs that judges or legal theorists might have as to the nature of judicial decisions and the objectivity of morality.

One problem with this argument is that there are many positivists who accept that morality is objective. Take Bentham, for instance. He thought that a hedonic calculus is possible and that the principle of utility is the true guide to our moral duties. Hobbes likewise thought his theory to be objectively true and that he could demonstrate what our moral responsibilities really are. For Hobbes, our moral duties are based on prudence and the need to escape the state of nature, but they are objective none the less. As Hart suggests, then, there is no necessary connection between positivism and the denial that moral standards are 'objective', though of course there is nothing *incompatible* between the two views either.[38]

A positivist who wishes to dispute Dworkin's claim that the integrity theory, unlike positivism, successfully eliminates the need for strong discretion in legal cases, and is morally and politically superior on that account, can, if his theory of morality permits him to do so, appeal to the non-objectivity of morality in response to Dworkin's attack. He can point out that the choice among Dworkinian constructive interpretations of law depends on moral judgments concerning what puts legal practice in its best moral light. But if morality is not objective, and there is no truth of the matter when it comes to moral judgments, it will not always be possible validly to choose one constructive interpretation as objectively better than all its rivals. This will be possible only when the dimension of 'fit' is sufficient to determine a uniquely superior theory. But in those cases where this is not so, i.e. in almost any hard case, we will be unable to define our existing legal rights in terms of the objectively best constructive interpretation of the settled law. The dimension of political morality will let us down. We will be unable to close off the possibility that judges will have strong discretion at the point where a choice must be made within this dimension.

[38] See Hart, 'Positivism and the Separation of Law and Morals', and d'Entreves, *Natural Law*, 176–7.

As noted, the above line of attack is open to those positivists who reject the objectivity of morals, or who deny that all moral questions have determinate answers. But once again, it is not their legal positivism which leads them necessarily in this direction. There may be a logical connection between the objectivity of morality and natural-law theory, but there is no such connection between positivism and any particular theory of morality.

There is a third possible ground for the view that positivists are necessarily committed to saying that whenever political morality is in play judges have discretion and therefore cannot be trying to discover the content of existing law. Writers often ascribe to all positivists, the following thesis about adjudication.

TA: Legal cases can be divided into two groups: (1) easy or textbook cases, where a uniquely right answer clearly and uncontroversially follows from what is clearly and uncontroversially valid law; and (2) all other cases, the hard cases, where the exercise of strong discretion is necessary because existing law has run out and fails to provide an answer.

In short, *TA* tells us that 'if someone's case is not clearly covered by ... [a valid] rule (because there is none that seems appropriate, or those that seem appropriate are vague, or for some other reason) then that case cannot be decided by "applying the law." It must be decided by some official, like a judge, "exercising his discretion".'[39] Now if *TA* truly is 'the positivist theory of adjudication', then of course the view of any positivist must be that a move to inherently controversial principles of political morality will necessarily bring with it the need for strong discretion. And the reason is not that the principles in question belong to political morality; the reason is that they are *controversial* in their application.

But why must *TA* be ascribed to a positivist? As we saw earlier in Chapter 3, although there are connections between positivism (a theory of law) and theories of adjudication, it is false that positivism, in any of its forms, leads directly to any particular theory of adjudication. But let us leave these reservations aside and concentrate instead on why someone might naturally ascribe *TA* to defenders of positivism. The only argument I can imagine would be one which utilized some version of the Argument From Function. The reasoning might go something like this.

[39] *Taking Rights Seriously*, 17.

legal system's
role in
setting questions
determinately
w certainty.

1. For the legal positivist, a primary function of legal systems is to settle and render determinate questions about how people are to behave and about when the public power is to be brought to bear upon them.

2. So a law just is, for the positivist, a peculiar sort of public standard (unlike, e.g. conventional standards of etiquette) which authoritatively and conclusively settles such questions.

3. Therefore, a law, in virtue of the function it is meant to serve, extends just so far as the clear guidance it provides.

4. Conclusion: Any decision where there is uncertainty and controversy about the existence or content of 'a law'—i.e. every decision in a hard case—could not, for the positivist, really be a decision about what is required by a law. This is so, once again, regardless of what judges and (misguided) legal theorists think of these decisions. The judges, for instance, may think they do not have strong discretion in such cases and that their decisions are not based on the exercise of strong discretionary judgment, but then they are just plain wrong about that.

5. Summary: If it is unclear what a law requires, it is clear, in the view of the positivist, that it fails to require anything at all, and that judges therefore have strong discretion whether they or anyone else believe that they do.

1)
There are at least two reasons why this extension of the Argument From Function will not work. First, the Argument From Function is itself unsound for a variety of reasons.[40] It should therefore not be employed to saddle the positivist with any particular theory of adjudication. But suppose my earlier objections to the Argument From Function are all misguided. There is a second reason for doubting the validity of its application in this context. Even if the positivist's theory were that a primary or essential feature of law is

NB
law in
general ③
under laws
good analysis

2) necessarily as described in the Argument From Function, it would be unfair to ascribe to him the fallacious inference that the same is therefore true of *individual laws*. The function of the army is to defeat the enemy; it hardly follows that the primary function of Private Bailey, chief cook and bottle-washer, is to do the same. Analogously, if an essential feature of a legal system is X, it fails to follow that the function of legal rule, R, is also X.

So even if a function of a legal system is necessarily as described, it in no way follows that the function of every law must be the same

---

[40] For details see Chapter 4 of this book.

and that inclusive positivism, which allows that sometimes determinations of law can depend on factors in political morality, must be excluded from the ranks of legal positivism. Of course, even if the validity of each and every law were to depend on factors in political morality because there is, for example, a charter which recognizes principles of political morality as tests for the validity of all subordinate legislation and legal decisions, it fails to follow that the function of settling issues authoritatively is thereby undermined. As noted in our earlier discussions, questions of political morality do have penumbras of uncertainty, and there may well be cases where two or more interpretations of a charter provision will seem equally good but better than all the rest. But it is a mistake to exaggerate the indeterminacy inherent in political morality. As argued, it is often quite clear, on any remotely plausible interpretation, what political morality, and thus a charter, requires. In such cases judges do not have strong discretion, nor need they necessarily feel the need to exercise strong discretionary judgment to settle the issues before them.

So there is nothing in positivism which seems to lead necessarily to *TA*. Nevertheless, it is understandable that *TA* should be linked with positivism. After all, it appears to be a thesis embraced by its leading contemporary proponent: H. L. A. Hart. As we shall see more fully in the next chapter, Hart seems to divide cases into two fundamental categories: core and penumbral. Core cases are clear cases, and clear cases are 'those in which there is general agreement that they fall within the scope of the [relevant] rule'.[41] In *The Concept of Law* and 'Positivism and the Separation of Law and Morals', Hart appears to ascribe such agreements to the fact that there are 'necessarily such agreements in the shared conventions of language',[42] but also seems explicitly to repudiate such a view later in 'Problems of the Philosophy of Law.' There he describes the view as an 'oversimplification', allowing that other factors, such as the rule's obvious or stated purpose, may settle the question of its application when its literal meaning proves insufficient.[43] What would have been a penumbral case on the earlier account might well turn out to be a core case on the 'Problems' account. On both views, however, core cases are easy cases where there is certainty and lack of controversy. Penumbral cases, *in which a strong, law-making discretion is required*, appear to be all the rest.

[41] 'Problems of the Philosophy of Law', 271.   [42] Ibid. 271.   [43] Ibid.

Yet as Dworkin is quick and surely right to point out, lack of clarity, certainty, and agreement in hard, penumbral cases does not entail a lack of a right answer and a consequent need for strong discretion.[44] On the contrary, it entails only that decisions in those cases cannot be arrived at mechanically or easily, but require the use of judgment, i.e. weak discretion. Irrespective of any disagreement, uncertainty or lack of clarity there might be in a hard case, the law, through possible means like Herculean or charter tests for validity, may in fact succeed in providing a uniquely right answer. Such a level of discovery might, of course, require considerable weak discretion, along with a good deal of hard thought and imagination. But there is no reason to think that there is no answer to be found just because there is uncertainty and controversy about what it might be. There is uncertainty and controversy over the question 'Does God exist?' It fails to follow that there is no uniquely correct answer to that question.

Of course, it is possible that a hard case in law where there is uncertainty and controversy does indeed lack a right answer determined by the law. As we saw earlier, there is reason to think that even Aquinas followed Aristotle in thinking that sometimes questions of justice must be settled by 'determinations of common notions', that is, through the exercise of strong discretionary judgment on the part of one with the authority to settle such questions. It might, for instance, be indeterminate whether a right to equality is violated if lawyers are required to be citizens of the country in which they practise their profession. I am not suggesting that this question is in fact indeterminate, only that it may be so, and that the uncertainty and controversy surrounding the *Andrews* case do not themselves entail that there was no right answer to the question it posed. They did not mean that the courts necessarily had strong discretion to settle the issue in a way which was not pre-determined by the moral tests for law recognized in the Charter. If those tests did in fact provide an answer, controversial though it might have been— and what in positivism commits one to the view that they could not have done so?—then in this and other hard cases like it, it is not necessarily true that the judge had strong discretion. He will have had it only if the hard penumbral case did lack a right answer, if, for instance, the moral principles of equality, together with the relevant institutional history in which those principles figured, failed to

[44] See, e.g. 'No Right Answer?', 76–84 and *Taking Rights Seriously*, 281–2.

single out one answer to the *Andrews* question, or because, as Mackie argues, morality is never an objective matter and moral questions never admit of objectively right answers. There is nothing in all this which is incompatible with legal positivism. So again we have no excuse for leaping to saddle all defenders of positivism with *TA*. This imposition is unjustified despite the fact that it does appear to be part of the theory of adjudication of one very noteworthy positivist.

So far we have been supposing an interpretation of the Discretion Argument according to which moral tests for law mean, for the positivist, that judges necessarily have strong discretion. But there is another possible interpretation according to which the exercise of strong discretionary judgment is necessary whenever moral tests are in play. On this interpretation, the argument runs as follows. Regardless of whether, in theory, a hard case always has a right answer, the complexity and difficulty of the (partly) moral questions raised in such a case mean that an ordinary non-Herculean judge would inevitably be led to the exercise of strong discretionary judgment. As with our sergeant above, he will be unable to choose an answer as the right one if he has no reasoned belief that it is one answer in particular. So whether right answers exist in Hercules' juridical heaven, ordinary judges would seldom be able to come to reasoned beliefs about what these are. They will therefore necessarily be led to exercise strong discretion. And in so doing they will often be creating new law.

This line of argument presents a natural route for the positivist to take in response to Dworkin's claim that his theory, unlike that of the positivists, does not entail the unavoidable exercise of strong discretionary judgment to settle hard cases. As we observed above, it could plausibly be replied that the exercise of such judgment would be inevitable if judges were to apply the Herculean decision procedure in hard cases. This would not be because the procedure and its constituent tests fail to provide legally correct answers which Hercules and God could discover. It would be due to the awesome difficulty real judges would face in trying to take that procedure on. It seems that real judges would often find the task so complex and baffling that they would, in the end, be forced to admit defeat in their attempts to discover the right answers it might provide. And as a consequence they would, in these cases, inevitably be led to the exercise of strong discretionary judgment. They would be led to choose answers which appear to them to be reasonable in the light of what appear to them to be reasonable social aims and purposes. They would, that is, choose not on the basis of standards which they believe to have institutional force over their decisions, but on the basis of standards which they themselves judge to be worthy of application. Any normative force these standards might have would be intrinsic to the standards themselves. They would be appropriate to apply not because of their connections with authoritative sources, but because they are good standards to apply.

The above represents a natural route for positivists to take in response to Dworkin's challenge. But as should now be abundantly clear, there is nothing in this line of argument to suggest (a) that whenever moral tests enter the picture the exercise of strong discretionary judgment is inevitable; (b) that the application of moral principles can never be part of an attempt to discover the existence or content of valid law; or (c) that inclusive positivism, which posits the possibility of such moral tests, is incoherent. The exercise of strong discretionary judgment may sometimes be required when moral tests are in play, but unless we think that there are never any answers to moral questions, and as we have seen there is nothing in positivism which leads to this view, there is no reason to suppose that such judgment is always required. If it is clear and uncontroversial that a Charter right is unreasonably infringed by subordinate legislation in a way that cannot be demonstrably justified in a free and democratic society, then a Canadian judge called upon to rule on this issue neither has nor needs to exercise strong discretion. Moral tests sometimes provide correct and uncontroversial answers to questions of legal validity. Inclusive positivism is therefore not an incoherent theory. It is possible for judges to discover positive law by way of arguments which include moral premises.

8. RAZ'S CHALLENGE

In conclusion we will consider one final argument against the claim that inclusive positivism is a coherent theory.[45] Upon drawing his distinction between the strong and weak social theses (in our terms,

---

[45] I am grateful to Professor Hart for bringing this possible objection to my attention.

between exclusive and inclusive positivism) Raz issues the following challenge to defenders of the latter.

Supporters of such a conception of the law have to provide an adequate criterion for separating legal references to morality, which make its application a case of applying pre-existing legal rules from cases of judicial discretion in which the judge, by resorting to moral considerations, is changing the law. I am unaware of any serious attempt to provide such a test.[46]

I would now like very briefly to make such an attempt. But first, an ambiguity in Raz's challenge must be noted. Does Raz want (a) a criterion for distinguishing cases where moral references are made and the judge *has* strong discretion, from those where such references are made but the judge does not *have* strong discretion? Or does he want (b) a criterion for distinguishing cases where moral references are made and the judge *exercises* strong discretion, from those in which such references are made but the judge does not *exercise* strong discretion?[47] Fortunately it matters not, for our purposes, which is desired. Both are easily provided once the ambiguity is appreciated and the distinction between having and exercising discretion is noted and understood.

Assume a jurisdiction in which the accepted tests for law have a moral component, say they incorporate principles of political morality such as one finds in the Canadian Charter. A case where these tests are in play and in which the judge has strong discretion will simply be one where those tests fail to determine a uniquely correct answer. This could be true for any number of reasons. It could be indeterminate, in theory, which of two interpretations of the relevant moral principles is correct and Thomistic determination is called for. Or, as some would argue, morality might not be an objective matter at all, in which case whenever a Charter right of political morality became relevant and could be understood only via moral reflection, the judge would have strong discretion. In either case his decision would constitute the creation of law, not its discovery, regardless of what he or anyone else thought. Again, whether a decision is in fact controlled by authoritative standards is independent, logically, of the beliefs of the decision-maker con-

---

[46] *The Authority of Law*, 47, n. 8.
[47] Raz's challenge provides yet another instance where the distinction between having and exercising discretion is not made but should be.

cerning this issue. It is possible for one's decision not to be fully controlled even if one believes it to be so and decides on that basis.

On the other hand, cases where principles of political morality are relevant and in which the judge does not have strong discretion will be cases where those principles do single out one answer, say, that the BC Law Society's citizenship requirement does unreasonably infringe Andrews' equality rights in a way which cannot be justified in a free and democratic society.[48] Of course, in such a case the judges could still have altered the law in deciding *Andrews*. They might have erroneously believed that they had strong discretion and decided accordingly, in a way which was different from what the law actually required. But this is not surprising. They might also have thought there was an answer determined by law but got it wrong. In either instance, the judges will have made a mistake, but their mistake might be an 'embedded' one or it might go undetected.

So there is little difficulty in providing a criterion in terms of which we can distinguish, *conceptually*, between references to morality which bring with them the having of strong discretion and those which do not and where, instead, pre-existing law fully controls the decision. As for how, *in practice*, one distinguishes such cases, it would seem that Dworkin is right in suggesting that we must simply examine each case on its own and come to a judgment concerning whether the law requires any particular answer and what that answer might be. One must, in other words, form a judgment competitive with those of the judges who decide(d) the case. If one's conclusion is that the law is (or was) indeterminate, and the judges therefore have (or had) strong discretion, then one's judgment will be what Dworkin calls an 'internally sceptical' judgment.[49]

In distinguishing cases where appeals to morality amount to or involve the exercise of strong discretion from cases in which this is not so, we have to look to the judges and how they decide. If a judge bases his decision on the premise that his interpretation of a Charter right is correct, and is therefore the one required by law, then his appeal to such a right is not discretionary. This is so even if he is wrong about that, and he does have strong discretion because there are at least two possible interpretations among which an undeter-

---

[48] I do not mean to suggest that this is the proper account of *Andrews*, only that it is a possible account.

[49] On internal and external scepticism, see *Law's Empire*, 78–85.

mined choice can be made. If, on the other hand, his decision is not based on the premise that his interpretation of the relevant Charter right is uniquely correct, and therefore the one required by law, then we have here a reference to morality which is discretionary. His choice from among the alternative interpretations which he thinks are left open by authoritative standards will be based on other non-authoritative standards. These are standards which he believes do not have institutional force over his decision but which are, given the circumstances, reasonable to apply none the less. He will view his appeal to such standards as a step beyond law, as the unavoidable exercise of strong discretionary judgment. And if Holmes is right, 'every judge consulting his own experience must be conscious of times when a free exercise of will, directed of set purpose to the furtherance of the common good, determined the form and the tendency of a rule which at that moment took its origin in one creative act'. Such cases will arise when the judge believes, accurately or not, that there is no uniquely correct interpretation of the relevant moral consideration(s). Or they will appear when he cannot honestly judge what that interpretation might be and as a result, perhaps reluctantly, gives up the futile attempt to seek it out, choosing instead a solution which seems to him to be appropriate even though, he believes, it is not determined by the standards which exert (only partial) control over his decision.

9. CONCLUSION

In the course of the last two chapters we have considered a wide variety of arguments which either have been or might be made in support of the claim that moral tests for law are inconsistent with legal positivism and that inclusive positivism is therefore internally incoherent. In each case we have found the argument wanting and have learned valuable lessons concerning the nature and commitments of legal positivism. As should now be painfully clear, one must be extremely careful in characterizing positivism.[50] The theory should be identified principally as a thesis concerning the conceptual separation of law and morality, as a denial of the natural lawyers' claim that legality, lawfulness, and legal validity are

[50] See the similar remarks of Hart in 'Legal Positivism'; Raz in *The Authority of Law*, 37ff.; and A. P. d'Entreves in *Natural Law*, 174ff.

always in some way or other and to some extent a function of moral validity, of the natural law.[51] One must not, of course, assume that this thesis is equivalent to the claim that necessarily, in no legal system, can the legal validity of any law ever depend on moral considerations. Inclusive positivism, as we have seen, is a plausible, coherent, and I think worthy version of positivism, one which has been held by many who have traditionally been thought of as defenders of that tradition, and which does not collapse into incoherence or into natural-law theory.

Our discussion has also shown that positivism should not be identified as a thesis concerning the values which law ought to pursue. It may well be true that, historically, philosophers classified as legal positivists have tended to stress the values of certainty, determinacy, stability, and the like, at the expense of other values, such as justice and fairness. They may even have been drawn in some cases to equate justice with what Aristotle called 'legal justice', that is, justice according to determinate rules, whatever their content might be.[52] This tendency might explain why some erroneously believe that 'The main thesis of legal positivism ... defines justice as what the law requires.'[53] This may have been true of Hobbes, for instance, who expresses some such view in Leviathan, chapter 30. But compare Hobbes' position with Hart's claim that any such thesis is wrong, 'unless "law" is given some especially wide meaning; for such an account of justice leaves unexplained the fact that criticism in the name of justice is not confined to the administration of the law in particular cases, but the laws themselves are often criticized as just or unjust'.[54]

It might also be that a strong concern for the values of certainty, determinacy, and the like explains the preoccupation of some positivists with content-neutral and, some might think, relatively

---

[55] Jules Coleman calls this thesis 'negative positivism'. I prefer to think of it simply as 'positivism' so as to capture and isolate what seems common to all varieties of positivism. In the end it may not matter which route is taken, so long as it is recognized that there are clearly different kinds of positivism and that inclusive positivism is one of them.

[52] See *Nicomachean Ethics*, V. 7, 1134b and 1137b.

[53] Arthur Danto, 'Human Nature and Natural Law', in S. Hook (ed.), *Law and Philosophy*, 187.

[54] *The Concept of Law*, 157.

determinate, pedigree tests for legal validity.[55] This could throw light on why some positivists advocate exclusive positivism. Yet as I hope our discussion of the Argument From Function shows, commitment to these values as somehow being primary or essential is in no way necessary to the theory of legal positivism.

Our investigation seems also to suggest that positivism should not be conceived as a theory necessarily committed to the view that a strong, law-making discretion is required whenever moral premises enter the picture. As a result, it cannot be held, on these grounds, that inclusive positivism is incoherent if it is presented as a positivistic account of the possible tests for determinations of law. It may well be true that sometimes when moral tests are in play judges have discretion or will feel the need to exercise discretionary judgment. But there is nothing in positivism itself to suggest that this is always inevitable. It is consistent with positivism to say that questions of political morality always have right answers, especially once these are placed within their proper 'linguistic, philosophic and historical contexts', and that there are always uniquely correct answers to the questions posed by moral tests. But it is also consistent with positivism to deny that there are always such answers, and to agree with Aquinas that principles of political morality sometimes require determination by one who has the authority to make such discretionary choices.

Finally, we now have reason to reject Dworkin's claim that positivism is undermined by the fact that principles of political morality often figure in determinations of law within Anglo-American legal systems. Indeed, there is reason to think that the defender of inclusive positivism can 'simply incorporate all of [Dworkin's] claims about legal practice, [to the extent that] they are sound, as refinements' of his own descriptive-explanatory theory of law.[56]

NB!

---

[55] I say 'some might think' because, as Raz points out, questions concerning source-based tests can be just as indeterminate as those involving questions of political morality. See Chapter 4 of this book.   NB

[56] *Taking Rights Seriously*, 346.

8

MORALS AND THE MEANING
OF LAWS

1. INTRODUCTION

Inclusive positivism has now been shown to be a coherent, plausible descriptive-explanatory theory of law which accords political morality a role in determining the existence and content of valid laws. As inclusive positivism suggests, principles of political morality are among the possible, though by no means necessary, bases for determinations of law. There is nothing in the concept of law itself which requires that political morality serve a determinative role. If it does serve some such role, this is only because the community has, through its variable legal practices, made this choice, and that choice could have been and might yet be different.

If all this is so, then a question naturally arises: Should our legal practices assign political morality the roles which inclusive positivism warrants as conceivable? Or should our practices be such as to make the existence and content of laws one thing, their merit or demerit another thing altogether? As noted earlier, Neil Mac-Cormick advocates the latter option. He wishes not only to show that there is considerable merit in (exclusive) legal positivism. He also wishes to demonstrate that there are practical advantages in having laws whose existence and content can always be determined independently of political morality. MacCormick defends both a descriptive-explanatory account of the nature of law and normative theories about how laws should be drafted and interpreted, i.e. normative theories of legislation and adjudication.[1] In this final chapter I shall provide reasons for accepting the contrary of Mac-Cormick's normative theory of adjudication. More specifically, I shall attempt to support the view that our legal practice should be such that the very meaning or content of our laws is to some extent

---

[1] Again, see 'A Moralistic Case For A-Moralistic Law?'

based on considerations of political morality. We have already seen why this is a conceptual possibility and why it is consistent with legal positivism. The aim now is to see whether this conceptual possibility should be realized in practice.

The approach to legal interpretation to be defended in this chapter is commonly associated with Lord Denning[2] but has historical roots in, e.g., *Heydon's Case*.[3] It has been variously termed 'purposive', 'liberal', 'functional', and 'instrumentalist'. Depending on the political or jurisprudential views of the commentator it has been said to embody 'the Grand style of judging'[4] or, alternatively, 'palm tree justice'.[5] The approach with which it is often contrasted is referred to as 'legalistic', 'literal', 'conceptualist', or 'formalistic', as an approach where the strict letter of the law must be respected even if its spirit, or standards of rationality or justice, are thereby violated. ,

My main objective, then, is to defend a fully normative theory regarding what our legal practices concerning the application and interpretation of legal rules should be. It is a theory according to which standards of political morality, often times the 'objects' which legal standards are introduced to protect, can figure to some degree in determining what the latter really mean and what impact they have upon the legal rights and responsibilities of litigants. As I have done several times in the past, I shall use the thoughts of H. L. A. Hart as my primary focus and starting point. I do so here for two reasons. First, the theory I wish to support can be profitably articulated and defended using tools and leads Hart has provided. Second, Hart's normative and descriptive-explanatory views on adjudication have been extremely influential among legal scholars. Yet it is not always realized that there are vital differences between, on the one hand, the classic view presented in *The Concept of Law* and 'Positivism and the Separation of Law and Morals', and on the other, the position hinted at in Hart's more recent article 'Problems of the Philosophy of Law'. I want both to bring these important

[2] See e.g. Denning, *The Discipline of Law*.

[3] (1584) 3 Co.Rep. 1a; 76 ER 637.

[4] K. Llewellyn, *The Common Law Tradition: Deciding Appeals*.

[5] In *Duport Steels Ltd.* v. *Sirs* [1980], Lord Scarman, contemplating a system of law in which Lord Denning's purposive, liberal approach to judging became widespread, had this to say. 'Justice in such [a society would be] left to the unguided, even if experienced, sage sitting under the spreading oak tree.' Dr J. Morris condemned Denning's approach to the interpretation of wills in an article entitled 'Palm Tree Justice in the Court of Appeal'.

differences to light and to show why the later view, which is very close to the position I wish to defend, is to be preferred. It may be that what I have called Hart's later view can, on closer reading, actually be found in his earlier writings. If so, then the aim is to show not that Hart's views have changed for the better, but that the standard interpretation of Hart's views on the role of legal rules in adjudication should be changed to reflect the much more plausible theory he actually holds.[6]

We will begin with a somewhat detailed discussion of Hart's early theory concerning the role of legal rules in adjudication and the necessity and desirability of judicial discretion. Following this, we will explore a number of difficulties raised by the theory and suggest how it might be usefully modified to avoid them. Next, several arguments which might be offered against the proposed modification will be sketched and criticized, with the hope that their rebuttal will facilitate acceptance of those modifications. Finally we will briefly examine reasons for supposing that our modified theory of adjudication is in fact Hart's current view, or the view which he meant all along to advocate.

2. HART'S EARLY THEORY

As we have already seen, on Hart's theory of law all legal systems consist of a master rule of recognition, which underlies and unifies the legal system by specifying criteria for validity which all the other laws of the system must meet, and all those rules which do in fact meet the requirements for validity exemplified in the rule of recognition. Hart's rule of recognition is a secondary, power-conferring, social rule. He distinguishes between primary and secondary rules and between rules which impose duties and those which create and regulate powers. Hart also identifies primary rules with duty-imposing rules and secondary rules with rules which confer powers. Primary rules, he suggests, require that we act or forbear from acting whether we wish to or not, whereas secondary rules confer powers which enable individuals to introduce new primary rules or in various ways to abolish or modify old rules, or 'deter-

---

[6] For an example of the standard view, see Fuller's 'Positivism and Fidelity to Law—A Reply to Professor Hart'. See also D. N. MacCormick, *H. L. A. Hart*, 124–6.

mine their incidence or control their operations'.[7] As noted in
Chapter 4, the primary/secondary and duty-imposing/power-confer-
ring distinctions are not one and the same, nor are they co-extensive.
Only some secondary rules confer powers, and all legal rules are in
one sense primary in so far as each serves as the object of secondary
rules of recognition and adjudication.[8]

In calling the rule of recognition a social rule, Hart means to
distinguish it from rules whose existence is a result of official, rule-
making action(s) taken in accordance with secondary rules which
establish and regulate this creative power. Unlike rules introduced
by the formal actions of people in authority, social rules arise in-
formally out of the complex practices of the members of the society
or group in which they exist. In the case of a rule of recognition its
existence is manifested in a complex general practice among the
officials of a legal system and the general population. The former
identify the valid rules of the system according to generally acknowledged and accepted criteria, while the latter acquiesce in, and
conform with, the results of the rule of recognition's use by the
officials.

In any event, for Hart the law of a particular legal system consists
of a social rule of recognition and all those valid rules which satisfy
the various criteria for validity that happen to be recognized in that
rule. Nothing other than this counts as law. There is no law behind
or above the law as Dworkin and defenders of classical natural-law
theory would have it. The law just is that determinate and limited set
of rules satisfying a socially constituted rule of recognition.
Furthermore, legal rights, duties and powers exist only to the extent
that these rules, interpreted and applied in accordance with the
relevant rules of adjudication, so specify.

In accepting this simple yet highly illuminating and influential
picture of law, one could easily be led to what might be termed 'the
formalist theory of adjudication': that the role of judges is, and
ought to be, nothing more and nothing less than to apply whatever
rules happen to be validated by the rule of recognition. This will
sometimes be difficult, say when a valid provincial law suggests one
answer while a valid federal law requires another. But in such instances, there will be other valid rules, like the Canadian para-

---

[7] *The Concept of Law*, 79.
[8] In the current discussion we will ignore these complications and present Hart's
views in the terms he chose to use in *The Concept of Law*.

mountcy rule, which ultimately settles what should be done. In cases where a valid rule's meaning is unclear, there will be valid 'canons of interpretation' which settle how the vague rule must be interpreted. In all instances, the valid rules themselves settle what is to be done and the judge's duty is exhausted by his obligation to apply these rules.

The formalist theory is obviously false. According to Hart its chief defect is that it fails to appreciate both the necessity and the desirability of judicial discretion in adjudicating legal cases under valid rules. We have already briefly encountered Hart's thoughts on this matter, but further, more detailed, discussion will prove useful at this juncture.

3. THE NECESSITY ARGUMENT

We will begin with Hart's argument for the claim that it is necessary that (strong) judicial discretion exist within a legal system comprised of a rule of recognition and the rules it validates.[9] Hart contrasts two methods of communicating general standards of behaviour. First there is the method of example, where an example or paradigm instance is provided and the one whose behaviour is to be governed by the standard is left to infer what it is that is being exemplified and required. Hart quickly shows how communication by this method 'may leave open ranges of possibilities, and hence doubt, as to what is intended, even as to matters which the person seeking to communicate has himself clearly envisaged'.[10] The shortcomings of this method are all too apparent to legal theorists who defend a theory of precedent which construes it as reasoning by example. The familiar and vexing questions are: What are the relevant features of the earlier cases? How do they bear on the instant

[9] Hart does not distinguish between exercising and having discretion, although he has expressed the view in private conversation that discussions of discretion should be respectful of the distinction. Where appropriate we will recast Hart's thoughts on judicial discretion to reflect this view.

[10] *The Concept of Law*, 122. Here we see the ambiguity between having and exercising discretion. That there are open possibilities suggests that the standard fails to control and that the decision-maker therefore has strong discretion. That there is doubt suggests only that the exercise of strong discretion will likely be called for. A standard can control even if there is doubt about whether it does, just as God may exist even though there is considerable doubt about whether He does.

case? Are there any relevant differences in terms of which the instant case can or must be distinguished from the earlier ones?

With this seemingly inferior method of example, Hart contrasts the more usual communication of general standards by 'explicit forms of language'.[11] This method might be thought 'clear, dependable and certain', but of course it is not always so.[12] It is here that Hart introduces his key notion of 'open texture', a concept first introduced by F. Waismann.[13]

In all fields of experience, not only that of rules, there is a limit, inherent in the nature of language, to the guidance which general language can provide. There will indeed be plain cases constantly recurring in similar contexts to which general expressions are clearly applicable ... where there is general agreement in judgments as to the applicability of the general terms ... but there will also be cases where it is not clear whether they apply or not.[14]

[H]owever smoothly they work over the great mass of ordinary cases, [they will], at some point where their application is in question, prove indeterminate; they have what has been termed an open texture ... uncertainty at the borderline is the price to be paid for the use of general classifying terms.[15]

Given this unavoidable feature of general terms, there is always the logical possibility that borderline or anomalous cases will arise in which it is simply indeterminate (or is it only unclear?) whether some particular fact-situation is covered by the general classificatory terms of the relevant legal rule. This will be so regardless of how precisely and unambiguously that rule has been expressed. Borrowing an example from Hart, we may suppose a rule prohibiting vehicles from a public park. The term 'vehicle' used to express this rule has what Hart calls a 'core of settled meaning'. It is clear to all competent users of the language that fully operational motor cycles, Ford Escorts and Mac trucks are vehicles and are thus legally prohibited by the rule from entering the park. 'General terms would be useless to us as a medium of communication unless there were such familiar, generally unchallenged cases'.[16] There will, however, be certain objects which do not fall within the core of settled meaning of the term 'vehicle'. For example, we might encounter a toy motor car, a motorized skateboard, or even 'a shell of a car with a rusty engine, no gear box, a roof like a sieve, and

---

[11] Ibid.   [12] Ibid.
[13] F. Waismann, 'Verifiability', in A. Flew (ed.), *Logic and Language*.
[14] *The Concept of Law*, 123.   [15] Ibid. 124–5.   [16] Ibid. 123.

several tires missing'.[17] In the latter case it might be argued that a vehicle must be capable of locomotion and that regardless of what else it might be, the dilapidated object in question has no such capability. Alternatively, it might be argued that it does have this capability, and that a little work would see that capability realized. In this, and each of the other instances noted above, we have objects which fall within the 'penumbra of uncertainty', where there are respectable reasons both for and against their inclusion within the scope of the term 'vehicle' and thus the rule in whose expression it is used. As Hart puts it, 'no firm convention or general agreement dictates its use, or, on the other hand, its rejection by the person concerned to classify'.[18] In these cases, Hart suggests, the rule's, and thus the law's, guidance runs out and it is the judge who must choose whether to subsume the entity or fact-situation under the rule. The judge's decision, not conventional agreement, determines whether the term is to apply. The judge must decide or determine by an act of fiat, guided no doubt by some view or other about reasonable social aims which might be furthered were the rule interpreted in his particular way, whether toy motor-cars or motorized wheelchairs are vehicles—or more precisely, shall be considered so for the purpose(s) of the rule. And, Hart adds, his conclusion, 'even though it may not be arbitrary or irrational is in effect a choice'.[19] This choice is to be based not upon what is required by an authoritative standard with institutional force, but rather upon a reasonable compromise among what appear to the judge to be reasonable social aims and purposes. It will therefore amount to the exercise of the judge's strong judicial discretion.

Hart's theory of language assumes that if there is lack of clarity and agreement on whether a term applies, it does not apply. He fails to distinguish (at least in his early writings) between uncertainty (an epistemic property) and indeterminacy (a logical property). If it is uncertain how a term applies, then it is indeterminate how it applies. This theory is, in effect, challenged by Dworkin who suggests that uncertainty does not entail indeterminacy and therefore the need for strong discretion. It entails only that judgment, i.e. weak discretion, is called for.[20] In discussing Hart's views on the need for discretion,

---

[17] *Smart* v. *Allan and Another* [1963] 1 QB 291.   [18] *The Concept of Law*, 123.
[19] Ibid. 124.

[20] For a discussion of semantic theories on which a term can apply despite disagreement and uncertainty concerning its application, see D. Brink, 'Legal Theory, Legal Interpretation and Judicial Review', esp. 111–29.

H's Necessity argument

we will assume that he has given good reasons for thinking that the *assume* application of rules is sometimes not merely uncertain but indeter- *indeterminacy.* minate as well. As will now be seen, however, even if we grant this assumption, the argument still fails to yield Hart's conclusion.

There is a good deal that can be said about Hart's Necessity ?, Argument. The first point is that the argument depends crucially on three further assumptions: (1) that general classificatory terms are open-textured and therefore sometimes indeterminate; (2) that if the meaning or scope of a general legal rule is indeterminate the law is therefore indeterminate and a presiding judge must consequently make a free choice among legally open alternatives; and (3) that the meaning or scope of a general legal rule is exhausted by the meaning or scope of its general classificatory terms. Each of these assumptions can be questioned.

Let us begin with assumption (1). It might be suggested that implicit in the use of every truly meaningful general term is a rule or agreed set of criteria used by those who employ and understand that term. This set of criteria, it might be urged, spell out necessary and sufficient conditions of that term's application. It will be conceded that these criteria are often extremely difficult to unearth, as philosophers who attempt to do so, e.g. Plato in his early dialogues, soon discover. Yet the discovery might be theoretically possible nevertheless, and it might be the duty of a judge always to try to make that discovery and to determine what the implicit criteria require in the way of the term's application. If so, there is no open texture and therefore no reason to think that judges must, of necessity, sometimes make free choices undetermined by the meaning of the rules they apply.

When one considers terms like 'brother', 'bachelor', and 'triangle', there is some initial plausibility in the suggestion that all general terms, at least those which are descriptive, can ultimately be defined in terms of necessary and sufficient conditions of correct application. But the plausibility vanishes when one considers other terms like 'horse', 'man', 'table', 'intention', 'cause', or 'reasonable', the last three of which figure in countless legal rules. With respect to these and many other terms utilized in the expression of legal rules, the following comments seem all too appropriate.

Wittgenstein's advice ... is peculiarly relevant to the analysis of legal and political terms. Considering the definition of 'game' he said, 'Don't say there must be something common or they would not be called 'games', but look and see whether there is anything common to all. For if you look at them you will not see anything common to all but similarities, relationships, and a whole series at that'.[21]

If the range of cases to which a general term may be applied are related by nothing stronger than family resemblances, or if, as Putnam and others argue, many descriptive terms connote 'cluster concepts',[22] then the possibility of our gathering together necessary and sufficient conditions of application must be very remote, and the possibility of it sometimes being indeterminate whether a case is covered by that term very strong indeed. And if many, if not most, general terms are of this nature, then it seems foolish to suppose that it is always possible to unearth necessary and sufficient conditions for the application of a general term and that judicial discretion can therefore be avoided.

Suppose, however, that the following reply is made. Some terms, like 'brother' and 'triangle' are not governed by family resemblance. Nor do they seem to connote cluster concepts or suffer from any other sources of indeterminacy. A brother is a male sibling, and a triangle is a closed, three-sided polygon. If we wish to eliminate strong discretion then all we need do is be careful in the terms we choose. We should choose terms like 'brother' and 'triangle' for which necessary and sufficient conditions do seem to be possible. Hence Hart's Necessity Argument is invalid.

There is little to this objection. In order to provide criteria of application for a general term one must, of course, employ other terms, and more often than not at least some of these will themselves be open-textured, governed by family resemblance and so on. It might be clear that a brother is a male sibling but it may be very unclear what it is to be a male or a sibling. When does a person who undergoes the long process involved in a sex change become, if ever some might say, a member of the opposite sex? There will undoubtedly be clear cases, but there will undoubtedly also be those which are not so clear.

But suppose all this is wrong, that necessary and sufficient conditions can always be found if one only looks long and hard enough and examines the appropriate paradigms. There is still an important point which has been overlooked but which was stressed by Waismann. Even if, by some chance, one could always discover a set of

---

[21] *The Concept of Law*, 234, citing *Philosophical Investigations*, i. 66.
[22] On cluster concepts, see H. Putnam, *Mind, Language and Reality*, 51–2.

features uniquely shared by all the present plain cases of a general term, this could never serve as an authoritative definition or criterion. 'We can never', as Waismann argued, 'exclude altogether the possibility of some unforeseen situation arising in which we shall have to [or want to] modify our definition.'[23] The fact that persons can now undergo sex changes with astounding success may, for instance, require that we reconsider our 'definition' of the term 'brother', a term which figures in many legal rules. Definitions are neither immutable nor absolutely authoritative, except perhaps in highly formalized languages such as Euclidean geometry which deal with abstract or ideal objects and notions. At best they are rough but helpful guides to what are, for present purposes, currently thought of by most people as plain cases; but they are often discarded or altered to accommodate new and unforeseen instances and circumstances. Since there is no supremely authoritative criterion to which a judge might appeal, but only a criterion perpetually open to the possibility of revision in light of new information and other kinds of advancements and changes, it follows that the judge may sometimes be required to make an undetermined choice in his decision whether to apply the term and thus the rule of which it is a part. The case before him might well be one which signals the need for a change in the hitherto acceptable definition or understanding of the general term.[24]

So Hart's first assumption, that open texture, or more broadly speaking semantic indeterminacy, is a recurring feature of general terms seems on reasonably sound footing.[25] His second assumption is that if the meaning of a legal rule is indeterminate, *the law* is indeterminate and a presiding judge must, as a consequence, make a free choice from among alternatives left open by the rule. But is this so? Consider the following possible objection.

It is quite conceivable that there should be a system of law in which seemingly indeterminate, anomalous cases are always referred back to a legislative source for settlement, and judges are permitted to decide plain or easy cases only. One is reminded here of the French Law of 16–24 August 1790, title 2, article 12 which (in

[23] 'Verifiability', 120.
[24] Some of the conditions under which this may occur will be discussed in further notes to this chapter.
[25] We will continue to use Hart's term 'open texture', but understand it to encompass whatever kinds of semantic indeterminacy there might be: vagueness, ambiguity, family resemblance, and so on.

rough translation) reads: 'Courts will address themselves to the legislature every time they believe it necessary to interpret a law.' The French Constitution of 1790, article 256 also says the following (again in rough translation): 'When, after the Supreme Court of Appeal has quashed the decision of a lower court, a second decision on the merits is appealed on the same grounds, the issue cannot be discussed in the Supreme Court of Appeal until it has been submitted to the legislature, which enacts a law binding on the Supreme Court of Appeal.' In both of these examples, it would seem that there is no need for judicial discretion: questions of indeterminacy are always dealt with by the legislature. Yet Hart's Necessity Argument purports to demonstrate that judicial discretion is an inevitable feature of all legal systems. The above legal system seems to furnish a counter-example to that argument. Yet another counter-instance might be found in a system in which only clear cases are held to be justiciable. Whenever there is indeterminacy in such a system, the case is simply dropped and there is therefore no need for strong discretion of any sort. In the French system, S1, there is no need for judicial discretion, even if the legislature's decisions are often discretionary. In the second system, S2, there would be no discretion of any kind.

This line of argument is not at all convincing. It is easy to see that strong judicial discretion would be necessary even within systems S1 and S2. Consider the following. The open texture of general terms entails that situations will arise in which it is indeterminate whether the meaning of a rule covers a particular fact-situation. These are cases which fall within the open-textured penumbra of meaning. In much the same way, it will sometimes be indeterminate whether a case falls within the penumbra, or alternatively whether it falls within the core of settled meaning. In short, it will sometimes be indeterminate whether a case is indeterminate. This will be so unless one wishes to claim that whenever there is even the tiniest and remotest of doubts as to the applicability of the term, the case automatically falls within the penumbra. But if this were true, it would follow that very few, if any, cases could be tried within S1 and S2. In almost any case one might imagine, there will be some grounds for a certain amount of Cartesian doubt. One could also be sure that litigants would point to these grounds whenever it was to their advantage to do so. If one is to assume, then, that S1 and S2 are even remotely viable legal systems, one must also assume that a

clear case could be one in which there is some remotely possible
Cartesian doubt about whether the fact-situation is covered by the
relevant term(s). But if this assumption is made, one must accept
that there will be borderline cases, wherever one wishes to draw the
line. Just as 'particular fact-situations do not await us already
marked off from each other, and labelled as instances of the general
rule', cases do not await us already marked off from each other as
either determinate or indeterminate. The cases shade into one
another. One individual might think that a toy motor car is clearly a
vehicle, another might think not, although he could very well
believe that it might be a vehicle. He simply thinks that it is not
obviously or indisputably so. A judge in such a case would be
forced, if he entertained both possibilities, to employ strong judicial
discretion and choose. He would be forced to decide either that the
case is a clear one, and thus that the child who is discovered driving
his toy car in the park has violated the rule, or that it is anomalous
or indeterminate, and thus that it is either non-justiciable or must be
sent back to the legislative source for settlement. Discretion will be
unavoidable in either case.

So if general classificatory terms often suffer from open texture
and there are no other considerations over and above the semantic
content of rules (and the discretion of the judges who apply them)
in terms of which questions of application may be conclusively
answered, it seems to follow that strong judicial discretion is a
necessary feature of law. This brings us to proposition (3), an
assumption which I do wish to contest. Hart's Necessity Argument presupposes that the scope of a legal rule is, and must be,
determined exclusively by the plain or ordinary meanings of the
general classifying terms used in its expression, so that if those
meanings provide insufficient guidance, the rule and thus the law
do so as well, and that a judge must of necessity resort to strong
judicial discretion. But is this a warranted assumption? It seems
not, as will be seen once we distinguish between the following
two questions:

(a) Does this rule apply to this fact-situation?

and

(b) Do the general terms used in the expression of this rule apply
    in virtue of their plain meaning?

The logically unavoidable open texture of general classifying terms entails indeterminacy in rules, and the consequent need for judicial discretion, only if one assumes that a negative or positive answer to (b) entails a corresponding answer to (a). But need this be the case? Is it not conceivable that a rule's content, its meaning and scope, could be determined by factors in addition to the meaning of its general terms, say by the generally understood or clearly stated purpose or aim of the rule, even when the meanings of the general terms used to express that rule fail us?

Fuller yrs ✓

Consider Hart's example once again: All vehicles are prohibited from the park. It is clear that toy motor cars, motorized skateboards and invalid wheelchairs fall within the open-textured penumbra of the term 'vehicle'. But suppose now that it is clearly understood by all (a) that the purpose or object of those who prescribed the rule was to further the policy of providing facilities for quiet, safe recreation; and (b) that this purpose should govern how the rule is to be interpreted and applied. Would it not at least make sense in this instance to claim that the rule obviously does not apply to motorized wheelchairs, that in this case the rule just is determinate despite open texture?

example where purpose of function of rule provides determinacy

Compare what we would be inclined to say in the following case. Suppose that my daughter is being particularly disagreeable. As punishment, I tell her to go to her room and not to come out for any reason during the next hour. In the meantime I leave for the store to buy groceries, during which time a fire breaks out at the house. I return within the hour to discover my daughter cowering in the corner of her room with smoke swirling about her head. After we both reach safety I ask her why she didn't leave her room when the fire broke out. She makes the following reply: 'But you told me not to leave my room for any reason.' Would it not be appropriate for me to say in response: 'When I told you not to leave for any reason I obviously didn't mean you to stay if your life was in danger!' Notice I didn't say: 'You should have disobeyed my instructions under these circumstances.' Rather, I said I didn't mean her to stay if her life was in danger. That's not what I meant when I told her what I did. In other words, what my instruction meant is a function of more than the plain meaning of the terms used in expressing it.

In communicating with one another we assume a whole range of beliefs and value judgments. We suppose that our listener shares certain beliefs and values and that what we say will be interpreted in light of these. In this instance, I assumed that my daughter would realize that her life is more valuable than carrying through on a minor punishment and that by 'any reason whatsoever' I did not mean to include avoiding a life-threatening fire. Many of these background beliefs and values in terms of which we communicate and understand one another can be attributed to 'common sense'. People, as people, share certain basic beliefs and values which form part of the interpretive background of communication. At the very least there is what John Rawls calls 'an overlapping consensus' on these matters.[26] Most people place a very high value on human life, and so I am not required to say explicitly in most contexts that such and such should be done, *unless your life is in danger*. It is, given our common values, simply understood that this is what is meant. Of course, there are also special contexts in which certain uncommon beliefs and values form the appropriate interpretive background. If, for example, my daughter is very small and has not yet come to realize or appreciate that saving her own life is of far greater value than doing exactly as Daddy says, then what I mean to convey to her might be better expressed by the verbal instruction: 'Stay in your room and don't come out for any reason unless you could really get hurt by staying.' Here the interpretive background is different and so the meaning of my instruction would not be conveyed to her were I simply to say: 'Stay in your room for an hour and don't come out for any reason.'

Legal rules are like my instruction(s) to my daughter. Their meaning is partly a function of an interpretive background of common beliefs and values, some of which find expression in legal principles. Legislators and judges assume this background for the purpose of determining what laws are established by the statutes and precedents they create. But unlike common everyday conversation, in which we assume whatever seems appropriate in the particular context in question, the law is an institutionalized, largely impersonal system in which varying degrees of importance are placed on clarity and the settled expectations which are engendered by clear standards. As Hart observes, legal systems compromise between two important social needs: the need for determinate rules which can easily and safely be applied by private citizens in their everyday

[26] See Rawls, 'Justice as Fairness: Political Not Metaphysical'; 'The Idea of an Overlapping Consensus'; and 'The Domain of the Political and Overlapping Consensus'.

lives without further guidance from legal officials; and the need to be flexible, to leave open for later settlement issues which can be properly appreciated and settled only when they arise in concrete cases. Sometimes a legal system will place far more weight on the first need and try to minimize the effect of interpretive backgrounds. In such instances 'too much is sacrificed to certainty and ... judicial interpretation of statutes or of precedent is too formal and fails to respond to the similarities and differences between cases which are visible only when they are considered in the light of social aims'.[27] At other times the appropriateness of appealing to a rich interpretive background will be acknowledged and the meaning or scope of statutes and precedents will be thought to depend on factors in addition to the plain meaning of a rule's terms. Which among the many approaches to legal interpretation is accepted and practised would appear to depend largely on secondary interpretation rules, or what are often termed 'canons of interpretation'. These can range from the 'literal rule' to the 'mischief rule', and vary not only from one system to the next, and from one time to the next within one and the same system, but also from one area of the law to the next. The relative certainty which one can sometimes get by using highly close-textured terms and minimizing interpretive background in ways recommended by the literal rule, may be more highly prized in criminal or contract law than in the law governing inadvertent negligence. Flexibility is perhaps more desirable when the consequences of a finding of liability are the payment of damages as opposed to a long stint in jail. In any event, just as rules of recognition vary depending on legal practice, sometimes recognizing moral factors, sometimes not, the considerations which help to determine the meaning or content of legal norms validated by a rule of recognition vary according to accepted legal practices and the secondary rules to which they give rise.

It is conceivable, though highly undesirable, that a legal system's interpretation rules should include *only* the literal rule of interpretation as it was enunciated by Chief Justice Jervis in *Abley* v. *Dale*. According to Jervis, 'if the precise words used are plain and unambiguous, in our judgment we are bound to construe them in their ordinary sense, even though it do lead, in our view, to an absurdity or manifest injustice'.[28] If this were considered the only rule appropriate for purposes of interpretation, then the interpretive back-

---

[27] *The Concept of Law*, 127.   [28] *Abley* v. *Dale* (1851) II CB 378.

ground would be very narrow indeed. It would also seem to follow from the open texture of general terms that judicial discretion would be necessary. If all that is relevant is the plain, ordinary meaning of the terms used to express a legal rule, and if these terms necessarily have open texture or suffer from other kinds of semantic indeterminacy, then free choices will be inevitable.

But suppose now that the system adopts, as most do, other secondary interpretation rules as well, rules according to which factors in addition to plain or literal meaning might determine the content of a legal rule. Say it includes the 'mischief rule' according to which the meaning of a rule is sometimes determined in part by the object or purpose of the rule, the mischief the lawmakers intended to rectify. This rule seemed to figure in the celebrated case of *Riggs* v. *Palmer*[29] where the question was whether the defendant, Elmer Palmer, was entitled to inherit under his grandfather's will, even though Elmer had murdered his grandfather to make the will operative and thus avoid disinheritance. The court expressed the following view.

[Handwritten margin notes: "Other Secondary interpretation rules"; "eg mischief rule"; "eg the object the makers intended in creating the rule."]

It is quite true that statutes regulating the making, proof, and effects of wills and the devolution of property *if literally construed*, and if their force and effect can in no way and under no circumstances be controlled or modified, give this property to the murderer (emphasis added).

It is a familiar canon of construction that a thing which is within the intention of the makers of a statute is as much within the statute as if it were within the letter; and a thing which is within the letter of a statute is not within the statute unless it be within the intention of the makers.

It was the intention of the law-makers that the donees in a will should have the property given to them. But it never could have been their intention that a donee who murdered the testator to make the will operative should have any benefit under it.

[I]n Smith's Commentaries, 814, many cases are mentioned where it was held that matters embraced in the general words of the statutes nevertheless were not within the statutes, because it could not have been the intention of the law-makers that they should be included.

It is clear that the court in *Riggs* has distinguished our two questions: whether a rule applies and whether the case falls within the core of settled meaning of the general terms used in expressing that rule. Judges are of course not alone here. Dworkin, for example,

[29] 115 NY 506, 22 NE 188 (1889). *Riggs* played a crucial role in Dworkin's early assault on Hart's theory of law. See *Taking Rights Seriously*, ch. 2.

provides a theory of interpretation in which the distinction plays a crucial role. For Dworkin it clearly does not follow from the thesis of open texture, or any other thesis about semantic indeterminacy, that judges have strong discretion. When the language of a legal rule fails to provide full guidance, Hercules will repair to his general interpretive theory and utilize its scheme of principles and policies to determine the right which has been created by the rule. The exact procedures Hercules will follow in determining the scope of that legal right will depend, according to Dworkin, on whether the rule finds its source in statute or previous judicial decision(s). The main difference is that in interpreting 'judicial enactments' Hercules must consider only argument of principle, not policy, as possible bases for the precedent. This is because judicial enactments, i.e. precedents, are justified only if they enforce existing rights established by legal principle. Judges, unlike legislators, may not create new rights in pursuance of policies or the goals they express. So if a precedent was decided correctly, and therefore has some force for the instant case, it must have been decided on principle not policy. So in interpreting it, Hercules will consider only those arguments which could have justified the precedent, i.e. he will consider only arguments of principle.

Not so in the case of statutory rules according to Dworkin. Legislators are free to pursue policy in exercising their law-making functions. As a result, it is appropriate, indeed necessary, to consider arguments of policy in interpreting statutory rules. Hercules will ask 'which arguments of principle and policy might properly have persuaded the legislature to enact just that statute.'[30] He must ask which of the various principles and policies which could reasonably be thought to justify the statute conflict with standards which must find their way into his general constructive interpretation of the law, if that theory is to provide a minimally adequate explanation and justification of the settled law. These must be excluded straight off. Those that are left, presumably, might properly have persuaded the legislators to enact the statute they did. Hercules must then determine which, among these remaining principles and policies, 'offers a better justification of the statute actually drafted'.[31] Dworkin holds, of course, that in theory there will always be a set of principles or policies in terms of which one can provide the statute with its best justification and explanation, i.e. its best constructive interpretation.

[30] *Taking Rights Seriously*, 108.   [31] Ibid. 109.

Left margin annotations: Yes, Herculean method of resolving indeterminacy

These will be standards which figure in Hercules' general constructive interpretation of his legal system; they could be, though
they will not likely be, standards which Hercules finds personally
unattractive, i.e., which conflict with principles in his theory of background political morality.

It should be stressed that Dworkin never requires that Hercules
ask which arguments of principle or policy did in fact persuade the
legislators (or the judges if the enactment is judicial) to enact the
rule that they did. There is no talk of attempting to decide in accordance with the actual aims or intentions of the legislators, as one finds
in *Riggs* and many other cases.[32] Rather, Dworkin suggests that
Hercules will ask which arguments might properly have persuaded
the enactors were they guided by their proper role in the legal/
political scheme. The emphasis is again placed on the judge's constructive interpretation of legal practice and not on speculation
about what is explicitly stated or generally agreed to have been the
actual aim of the enactment. In Dworkin's view it is quite appropriate for Hercules (and other judges presumably) to decide a case
one way even though the intentions of the enactors clearly were, or
are, that it be decided in some other way. On Dworkin's theory they
might have got their institutional duty all wrong.

So for Dworkin, when a legislature or court enacts a legal standard it does something far more than create a standard the scope of
which is entirely a function of the 'shared conventions of language'.
The standard created by that institutional event extends, at the
moment of enactment, to all those cases in which the standard,
properly interpreted, applies. And whether a particular interpretation is proper will depend, at least in a hard, penumbral case, on
whether the enactment, thus interpreted, would advance those principles or goals which provided the standard with its best justification. Dworkin clearly distinguishes between our two questions:
whether a rule applies to a particular case and determines a result,
and whether the general and possibly open-textured terms used in its
expression apply in virtue of their agreed, plain meanings. It is
unclear to me (a) whether Dworkin thinks that legal rules must, in
all systems, at all times, be interpreted as Hercules interprets them;
or alternatively (b) whether Hercules' procedure is thought to rep-

---

[32] As noted earlier, Dworkin strenuously objects to any theory according to which
interpretation in law is a matter of discovering the historical intentions of legislators
and judges. See *Law's Empire*, 317–27.

resent only one among possibly many practices of interpretation, a procedure which Dworkin no doubt thinks is both desirable and representative of current practice within modern, Anglo-American legal systems, but which might be different. My claim, following Hart, that courts can pursue, and have pursued, various interpretive practices depending on the secondary interpretation rules accepted within their legal systems, is inconsistent with (a) but perfectly compatible with (b).

I conclude (i) that the plain meaning of the terms used in expressing a legal standard is not the only factor which can, or has been thought to, determine its meaning or scope, and (ii) that the connection between the settled, plain meaning of a rule's terms and the meaning, content, or scope of the rule itself depends on secondary interpretation rules accepted by the judges of the system.[33] We do seem to have a choice in how we determine the meaning, scope, and effect of our legal rules, and different choices do seem to have been made. Discretion may be necessary in all legal systems, but Hart's simple appeal to the semantic thesis of open texture is clearly not enough to show that this is so. Whether another argument, sensitive to the points made above, can be fashioned to show the necessity of strong judicial discretion is a question which we will not explore here. It is likely, however, that whatever the interpretive background appropriate to a particular legal system, or a particular court deciding a particular case in a particular area of law, indeterminacy will be encountered somewhere along the line. The objects or purposes of legal rules, the most common items appealed to in addition to plain meaning in determining what a rule really means, often conflict and are incommensurable with one another. If so, then, there will likely be room, at some stage, for a judge's free exercise of choice among logically open alternatives.

NB

4. THE DESIRABILITY ARGUMENT

It is now time to consider Hart's argument for the claim that the having and exercising of strong judicial discretion is a highly desirable feature of legal systems. We have already encountered this argument in earlier discussions of the concept of strong discretion. But it is necessary to consider it once again, to see how it can be

[33] It is on the acceptability of (ii) that I may part company with Dworkin.

H'S ~~ ~~ Desirability argument.

W's main point

extended to support the main conclusion we wish to establish: that it is desirable that the meaning of legal standards should sometimes be a function of factors in addition to plain meaning.

The Desirability Argument begins with the familiar premise that creators of rules do not, and for all practical purposes cannot, anticipate all the possible fact-situations to which their general rules will, or might reasonably, be thought to apply. Nevertheless, they can and probably do anticipate certain clear cases, e.g., the operators of noisy motor cars and motor cycles taking Sunday drives through the public park. They know that this sort of fact-situation either will or is very likely to arise, and their aim or intention is to secure peace and quiet in the park by excluding such vehicles. But what of the unanticipated cases? In Hart's view, the aims or intentions of the legislators in these cases are indeterminate. The legislators 'have not settled, because [they] have not anticipated, the questions which will be raised by the unenvisaged case when it arises'.[34] Yet if their rule is so clear and determinate in meaning that it dictates results in all (or even nearly all) conceivable cases, the legislators would have blindly committed themselves and the judge to a particular result in the unanticipated case. 'The rigidity of our classifications will thus war with our aims in having or maintaining the rule.'[35] It is better, however, that this not be blindly predetermined and that the question of what is to be done be left to the informed discretion of judges who can more fully appreciate and rationally settle them when they arise in concrete cases. The open-textured penumbra of general terms allows for this possibility. So both judicial discretion and open texture are desirable features of law.

As with the Necessity Argument there is a good deal that can be said in response to the Desirability Argument. Once again, we shall restrict ourselves to a few pertinent comments.

The first point to be made about the argument is that it seems to fail, as it stands, to demonstrate that judicial discretion is a good thing to have. Even if one were to accept, as proven, the claim that some form of strong discretion is desirable when rules are applied to concrete cases, it has yet to be shown that the desirable form is judicial discretion. Ideally perhaps the delicate balancing of social aims and purposes which Hart's theory requires would be better left, as in S1 above, to a more representative and responsible body such

---

[34] *The Concept of Law*, 126.   [35] Ibid. 126–7.

as a legislature. If, as members of democratic societies, we are hesitant to allow non-representative individuals like judges and monarchs to set laws and decide thereby how citizens will be dealt with by the legal system, we should be equally hesitant to allow them the power to decide what shall be done in hard cases where those laws prove indeterminate.

Perhaps the most obvious reply to this first objection is to concede that judicial discretion does seem to compromise democratic ideals. The ideal situation might be one where all judicial decisions clearly follow, in conjunction with the facts of cases, from decisions made by democratic bodies. Yet it is often the case that ideals and ideal procedures cannot be successfully realized in practice, and that we meet with considerable misfortune and failure if we strive for the ideal in our less than perfect world. To take a familiar example, Plato may well have been right in claiming that government by enlightened, wholly impartial, and benevolent philosopher-kings would be the ideal. Yet even if this is so, it remains true that the results, in terms of utter mismanagement and tyranny, of striving to implement such a system within our highly imperfect world would be far from welcome. The results would be far less desirable than those forthcoming from representative democracy with all its obvious limitations and imperfections.

Similar considerations apply to the choice between judicial and legislative discretion. We might grant that within an ideal world in which legislators have sufficient time and energy to deal properly with hard cases, it would be better if they, and not judges, performed the delicate balancing of social aims, purposes, and principles such cases typically require. But of course in our less than perfect world, legislators have neither the time nor the energy to acquaint themselves adequately with all the facts and all the implications of all hard cases. Even if they were somehow able to make the necessary time, there is little doubt that the wheels of government and justice would be forced to turn far more slowly than we should find acceptable. So given these practical considerations, it seems to follow that judges and not legislators are our best hope in dealing with hard, penumbral cases. It thus follows, in light of Hart's arguments, that the exercise of strong judicial discretion is indeed a desirable thing to have within legal systems. Even if we could somehow eliminate the necessity for judicial discretion this would not be a good thing.

There is, however, one further important point to be made about

Hart's Desirability Argument. This is not so much an objection as a suggestion that the argument fails to go far enough in drawing the implications of the premises Hart has provided. Consider the following. Hart has convincingly argued, against those with formalist leanings, that the possibility of blindly committing ourselves to unreasonable results in unanticipated cases is a sufficient reason for framing legal rules in loose, open-textured terms, even if we did have at our disposal logically closed-textured terms with no penumbras of indeterminacy. We must, if we are to avoid unanticipated absurdities and other undesirable results, leave our judges room to manœuvre when they apply legal rules to concrete cases. When we frame rules in this way we pay a high price in terms of certainty, predictability, and to some extent perhaps, fairness, in the consistent application of public rules of conduct. But this is often a price well worth paying. My question for Hart is this. The possibility of unwanted results serves as a sufficient reason for preserving the penumbra even if it could be eliminated altogether. Why does this possibility not also serve as a sufficient reason for following the interpretive practice of not considering a rule applicable when, unfortunately, the plain meanings of the general terms used in its expression call for a clearly absurd, manifestly unjust, or otherwise undesirable, result—a result which we could have avoided if, by some stroke of luck, the case had fallen within the penumbra? In other words, cannot the Desirability Argument be extended to what we will call 'plain-meaning cases', cases which do not fall within the open-textured penumbra of the rule's general terms, but rather their core of settled meaning? In short, can the argument not be extended to cases like *Riggs*?

It is clear to me that it can, and that we should not hesitate to pursue the interpretive practices that are suggested by this extension. It is likely, however, that early Hart, the author of *The Concept of Law* and 'Positivism and the Separation of Law and Morals', would be extremely reluctant to pursue this course. To allow that a rule might not apply even though the plain meaning of the terms used to express it call for application would be to 'assert mysteriously that there is some fused identity between the law as it is and as it ought to be . . . that all legal questions are fundamentally like those of the penumbra. It [would be] to assert that there is no central element of actual law to be seen *in the core of settled meaning which rules have*.'[36]

The question I now propose to investigate is this. What arguments

[36] 'Positivism and the Separation of Law and Morals', 29, emphasis added.

might be given to block my proposed extension of the Desirability Argument to plain-meaning cases? In the following two sections I shall consider three standard arguments each of which ultimately fails.

Objections to proposed extension of Desirability Argument

5. THE INTENTION ARGUMENT

Perhaps the following fairly familiar argument would be advanced. There will admittedly be plain-meaning cases which we or a judge might wish to see excluded from the scope of a legal rule in order to give effect to its agreed or stated purpose, or to avoid perceived absurdity or manifest injustice. Nevertheless, it is the proper function of the judiciary in a constitutional democracy to render decisions which accord with the wishes or intentions of the elected legislators, whenever, that is, it is clear what these are, and even when doing so might seem self-defeating or clearly unreasonable or repugnant to the judges' sense of justice. Recall the words of Jervis CJ in *Abley* v. *Dale* that 'if the precise words used are plain and unambiguous, in our judgment we are bound to construe them in their ordinary sense, even though it do lead, in our view of the case, to an absurdity or manifest injustice'. Since the cases in question are all, *ex hypothesi*, plainly covered by the general terms used to express a legal rule, the wishes or intentions of the legislators must have been those which will be respected only if the rules are applied. An argument of this form seems to have been advanced by Justice Tindal in *Sussex Peerage Case*,[37] where he states that if 'the words of the statute are themselves precise and unambiguous, then no more can be necessary than to expound those words in their natural and ordinary sense. The words themselves alone do, in such case, best declare the intention of the lawgiver.' Viscount Simonds would no doubt have concurred. In *Magor and St Mellons RDC* v. *Newport Corporation*[38] he stated, in response to an invitation to construe a statute in a way other than was suggested by literal meaning: 'It appears to me to be a naked usurpation of the legislative function under the thin disguise of interpretation.'

So what can be said about the Intention Argument? There are a host of reasons for thinking it is unsound, despite its popularity.

First, the most obvious point against the Intention Argument is

[37] (1844) 11 Cl. & F. 84.   [38] [1952] AC 189.

that it applies only to statutory law and completely ignores the vast body of rules instituted and developed by the courts themselves. Why should the intentions of an earlier judge, who is usually no less responsible to the electorate than the judge deciding the present case, govern how a precedent is to be interpreted, or how a statute is to be understood if, as is usual, judicial interpretations of statutes themselves have the effect of precedent? A judge, or even a small group of judges on an Appeal Court, are no more likely than a full legislature to have anticipated all the fact-situations to which the plain meaning of their rulings might reasonably be thought to apply. So allowing later judges to interpret those rulings in light of what would be self-defeating, absurd, or manifestly unjust in the instant case, seems a very reasonable course to pursue.

Second, the Intention Argument falls prey to the many objections to 'intentionalism' referred to and discussed in Chapter 5. How does one meaningfully ascribe intentions to a disparate body like a legislature? Why should we think, in any case, that their intentions should govern how the public rules they enact must be interpreted? Recall Dworkin's theory that a legal rule creates a right which is in part a function, not of the arguments of principle or policy which did in fact persuade the legislators to enact the statute they did, but rather the arguments which provide the statute with its best justification. As noted earlier, there is little reason to think that what did persuade the legislators, on the one hand, and what would have persuaded them had they decided in accordance with the best interpretive theory of the law, on the other, will always be identical. But if so, then on one plausible theory of interpretation the actual intentions of legislators have little probative force. And even if we disagree with Dworkin on what does count in interpreting legal rules, the question still remains: Why should our legal rules continue to be governed by the intentions of possibly long-dead legislators who could not always have anticipated what the literal meaning of their rules would seem to require in future cases?

A third and related point revolves around an ambiguity in the term 'intention'. The Intention Argument is insensitive to the difference between what Gerald MacCallum has called 'particular' and 'general' legislative intentions.[39] The former refers to the sense

---

[39] MacCallum, 'Legislative Intent', 754ff. Others distinguish between abstract versus specific or concrete intentions. See e.g. Dworkin, *Law's Empire*, and Brink, 'Legal Theory, Legal Interpretation, and Judicial Review'.

in which the legislators intended particular words to be understood (what they meant by those words), while the latter refers to the purpose(s) or aim(s) they intended to secure in framing the rule they did (what they meant to achieve). Given this useful distinction, the obvious question is: Which of these two very different sorts of intentions must be respected by judges in interpreting legal rules? If one answers that the particular intentions must always be respected, then the question automatically arises why, given Hart's argument, we should not be willing to allow judges to ignore those particular intentions when doing so is a necessary condition, say, of fulfilling or not frustrating the legislators' general intentions? And if we assume, as the court seemed to in *Riggs*, that among the intentions of legislators is that application of their rules should not lead to clear absurdity or manifest injustice, then we seem to have an argument for discounting particular intentions in such cases. We have a strong argument for following the practice of denying the applicability of legal rules under these conditions, even in plain-meaning cases.

If, on the other hand, it is answered that the role of the judiciary is to abide by the general intentions of the legislators, then, quite obviously, the judge's task will sometimes require the non-application of rules in plain-meaning cases. As noted, this seems to have been the view of the court in *Riggs*. It is also the view of Lord Denning who said, in *Engineering ITB* v. *Samuel Talbot Ltd* (1969), that 'We no longer construe acts according to their literal meaning. We construe them according to their object or intent.'[40] The Canadian Supreme Court echoed these thoughts when reflecting on how to approach the *Canadian Charter of Rights and Freedoms*. Recall the words of Dickson CJ that 'The meaning of a right or freedom guaranteed by the Charter [is] to be ascertained by an analysis of the purpose of such a guarantee: it [is] to be understood, in other words, in the light of the interests it was meant to protect.'[41]

A fourth and perhaps the most serious objection to the Intention Argument is that it seems to rest on the assumption that the plain meanings of the terms used to express a legal rule are an infallible indicator of the intentions of the legislators. But this assumption is false. Consider a rule requiring that all transport vehicles pay a road tax of $100. Given the plain, ordinary meaning of 'transport vehicle', cargo airplanes are subject to the tax. Nevertheless, I take

---

[40] *Engineering ITB* v. *Samuel Talbot Ltd.* (1969) 2QB 270 at 275.
[41] *R.* v. *Big M Drug Mart*, [1985] 1 SCR 295 at 344.

it, we may safely assume that the legislators did not mean or intend that they be subject to a road tax. This could have been neither their general nor their particular intention. Of course it is true that if, in issuing a rule, legislators commit us to all results which accord with the plain meaning of the terms used, then they may be said to have committed us, regrettably and perhaps foolishly, to holding cargo airplanes subject to the tax. But it is not true that they could be said thereby to have intended or meant that this be so when they issued their rule. Their response to any suggestion that they had would no doubt be to say: 'When we said "transport vehicles" we obviously did not mean to include cargo airplanes!' Compare my reaction to my daughter who, when told not to come out of her room for any reason, stays there despite the fire which threatens her life: 'I obviously didn't mean you to stay if your life was being seriously threatened!'

True, it might be replied. The plain meaning of the terms used in the expression of a legal rule do not necessarily function as an infallible indicator of the particular or general intentions of legislators. It does, nevertheless, constitute the best evidence we have as to what those were or now are. Consider the following variation on the Intention Argument. The cases under consideration are all, *ex hypothesi*, plain-meaning cases. It follows that, for any particular case one happens to choose, the hypothesis that it was anticipated and that it was intended or meant to be included within the scope of the rule is far more likely than the hypothesis that it was not. Legislators (we will continue to ignore judge-made law here) must be assumed to be reasonably intelligent and capable users of the language in which they frame their rules. It is reasonable to assume, therefore, that they were well aware of the plain-meaning cases and intended that they be included within the scope of their rules. Hence it is far more likely, though admittedly not certain—but where in law does one ever have absolute certainty?—that judges will respect the intentions of the legislators if they always apply legal rules in plain-meaning cases.[42]

Though this modification of the Intention Argument is more plausible than the original, it too is unconvincing. Granted, one must not forget that the cases under consideration are all plain-meaning cases. But one must also remember that they are all such that 'we

[42] An argument of this form is advanced by MacCormick in *Legal Reasoning and Legal Theory*, 204.

would wish to exclude [them] in order to give effect to reasonable social aims'. Indeed, the aims which prompt this wish are sometimes those for the sake of which the rule obviously was fashioned. Given the nature of these cases, and given that legislators realize that judges too are reasonably intelligent and competent users of the language who, like other competent members of the language community, are reasonably well aware of the plain meanings of most terms, it seems at least as likely that the legislators failed to anticipate these particular cases and that they did not, therefore, intend or mean them to be included within the scope of their rules. Otherwise they would have expressed their rules differently, in ways such that plain meaning did not lead to these obviously unwanted results.

Of course all this assumes that the legislators' intentions are fixed by plain meaning. Yet as we saw earlier, we assume, in communicating with each other, an interpretive background of common beliefs and values. Recall, again, the case of my child in the burning bedroom. I did not intend or mean what is suggested by a strictly literal interpretation of the words I chose to communicate my instruction. I assumed that my words would be interpreted in the light of the fact that my daughter's life, indeed human life in general, is more valuable than the blind following of orders construed strictly and literally. If legislators assume that their words will be interpreted in light of moral and other practical values, serious violation of which would lead in the instant case to clear absurdity or manifest injustice, then we have very little reason indeed to think that they intended the absurd or manifestly unjust results to which an overly literal interpretation of their rules would lead. Their response to any suggestion that they had would undoubtedly be to say: 'That's obviously not what we meant when we passed that rule!'

So even this weaker version of the Intention Argument seems destined to failure. Indeed, since the plain meanings of a rule's general terms do, in the kind of case we have been considering, suggest results which in all probability conflict with the intentions of the legislators, the argument, so far as it has any plausibility at all, would seem to justify non-application of rules in those cases. We would do well, then, to consider another line of argument.

6. THE RULE OF LAW ARGUMENT 1

A second popular argument which might be used against my proposed extension of the Desirability Argument to plain-meaning cases appeals to the value of law according to rules. Contrasted with this is the disutility of law according to people and their possibly fluctuating, idiosyncratic, and erroneous views concerning justice. The argument might go something like this.

To allow that legal rules might not apply in plain-meaning cases would be to undermine totally the pursuit of the rule of law. In fact it would be to play directly into the hands of legal realism and its modern variant, the Critical Legal Studies Movement, forms of rule scepticism according to which there are in actual fact no binding rules at all and judges simply decide cases on grounds of their own choosing. These grounds might be political, moral, or personal. Judges only pretend to be following rules when what they are in fact doing is rationalizing their blatant, and often abusive and reactionary exercise of political power. If it were within a judge's legal power to consider a plain-meaning case outside the scope of a legal rule, whenever in his view its exclusion would seem desirable, then he could not, with any sense whatsoever, be said to be bound by those rules. He would never, to use Raz's terminology, be at the executive stage where exclusionary reasons have replaced deliberative reasons for action and the careful balancing which these require. In short, we would have no legal rules at all.

One is reminded in this context of a similar potential problem which emerged from the notorious Practice Statement of 1966. As noted earlier, prior to 26 June 1966, the British House of Lords had considered itself bound by its own precedents, that is, bound by the rulings it had made and used to decide earlier cases. In the view of the pre–1966 Court, its own precedents had overwhelming institutional force over its later decisions. On 26 June, however, Lord Gardiner revealed the Lords' intention to modify their legal practice, and 'while treating former decisions of [the] House as normally binding, to depart from a previous decision when it appear[ed] right to do so'.[43] In other words, the Lords were taking it upon themselves to lessen considerably the institutional force of their own earlier decisions. That force would no longer be (nearly) absolute but could be overcome. One of the more intriguing questions raised by

[43] Cited in Cross, *Precedent in English Law*, 109.

Lord Gardiner's statement concerns the meaning of the phrase 'when it appears right to do so'. It is clear that a rule from which one is free to depart *whenever it appears right to do so*, cannot be in the slightest bit binding. Indeed, it may be no rule at all. A rule from which one may depart whenever it appears right to do so, seems to exclude no competing considerations whatsoever, to have no exclusionary force at all; yet having at least some degree of exclusionary force seems to be a defining feature of rules.

This point is a familiar one in moral philosophy and is sometimes used to attack certain forms of rule utilitarianism. If, on each occasion in which a so-called moral rule's application were at issue, one were able justifiably to depart from the rule if it appeared right to do so, i.e., if departure would result in more net utility than application, then rule utilitarianism reduces in effect to act utilitarianism. One is left judging each case on its own merits.[44] Similarly, if a judge were able to consider a plain-meaning case outside the scope of a legal rule on the grounds that his so considering it would further the purpose(s) of the rule or avoid absurdity or repugnance, then his task would not be to apply rules of law, but in effect to render decisions which further reasonable social aims in ways which are neither absurd nor unjust. This is exactly what some realists claim the judges are really trying to do, despite any rhetoric to the contrary. It follows that if we are to have the rule of law, and are not to surrender to legal realism, then there must, as a matter of logic, be cases in which the application of legal rules is not at the option of the judge who is to apply them, and these are the plain-meaning cases. Once we abandon rules in plain-meaning cases we have no way of avoiding the radical indeterminacy associated with realism and the Critical Legal Studies Movement.

The defect in the Rule of Law Argument 1 lies in its final step. It is undeniable that meaningful rule following, and thus the very possibility of the rule of law, require that there be at least some cases where application is not at the option of the rule-applier. Otherwise, no move has been made away from Raz's deliberative stage and the rule has no institutional force whatsoever. It does not follow, however, that these cases are necessarily co-extensive with the class of all plain-meaning cases. We do have other options. Consider the English House of Lords again. As became clear in the months and

---

[44] For discussion of this point see R. M. Hare, *Freedom and Reason*, 130–6 and David Lyons, *Forms and Limits of Utilitarianism, passim.*

years following the Practice Statement, the Lords had intended to depart from their own precedents only under very special circumstances. In *Knuller Publishing and Promotions Ltd* v. *Director of Public Prosecutions*[45] for example, the court refused to overturn its earlier decision in *Shaw* v. *Director of Public Prosecutions*.[46] Lord Reid had this to say: 'In the general interests of certainty in the law we must be sure that there is some very good reason before we act.' In *Miliangos* v. *George Frank (Textiles) Ltd*[47] the Lords again hesitated to depart from their precedents, suggesting that they would depart only when failure to do so would lead to 'great injustice', the implication being that mere injustice would not suffice. Yet another example: in *Fitzleet Estates Ltd* v. *Cherry*[48] Viscount Dilhorne said: 'If the decision in the *Chancery Lane Case* was wrong, it certainly was not so clearly wrong and productive of injustice as to make it right for the House to depart from it.'

There are, in fact, many options which could be pursued in limiting, though not eliminating, the binding force of legal rules. Suppose the practice is to consider legal rules applicable and binding in all plain-meaning cases, except where it is obvious that application would severely frustrate the very objectives the enactors sought to realize by prescribing the rule they did. It would still make perfectly good sense to speak in terms of binding rules and meaningful rule following. It would make sense because there would remain binding standards which determine inescapable results in the vast majority of plain-meaning cases. These would include all those plain-meaning cases in which reasons other than frustration of the rule's objectives argue strongly in favour of non-application. Suppose the clear aim of imposing a road tax on transport vehicles is to shift the cost of road repairs to those most responsible for deterioration of the province's highways. That objective might be employed to defend the exclusion of cargo airplanes. But it could not be used to exclude, say, independent truckers upon whom the extra tax might, for other reasons, impose an unfair burden, and who a judge might therefore wish to see excluded from the scope of the rule.

Suppose, on the other hand, the practice is to follow a version of the golden rule of interpretation according to which a rule applies in all plain-meaning cases unless this 'leads to [any] manifest ab-

---

[45] [1973] AC at 455.   [46] [1962] AC 220.   [47] [1976] AC 443.
[48] All ER 996, 1000.

surdity or [moral] repugnance'.[49] Here any absurdity or moral repugnance will do: we are not restricted to absurd or repugnant frustrations of the rule's objective(s). Again, meaningful rule following seems possible. To warrant exclusion of a plain-meaning case from the scope of a legal rule, it must be shown that our including it would be, not merely undesirable, unreasonable, or unjust, but manifestly absurd or morally repugnant. Under such a practice one might justify excluding cargo airplanes but perhaps not independent truckers. It might be somewhat unjust to impose the extra tax upon a group struggling for economic survival and who already contribute more than enough through the fuel taxes they are required to pay; it might not, however, be manifestly unjust or otherwise repugnant to do so, as it would have been had Elmer Palmer been allowed his ill-gotten gains.

With the golden rule we of course have moral factors determining the very meaning and scope of legal rules, the very possibility and desirability of which we have been considering in this chapter. That the golden rule does have a history within Anglo-American legal systems suggests that the (contingent) fusion of law and morality which inclusive positivism contemplates as possible has extended, historically, not only to determinations of legal validity, as in the Charter challenges discussed in Chapter 5, but to determinations of the meaning or content of valid laws, as in *Riggs*. We have here further evidence in favour of inclusive positivism and against exclusive positivism whose rendering of cases like *Riggs* must be as forced and counter-intuitive as its rendering of *Andrews* and *Morgentaler*.

It is clear that we can rationally restrict the range of factors which place a plain-meaning case outside the scope of a legal rule, and that some of these might be moral factors like manifest moral repugnance or gross injustice. We have logically possible options besides (a) allowing the exclusion of plain-meaning cases on *any* reasonable ground whatsoever, in which case there are no binding rules with institutional force over judges' decisions; and (b) allowing their exclusion on *no grounds whatsoever*. It follows that we are not faced with the unpalatable dilemma of considering rules applicable in each and every plain-meaning case, or falling prey to the kind of radical indeterminacy which, according to legal realists, plagues all attempts to pursue the rule of law. There are middle

---

[49] B. Parke in *Becke* v. *Smith* (1836).

courses and its failure to appreciate them renders Rule of Law Argument 1 unsound.

7. THE RULE OF LAW ARGUMENT 2

In light of the above, it is clear that one cannot successfully block my proposed extension of Hart's Desirability Argument to plain-meaning cases by arguing that it would result in the total abandonment of the rule of law. But perhaps there is a more plausible way of formulating the Rule of Law Argument. Perhaps the point is not that we must, as a matter of sheer logic, have our rules apply in all plain-meaning cases if we are to have the rule of law. The point may be that it is desirable, all things considered, that we do so. If we interpret legal rules in such a way that they do not apply even though the plain, ordinary meanings of their terms make them clearly applicable, then great uncertainty and instability is the result. Citizens will never know where they stand under the law. There are, to be sure, plain-meaning cases, like *Riggs*, in which clearly desirable social aims argue strongly in favour of non-application. But there are other more general social aims, like certainty, predictability, and fairness, which argue strongly in favour of interpreting legal rules as applying in all plain-meaning cases. And the number of times and the extent to which the latter aims outweigh the former is such that it is better, in the long run, if rules are conceived as extending to all plain-meaning cases. We are far better off if our secondary interpretation rules require application in all such cases.

Support for this line of argument is gained when one considers that the ordinary private citizen cannot be presumed always to know the various social aims and purposes for the sake of which legal rules are or might be fashioned, or the standards of justice and rationality in terms of which a judge might attempt to justify non-application in a plain-meaning case. We are on far safer ground, however, if we presume that, as a member of the language community, the ordinary citizen is reasonably well aware of the plain meaning of words used within that community. Thus if rules are always interpreted and applied in accordance with plain meaning, we have a reasonable chance of fulfilling the need for rules which individuals can apply for themselves without official guidance from judges or the weighing up of social, political, and moral factors. If, on the other hand, the scope of a legal rule may at any time depend on various controversial, and to the private citizen possibly unknown, views concerning reasonable social aims and purposes, or manifestly absurd and repugnant results, then our chances of fulfilling this crucial need are substantially, and perhaps unacceptably, reduced.[50]

Rule of Law Argument 2 represents the most powerful objection to the proposed extension of the Desirability Argument to plain-meaning cases. But there are at least three important considerations weighing against it.

First, the argument exaggerates the extent to which there is widespread agreement on plain meanings, and thus the extent to which clear guidance is forthcoming if the scope of a rule is always taken to depend exclusively on the literal meaning of the terms used to express it. As stated in paragraph 30 of the 21st Report of the English Law Commission, 'to place undue emphasis on the literal meaning of the words of a provision is to assume an unattainable perfection in draughtsmanship' ... Such an approach ignores the limitations of language, which is not infrequently demonstrated even at the level of the House of Lords when Law Lords differ as to the so-called "plain meaning of words".'[51]

This sort of controversy over 'plain meaning' is nicely illustrated in *Re Rowland* where a major controversy arose over the meaning of the term 'coincide'.[52] A young doctor and his wife had gone on vaca-

---

[50] Gerald Postema argues that it is a characteristic feature of law that it provides a focus for the expectations of parties engaged in various complex patterns of social interaction. These include interactions among citizens (e.g. adjacent landowners or contractors), among citizens and law-applying officials (e.g. judges), and among law-applying officials themselves. As Postema argues, it is important that these various groups be co-ordinated in their expectations concerning how the others will interpret the rules administered by the law-applying officials. This raises co-ordination problems which, it might be argued following Postema, can be solved only if interpretations of legal rules do not depend on anything other than plain meaning. This is something which all the parties can be expected to know. But as will be seen shortly, there is little reason to think that only plain meaning can serve to focus expectations in the ways Postema requires. For Postema's account of the co-ordinative function of (effective) legal practice, see his 'Coordination and Convention at the Foundations of Law'.

[51] Cf. *London North-Eastern RY.* v. *Berriman [1946]*.

[52] [1963] Ch. 1. This case did not involve the interpretation of a statute or precedent but rather that of a will. But similar considerations apply in this area of the law, as they do in other areas, like contracts. The courts also seem to have pursued a corresponding variety of practices in construing or interpreting these legal instruments, and seem to have offered similar arguments for and against liberal and literal approaches to interpretation. On this see e.g. Lord Denning, *The Discipline of Law, passim.* and *Justice, Lord Denning and the Constitution*, P. Robson and P. Watchman (eds.), *passim*.

tion in the South Seas. Before leaving each had a will drawn up. The doctor made a bequest 'in the event of my wife's death preceding or coinciding with my own death', while she made a similar provision. During their vacation they ventured to sea in a vessel which disappeared without a trace, though one body and some wreckage was later discovered. The conclusion of the court was that the boat had gone down suddenly with all hands lost. The question before the Chancery Court was: Did the death of the wife 'coincide' with that of her husband? Two of the three judges, together with counsel Mr Knox, agreed that there was absolutely no reason to believe that the deaths had coincided. Lord Denning thought this absurd, and his reasons are well worth quoting in full.

One way of approach, which was much favoured in the nineteenth century, is to ask yourself simply: what is the ordinary grammatical meaning of the word 'coincide' as used in the English language? On that approach, the answer it is said is plain: it means 'coincident in point of time'. And that means, so it is said, the same as 'simultaneous' or 'at the same point in time'. So instead of interpreting the word 'coincide', you turn to interpreting the word 'simultaneous'. And at that point you come upon a difficulty because, strictly speaking, no two people ever die at exactly the same point of time. Or, at any rate, no one can ever prove that they do ...

... I asked Mr. Knox whether deaths are simultaneous when an aircraft crashes on a mountainside and all its occupants are killed. He said they were not, because one might have died a little while after the others. To be simultaneous, there would have to be proof that they died simultaneously at the same instant, and such proof would rarely be available. I must confess that, if ever there were an absurdity, I should have thought we have one here. It is said that when an aircraft explodes in mid-air, the deaths of the occupants coincide; but when it crashes into a mountainside, they do not! The supporters of this argument invoke as their authority 'the ordinary man'. He would, I suggest, be amazed to find such a view attributed to him. Yet it is the argument, as I understand it, which urges that in this case the deaths of Dr. Rowland and his wife did not coincide.

Denning went on to invite his colleagues to ignore the ordinary, plain meaning of 'coincide' (as they understood it) and to consider instead what the doctor obviously meant by 'coincide' and what he meant to achieve by including the provision he did. In other words, he asked them to consider the wider interpretive background in which more than the a-contextual, plain meaning of individual terms governs what a will means, as is often true in the case of precedents and statutes, and was true in the example of my daughter's instruction to stay in her room. Denning's colleagues declined the invitation, however, choosing instead to 'interpret' the will in accordance with what they, unlike Denning, thought to be the plain meaning of 'coincide'. Russell LJ for the majority put it this way:

The testator's language does not fit the facts of the case, so far as they are known. To hold otherwise would not, in my judgment, be to construe the will at all: it would be the result of inserting in the will a phrase which the testator never used. ... There is no jurisdiction in the Court to achieve a sensible result by such means.

So not only did the Court disagree with Denning's assessment of the so-called plain meaning of 'coincide', they refused to consider anything more than this element in their attempt to provide the will with a sensible interpretation. The result was an interpretation with respect to which any reasonable person would have likely responded by saying: 'When I said "coincide" that's obviously not what I meant!'

A second objection to Rule of Law Argument 2 is that it overstates the degree to which legal systems are in fact committed to interpreting their rules in accordance with plain, ordinary meaning. Presumably by 'plain or ordinary meaning' is meant the meaning ascribed to the rule and its terms by ordinary people in ordinary, everyday contexts. It is this type of meaning which is in play when we say: 'He tried to force the door open.' To be contrasted with this plain, ordinary meaning of the term 'force' is the technical meaning it bears when employed in specialized contexts, as when a physicist says: 'The force communicated by the particle is equal to its mass times its acceleration.'

The kind of guidance presupposed in Rule of Law Argument 2 requires that rules be interpreted in terms of the ordinary, plain meaning of their constituent terms, a kind of meaning with which ordinary citizens can be expected to be familiar. But it is not at all uncommon for special, legal meanings to be ascribed to terms and phrases in law and for these to diverge considerably from everyday meaning. Consider the case of *Fisher* v. *Bell* which serves to illustrate how different legal meaning can be from ordinary meaning.[53] The English 'Restriction of Offensive Weapons Act' (1959) had made it an offence to 'offer for sale' flick knives. The court was called upon

[53] [1961] 1 QB 394.

to decide whether a merchant who had displayed such weapons in his shop window had violated the Act. On the plain, ordinary meaning of 'offer for sale', the Act had clearly been violated. The court, nevertheless, ruled in favour of the vendor, ascribing to the phrase 'offer for sale' the strictly legal, technical meaning it has under the law of contract. They ruled that there had, in this case, been only an 'invitation to treat'. In other words, there had been an invitation to make an offer to purchase, not an offer to sell. Now, if we can live with such technical, and to the ordinary, reasonable man, probably obscure and mysterious 'legal meanings', then why should we fear exclusion of plain-meaning cases where failure to exclude leads to obvious frustration of the rule's purpose, or to manifest absurdity, moral repugnance, or grave injustice? Our commitment to rules understood only in terms of plain meaning is at present not nearly as strong as might be thought.

A third objection to Rule of Argument 2 is that it seems to exaggerate the degree of instability introduced if the scope of legal rules is sometimes taken to depend on factors other than the plain, literal meaning of the terms used in their expression. It assumes that great uncertainty, instability, and the absence of clear guidance would result if, for instance, it were generally recognized that rules do not apply in plain-meaning cases where application would be clearly and demonstrably self-defeating or unreasonable, or manifestly absurd, repugnant, or unjust. This assumption is highly questionable.

Recall our earlier discussions of the Argument From Function, where we considered a similar objection to the proposal that legal validity should sometimes be a function of whether a rule conforms with Charter provisions, like a right to equality or liberty. We noted that pedigreed rules, whose validity and content are a function of non-moral factors, are nevertheless subject to considerable controversy over their proper interpretation, indeed over the very procedures to be used in trying to understand them and what they imply for legal cases. We also noted that pedigreed rules sometimes conflict with one another and have 'gaps'. It was further pointed out that moral questions, even within pluralistic societies like Canada, Britain, and the United States, sometimes admit of easy resolution. Is it any less difficult to know in advance that the deaths of its occupants coincide when an aircraft explodes in mid-air, but do not when it crashes into a mountainside, than it is to determine that it is morally repugnant to allow Elmer Palmer his ill-gotten gains? I should think not. One can grant that there is a limit to common agreement over moral repugnancies, absurdities, and injustices. But there is also a limit to any reasonable disagreements that might arise. Surely we are on safe ground if we suppose that the private citizen's and law-applying official's ability to detect plain-meaning cases in which applying a legal rule would, by all accounts, be manifestly absurd, repugnant, or unjust is no less than his ability to detect plain-meaning cases themselves. There is, to use Rawls' phrase once again, a considerable overlapping consensus on such matters. It may be perfectly obvious that a cargo airplane is within the ordinary or plain meaning of the description 'transport vehicle', though whether it is within the legal meaning of this phrase, supposing there is one, is another matter altogether. It is no less obvious that it would be absurd to impose a road tax on such a vehicle. It may have been patently obvious that Elmer Palmer, murderer, qualified as donee under the plain meaning of the New York statutes governing wills; it was and continues to be equally obvious that it would be manifestly repugnant and unjust to allow him his inheritance.[54] If this is correct, then it is clear that one encounters no great loss of certainty, stability, and guidance if it is widely understood that, in plain-meaning cases such as these, the rules do not determine the results that plain meaning suggests, that the interpretive background through which such rules are to be understood includes shared beliefs concerning what is manifestly absurd or morally repugnant or unjust. Indeed, given that one loses very little, if anything, and given the distinct possibility that manifestly self-defeating, absurd, or repugnant results will be encountered if one does not follow this interpretive practice, it seems clearly preferable, all things considered, that we follow the court in *Riggs* and do not conceive of our legal rules as extending to all plain-meaning cases.

---

[54] Cf. *Schobelt* v. *Barber* [1967] 1 OR 349, 60 DLR (2d) 519 (Ont. HC), a case similar to *Riggs*. Here the question was whether a man who had murdered his wife could assume sole title to a home they had owned jointly. The court accepted the submission that it was obviously repugnant that the defendant 'should be able to accelerate the law to his own ends'. But it was unwilling to pursue the 'liberal' approach of the court in *Riggs* and interpret the relevant legal rules so as to avoid the manifest repugnance. So much the worse for the Ontario Court.

8. LATER HART

Despite the above, it is likely that early Hart would have been loathe to accept my proposed extension of the Desirability Argument. In his early writings, Hart wishes to tie cases where the law does speak and determine legal rights, duties and powers to the core of settled meaning possessed by terms used in the expression of legal rules. Cases where the law's guidance runs out and judicial discretion is necessary and acceptable are, on the other hand, tied to the open-textured penumbra. Hart seemed to think that this particular line of division was required by the separation of law and morals. To allow standards determining absurdities, moral repugnancies and injustices into our interpretive background would be to 'assert mysteriously that there is some fused identity between the law as it is and as it ought to be ... that all legal questions are fundamentally like those of the penumbra ... that there is no central element of actual law to be seen in the core of settled meaning which rules have'.[55] Yet as we have seen, the partial fusion which Hart feared does not result in the unsettling of settled law, any more than it somehow transforms legal questions into unanswerable moral questions. Moral questions often have determinative answers, and morally undesirable but valid legal rules will, if the approach herein defended is followed, still have to be applied. Few legal rules are ever manifestly self-defeating, absurd, or morally repugnant, in their application, though many are often unreasonable or morally undesirable to lesser degrees. The result is that there will be countless plain meaning cases which a judge might wish to see excluded from the scope of a legal rule in order to give effect to reasonable social and moral aims. Yet given the interpretive approach defended here, most of these will also be cases where the judge will be forced to follow plain meaning. He will be forced to accept the morally undesirable or unreasonable results of the rule's application because these are not so undesirable or unreasonable that applying them would be manifestly absurd or morally repugnant. The separation of law and morals would be preserved, then, despite the modest role assigned to standards of rationality and morality in determining the content of valid legal rules.

So how has the Hartian view sketched and criticized above been

---

[55] 'Positivism and the Separation of Law and Morals', 29.

altered?[56] The most important change is that the notion of open texture seems to have been replaced with the notion of 'relative indeterminacy'. In distinguishing between clear and unclear cases, between the core of settled law (not meaning) and the penumbra of uncertainty, Hart now writes:

> The clear cases are those in which there is general agreement that they fall within the scope of a rule, and it is tempting to ascribe such agreement simply to the fact that there are necessarily such agreements in the shared conventions of language. But this would be an oversimplification because it does not allow for the special conventions of the legal use of words, which may diverge from their common use, or for the way in which the meaning of words may be clearly controlled by reference to the purpose of a statutory enactment which itself may be either explicitly stated or generally agreed.[57]

So Hart now wishes to allow that the explicitly stated or generally agreed purpose of a rule can be used to determine whether a case clearly falls within its scope, and thus within the central element of settled law established by the rule. Hart seems here to be acknowledging the role of an interpretive background containing more than the plain meaning of terms. This background includes not only special conventions and understandings concerning the legal meanings of terms, but assumptions concerning the purposes for which rules are fashioned. Sometimes, as he says, the purpose or aim of a rule is explicitly stated in the rule, e.g. in the preamble of a statute. At other times, the purpose may be inferred, from the language chosen to express the rule, the climate in which it was introduced, and presumably common assumptions about what sorts of things of value it is reasonable to pursue by enacting rules of the kind in question. It is often because we know the kinds of things people want and need that we are able to determine what a rule is for and therefore how it is to be interpreted. I know that protection from bodily harm and death is something people generally want, and in light of this I am able to determine, without being told so explicitly, that rules against the unlicensed, private possession of fully automatic weapons have been introduced largely for this purpose. As we saw earlier, knowledge of such common values and

---

[56] Or how does it misrepresent what has all along been Hart's view? We will continue to assume that there has been a change in Hart's position, though again, it may be that the position sketched below is in fact the view he always held.

[57] 'Problems of the Philosophy of Law', 271.

beliefs forms part of the interpretive background which must often be utilized in interpreting such rules.

On Hart's new account even if the open texture of the terms used in the expression of a rule causes indeterminacy, this can sometimes be overcome by an appeal to other factors. If it is clear that the obvious or stated purpose of a rule would be satisfied only if the rule were taken not to apply in a case involving open texture, then the rule just does not apply in that case. The law provides full guidance, the rule determines a legally binding result, despite open texture. Hart puts the point this way:

It is of crucial importance that cases for decision do not arise in a vacuum but in the course of the operation of a working body of rules, an operation in which a multiplicity of diverse considerations are continuously recognized as good reasons for a decision. These include a wide variety of individual and social interests, social and political aims, and standards of morality and justice; and they may be formulated in general terms as principles, policies, and standards. In some cases only one such consideration may be relevant, and it may determine a decision as unambiguously as a determinate legal rule.[58]

On this more sophisticated view, it would seem that not all clear cases where the law does determine inescapable results are plain-meaning cases.

Hart's appeal to purpose in determining where the core of settled law lies has some other significant consequences for our earlier discussion. We considered above the distinct possibility that having to apply rules in all plain-meaning cases would sometimes lead to manifestly absurd or morally repugnant results, indeed, to results which sometimes seriously conflict with our very aims in having the rule. This possibility, I argued, seemed to create problems for Hart's early view, which wisely recognizes the need for flexibility, and yet ties the scope of legal rules to plain-meaning cases. I argued further that these unfortunate results could largely be avoided, at minimal cost and without violating the main premises of legal positivism, if it were acknowledged that the scope of a legal rule does not necessarily extend to each and every plain-meaning case. In that Hart now wishes to agree with Fuller that the 'meaning of words may clearly be controlled by reference to the purpose of a statutory enactment', it is not unreasonable to suppose that he might accept my suggestion

---

[58] Ibid.

and thereby avoid the problems detected.[59] If applying a rule in a plain-meaning case, say *Riggs*, would lead to manifest absurdity or moral repugnance, then that case just might not, given the appropriate secondary interpretation rules and the interpretive background it requires us to assume, be a case in which the rule applies. Granted it might be considered such a case, but this is not necessary.

If Hart were to accept this latter suggestion, then we could ascribe to him the following three theses:

1. It is not necessarily true that all the cases in which the law determines results are plain-meaning cases (purpose, e.g. might settle any indeterminacy arising from open texture).

2. It is not necessarily true that all plain-meaning cases are ones in which the law determines the result recommended by plain meaning (plain meaning, e.g., may conflict seriously with the agreed purpose of the rule, or plain meaning may suggest a result which is manifestly absurd, repugnant, or unjust).

3. It is not necessarily true that all plain-meaning cases are ones in which the law is determinate (it may, e.g., be indeterminate whether the injustice caused by a literal interpretation of the rule is sufficient to warrant excluding the case from the scope of the rule, and the exercise of strong discretionary judgment is required to settle that question).

Whether in the end these are conclusions which Hart would be willing to accept is an open question. Were he to do so, then his current view would be very different from the early, more familiar view, according to which all plain-meaning cases are necessarily cases fully controlled by law and vice versa. But the more important question is whether conclusions 1—3 are ones *we* should be willing to accept. If my critique of Hart's early view is sound, then it is clear that we should. We have ample reason to accept that these conclusions are not merely consistent with inclusive positivism, but characterize legal practices we would be wise to pursue.

---

[59] The role of purpose in interpreting rules was stressed by Fuller in, e.g., 'Positivism and Fidelity to Law—A Reply to Professor Hart'. At one point Fuller asks: '[I]s it really ever possible to interpret a word in a statute without knowing the aim of the statute?' Fuller's suggestion is too strong. We should grant that the terms of a rule can, and perhaps must, sometimes be interpreted in light of its purpose without agreeing that this is always true. In the absence of an expressly stated or agreed aim of a statute it must be possible to interpret its relevant classifying terms independently of knowing its purpose. This must be possible at least to the extent that one can identify standard or paradigm instances of the relevant terms. Otherwise how could one even begin to formulate conjectures as to the statute's purpose? This objection to Fuller's thesis was first made by R. Wasserstrom in *The Judicial Decision*, 180.

REFERENCES

Aquinas, St Thomas, *Summa Theologica* (many editions).

Aristotle, *Nichomachean Ethics* (many editions).

Attwell, E., (ed.), *Perspectives in Jurisprudence* (Glasgow: University of Glasgow Press, 1977).

Austin, J., *The Province of Jurisprudence Determined*, H. L. A. Hart (ed.) (London: Weidenfeld & Nicholson, 1954).

—— 'A Positivist Conception of Law', in J. Feinberg and H. Gross (eds.), *Philosophy of Law* (4th edn.). This is taken from *The Province of Jurisprudence Determined*, Lectures 1 and 4. All page references to Austin's work are to this reprint.

Baum-Levenbrook, B., 'Discretion and Dispositive Concepts', 9 *Canadian Journal of Philosophy* (1979), 613.

✗ Bayles, M., 'What is Jurisprudence About? Theories, Definitions, Concepts, or Conceptions of Law?', 18 *Philosophical Topics*, no. 1 (1990), 23.

—— 'Hart vs. Dworkin', 10 *Law and Philosophy*, no. 4 (1991), 349.

Bentham, J., 'A Fragment On Government', in 1 *The Collected Works of Jeremy Bentham* (London, Bowring edn., 1843).

—— 'Anarchical Fallacies', in 2 *The Collected Works of Jeremy Bentham* (London, Bowring edn., 1843).

Berkeley, G., *A Treatise Concerning the Principles of Human Knowledge* (many editions).

Black, W. W., 'Canadian Charter of Rights and Freedoms', in J. Magnet (ed.), *Constitutional Law of Canada*.

Bork, R., 'Neutral Principles and Some First Amendment Problems', 47 *Indiana Law Journal* (1971), 1.

Brandt, R. B., *Hopi Ethics: A Theoretical Analysis* (Chicago: University of Chicago Press, 1954).

—— *Ethical Theory* (Englewood Cliffs, NJ: Prentice-Hall, 1959).

—— *A Theory of the Good and the Right* (Oxford: Oxford University Press, 1979).

Brink, D., 'Legal Positivism and Natural Law Reconsidered', 68 *The Monist*, no. 3 (1985), 364.

—— 'Legal Theory, Legal Interpretation, and Judicial Review, 17 *Philosophy and Public Affairs*, no. 2 (1988), 105.

Brode, P., *The Charter of Wrongs: Canada's Retreat From Democracy* (Toronto: The Mackenzie Institute, 1990).

Burton, S., 'Ronald Dworkin and Legal Positivism', 73 *Iowa Law Review* (1987–8), 109.

Calkins, M. (ed.), *Berkeley Selections* (New York: C. Scribner's Sons, 1957).

Cardozo, B., *The Nature of the Judicial Process* (New Haven, Conn.: Yale University Press, 1921).

Clark, S. and Simpson, E. (eds.), *Anti-Theory in Ethics and Moral Conservatism* (Albany: State University of New York Press, 1989).

Coleman, J., 'Negative and Positive Positivism', 11 *Journal of Legal Studies* (1982), 139.

—— and Paul, E. (eds.), *Philosophy of Law* (Oxford: Blackwell's, 1987).

Cross, Sir R., *Precedent in English Law* (3rd edn.) (Oxford: Oxford University Press, 1977).

Danto, A., 'Human Nature and Natural Law', in S. Hook (ed.), *Law and Philosophy*.

Denning, L. J., *The Discipline of Law* (London: Butterworth's, 1979).

d'Entreves, A. P., *Natural Law* (London: Hutchinson, 1951).

Dworkin, R. M., 'Judicial Discretion', 60 *Journal of Philosophy* (1963), 624.

—— 'No Right Answer?' in P. Hacker and J. Raz (eds.), *Law, Morality and Society: Essays in Honour of H. L. A. Hart*, 58.

—— *Taking Rights Seriously* (2nd edn.) (Cambridge: Harvard University Press, 1978).

—— *Law's Empire* (Cambridge: Harvard University Press, 1986).

—— 'From Bork to Kennedy', 34 *New York Review of Books*, no. 20 (1987), 36.

Dyzenhaus, D., *Hard Cases in Wicked Legal Systems: South African Law in the Perspective of Legal Philosophy* (Oxford: Clarendon Press, 1991).

Edwards, P. (ed.), *The Encyclopedia of Philosophy* (New York: Macmillan, 1967).

Feinberg, J. and Gross, H. (eds.), *Philosophy of Law* (3rd edn.) (Belmont, Calif.: Wadsworth, 1986).

—— (eds.), *Philosophy of Law* (4th edn.) (Belmont Calif.: Wadsworth, 1991).

Feynman, R. P., *'What Do You Care What Other People Think?': Further Adventures of a Curious Character* (New York: W. W. Norton, 1988).

Finnis, J., *Natural Law and Natural Rights* (Oxford: Clarendon Press, 1980).

Flew, A. (ed.), *Logic and Language: First Series* (Oxford: Blackwell's, 1968).

Frankena, W. W., 'On Defining and Defending Natural Law', in S. Hook, (ed.), *Law and Philosophy*.

Frege, G., 'The Thought: A Logical Inquiry', in P. F. Strawson (ed.), *Philosophical Logic*.

Fuller, L. L., 'Positivism and Fidelity to Law—A Reply to Professor Hart', in J. Feinberg and H. Gross (eds.), *Philosophy of Law* (4th edn.). All page references are to this reprint. The original appeared in 71 *Harvard Law Review* (1958), 630.

Gavison, R. (ed.), *Issues in Contemporary Legal Philosophy: The Influence of H. L. A. Hart* (Oxford: Clarendon Press, 1987).

Gilligan, C., *In A Different Voice: Psychological Theory and Women's Development* (Cambridge, Mass.: Harvard University Press, 1982).

Goldsworthy, J. D., 'The Self-Destruction of Legal Positivism', 10 *Oxford Journal Of Legal Studies*, no. 4 (1990), 449.

Gray, J. C., *The Nature and Sources of the Law* (New York: Macmillan, 1921).

—— 'A Realist Conception of Law', in J. Feinberg and H. Gross (eds.), *Philosophy of Law* (3rd edn.).

✶ Green, L., 'The Political Content of Legal Theory', 17 *Philosophy of the Social Sciences* (1987), 15.

Hacker, P. and Raz, J. (eds.), *Law, Morality and Society: Essays in Honour of H. L. A. Hart* (Oxford: Clarendon Press, 1977).

Hare, R. M., *Freedom and Reason* (Oxford: Oxford University Press, 1963).

—— *Moral Thinking: Its Levels, Method and Point* (Oxford: Clarendon Press, 1981).

Hart, H. L. A., 'Positivism and the Separation of Law and Morals', in J. Feinberg and H. Gross (eds.), *Philosophy of Law* (4th edn.). All page references to this article are to this reprint. The article originally appeared in 71 *Harvard Law Review* (1958), 593.

—— *The Concept of Law* (Oxford: Clarendon Press, 1961).

—— 'Legal Positivism' in P. Edwards (ed.), 4 *The Encyclopedia of Philosophy*, 418.

✳ —— *Essays on Bentham: Jurisprudence and Political Theory* (Oxford: Clarendon Press, 1982).

—— 'Commands and Authoritative Reasons', in H. L. A. Hart, *Essays on Bentham: Jurisprudence and Political Theory*, 243.

—— *Essays in Jurisprudence and Philosophy* (Oxford: Clarendon Press, 1983).

—— 'American Jurisprudence Through English Eyes: The Nightmare and the Noble Dream', in H. L. A. Hart, *Essays in Jurisprudence and Philosophy*, 123.

—— 'Lon L. Fuller: The Morality of Law', in H. L. A. Hart, *Essays in Jurisprudence and Philosophy*, 343.

—— 'Comment' in R. Gavison (ed.), *Issues in Contemporary Philosophy: The Influence of H. L. A. Hart*.

Hogg, P., *Constitutional Law of Canada* (2nd edn) (Toronto: Carswell, 1985).

Holmes, O. W., *Collected Legal Papers* (London: Constable & Co. Ltd., 1920).

Hook, S. (ed.), *Law and Philosophy* (New York: New York University Press, 1964).

Hutchinson, A and Monohan, P. (eds.), *The Rule of Law: Ideal or Ideology* (Toronto: Carswell, 1987).

Hume, D., *A Treatise of Human Nature*, L. A. Selby-Bigge (ed.) (Oxford: Clarendon Press, 1973).

Kelsen, H., *The Pure Theory of Law* (Berkeley Calif.: University of California Press, 1967).

Kohlberg, L., *Essays on Moral Development* (San Francisco: Harper & Row, 1984).

Llewellyn, K., *The Common Law Tradition: Deciding Appeals* (Boston: Little, Brown & Co., 1960).

Lyons, D., *Forms and Limits of Utilitarianism* (Oxford: Clarendon Press, 1965).

—— 'Principles, Positivism and Legal Theory', 87 *Yale Law Journal*, (1977), 415.

—— 'Moral Aspects of Legal Theory', 7 *Midwest Studies in Philosophy*, (1982), 245.

—— 'Derivability, Defensibility and the Justification of Judicial Decisions', 68 *The Monist*, no. 3 (1985), 325.

—— 'Comment', in Gavison R. (ed.), *Issues in Contemporary Legal Philosophy: The Influence of H. L. A. Hart*.

—— 'Constitutional Interpretation and Original Meaning', in J. Coleman and E. Paul (eds.), *Philosophy of Law*.

MacCallum, G., 'Legislative Intent', 75 *Yale Law Journal* (1966), 754.

MacCormick, D. N., *Legal Reasoning and Legal Theory* (Oxford: Clarendon Press, 1978).

—— *H. L. A. Hart* (Stanford, Calif.: Stanford University Press, 1981).

—— 'A Moralistic Case For A-Moralistic Law?', 20 *Valparaiso Law Review*, no. 1 (1985), 1.

—— 'Comment', in Gavison, R. (ed.), *Issues In Contemporary Legal Philosophy: The Influence of H. L. A. Hart*.

—— 'Reconstruction After Deconstruction: A Response to CLS', 10 *Oxford Journal of Legal Studies*, no. 4 (1990), 539.

Mackie, J. L., 'The Third Theory of Law', 7 *Philosophy and Public Affairs*, no. 1 (1977), 3.

Macmillan, Lord M. J., 'Law and Ethics', in *Law and Other Things* (Cambridge: Cambridge University Press, 1948).

Magnet, J. E. (ed.), *Constitutional Law of Canada* (Toronto: Carswell, 1987).

Mill, J. S., *On Liberty* (London: Shields edn., 1859).

Moles, R., *Definition and Rule in Legal Theory: A Reassessment of H. L. A. Hart and the Positivist Tradition* (Oxford: Blackwell's, 1987).

See p. 126 ⇒ in text for misreading of Part

Moore, G. E., *Principia Ethica* (Cambridge: Cambridge University Press, 1903).

Morris, J., 'Palm Tree Justice in the Court of Appeal', 82 *Law Quarterly Review* (1966), 196.

Munzer, S., 'Validity and Legal Conflicts', 82 *Yale Law Journal* (1973), 1140.

Nowell-Smith, P. H., 'Dworkin v. Hart Appealed: A Meta-Ethical Inquiry', 13 *Metaphilosophy*, no. 1 (1982), 1.

Perry, S., 'Judicial Obligation, Precedent and the Common Law', 7 *Oxford Journal of Legal Studies*, (1987), 221.   *critique of Raz's exclusionary reasons for action*.

Postema, G., 'Coordination and Convention at the Foundations of Law', XI *Journal of Legal Studies* (1982), 165.

—— 'The Normativity of Law', in R. Gavison (ed.), *Issues in Contemporary Legal Philosophy: The Influence of H. L. A. Hart*.

Putnam, H., *Mind, Language and Reality* (Cambridge: Cambridge University Press, 1975).

Radbruch, G., *Rechtsphilosophie*, E. Wolf and H. Schneider (eds.) (Stuttgart: K. F. Koehler Verlag, 1973).

Radcliffe, L., *The Law and Its Compass* (Evanston, Ill.: Northwestern University Press, 1960).

Rawls, J., 'Two Concepts of Rules', 64 *Philosophical Review*, (1955), 3.

—— 'Justice as Fairness: Political Not Metaphysical', 14 *Philosophy and Public Affairs* (1985), 223.

—— 'The Idea of an Overlapping Consensus', 7 *Oxford Journal of Legal Studies*, (1987), 1.

—— 'The Domain of the Political and Overlapping Consensus', 64 *New York University Law Review*, no. 2 (1989), 233.

Raz, J., 'Legal Principles and the Limits of Law', 81 *Yale Law Journal*, no. 5 (1972), 823.

—— *The Authority of Law* (Oxford: Clarendon Press, 1979).

—— *The Concept of a Legal System* (2nd edn.) (Oxford: Clarendon Press, 1980).

—— 'The Problem About the Nature of Law', 21 *University of Western Ontario Law Review* (1983), 203.

—— 'Authority and Justification', 14 *Philosophy and Public Affairs*, no. 1 (1985), 3.

—— 'Authority, Law and Morality', 68 *The Monist*, no. 3 (1985), 295.

—— *The Morality of Freedom* (Oxford: Clarendon Press, 1986).

Rehnquist, W., 'The Notion of a Living Constitution', 54 *Texas Law Review* (1976), 693.

Rest, J., *Moral Development: Advances in Research and Theory* (New York: Praeger 1986).

Richards, D., 'Constitutional Interpretation, History and the Death Penalty: A Book Review', 71 *California Law Review*, (1983), 1372.

Robson, P. and Watchman, P. (eds.), *Justice, Lord Denning and the Constitution* (Westmead: Gower Press, 1981).

Ross, Sir D., *The Right and the Good* (Oxford: Oxford University Press, 1930).

Sartorius, R., 'Social Policy and Judicial Legislation', 8 *American Philosophical Quarterly* (1971), 151.

Shiner, R., 'The Metaphysics of Taking Rights Seriously', 12 *Philosophia*, nos. 3–4, (1983), 223.

Simpson, E., *Good Lives and Moral Education* (New York: Peter Lang, 1989).

Smith, A., *The Theory of the Moral Sentiments* (Oxford: Clarendon Press, 1976).

Soper, E. P., 'Legal Theory and the Obligation of a Judge: The Hart/Dworkin Dispute', 75 *Michigan Law Review* (1977), 477.

—— *A Theory of Law* (Cambridge, Mass.: Harvard University Press, 1984).

—— 'Dworkin's Domain', 100 *Harvard Law Review* (1987), 1166.

—— 'Legal Theory and the Claim of Authority', 18 *Philosophy and Public Affairs*, no. 3 (1989), 214.

Strawson, P. F. (ed.), *Philosophical Logic* (Oxford: Oxford University Press, 1967).

Summers, R., *Lon L. Fuller* (Stanford, Calif.: Stanford University Press, 1984).

Tapper, C., 'A Note on Principles', 34 *Modern Law Review* (1971), 628.

Ten, C. L., 'The Soundest Theory of Law', 88 *Mind* (1979), 352.

Tur, R., 'Positivism, Principles and Rules', in E. Attwell (ed.), *Perspectives in Jurisprudence*.

Ullmann, W., *The Medieval Idea of Law* (London: Methuen, 1946).

Waismann, F., 'Verifiability' in A. Flew (ed.), *Logic and Language: First Series*.

Waluchow, W. J., 'Review of *Justice, Lord Denning and the Constitution*', 2 *Canadian Philosophical Reviews* (1982), 294.

—— 'Strong Discretion', 33 *The Philosophical Quarterly*, no. 133 (1983), 321.

—— 'Hart, Legal Rules and Palm Tree Justice', 4 *Law and Philosophy* (1985), 41.

—— 'Herculean Positivism', 5 *Oxford Journal of Legal Studies*, no. 2 (1985), 187.

—— 'Review of *Definition and Rule in Legal Theory: A Reassessment of H. L. A. Hart and the Positivist Tradition*', 8 *Canadian Philosophical Reviews* (1988), 181.

——The Weak Social Thesis', 9 *Oxford Journal of Legal Studies*, no. 1 (1989), 23.

——'Charter Challenges: A Test Case For Theories of Law', 29 *Osgoode Hall Law Journal*, no. 1 (1990), 183.

Wasserstrom, R., *The Judicial Decision* (Stanford: Stanford University Press, 1961).

Wittgenstein, L., *Philosophical Investigations*, trans. G. E. M. Anscombe (New York: Macmillan, 1953).

Wollheim, R., 'Natural Law', in P. Edwards (ed.), 5 *The Encyclopedia of Philosophy*, 450.

TABLE OF CASES

A.-G. Ca (employment of Japanese) .... 172n.

A.-G. Ontario v. Policy-holders of Wentworth Insurance Co ...... 172n.

A.-G. Quebec v. Blaikie .... 41n.

Abley v. Dale 246, 254

Andrews v. Law Society of B.C.   122, 139, 149–64, 167, 169, 208, 228, 262

Becke v. Smith (1836) 35, 262

Duport Steels Ltd. v. Sirs .... 233n.

Edwards v. A.-G. Canada .... 41n.

Engineering ITB v. Samuel Talbot Ltd. 256

Fisher v. Bell 266–7

Fitzleet Estates Ltd. v. Cherry 261

Henningsen v. Bloomfield Motors 167, 169

Heydon's Case 233

Hunter v. Southam Inc. .... 67n.

Knuller Publishing and Promotions Ltd. v. Director of Public Pros-
ecutions 261

Law Society of B.C. v. Andrews .... 122n., 149n.

Law Society of Upper Canada v. Shapinker .... 67n.

Lochner v. New York 68

London North-Eastern Ry. v. Berriman .... 264n.

MacPherson v. Buick .... 200n.

Magor and St Mellons RDC v. Newport Corporation 254

Marbury v. Madison 66

Miliangos v. George Frank (Textiles) Ltd. 261

Nash v. Tamplin and Sons Brewery Ltd. 37

Norton v. Shelby County 160

Olympic Oil and Cake Co. Ltd. v. Produce Brokers Ltd. 37, 38, 57

R. v. Big M Drug Mart 67n., 144–5, 256

R. v. Oakes 153, 155

Re Bozanich .... 172n.

Re Rowland.. 264–6

Regina v. Morgentaler, Smoling and Scott 116, 155–6, 161–4, 167,
169, 208, 262

Reference re s92(4) of the Vehicles Act 1957 (Saskatchewan) ...... 172n.

Riggs v. Palmer 167, 169, 247, 253, 256, 262, 263, 268, 272

Royal Bank of Canada v. Larue 172

Schenck v. United States .... 172n.

Schobelt *v.* Barber .... 268n.

Shaw *v.* Director of Public Prosecutions 261

Smart *v.* Allen and Another 122, 237–8

Sussex Peerage Case 254

Tennant *v.* Union Bank of Canada .... 172n.

Terminiello *v.* Chicago .... 172n.

Thompson Newspapers Ltd. *v.* Canada (Director of Investigation and
Research Restrictive Trade Practices Commission) 145

INDEX

adjudication, theory of:
  connections with theory of law
    65–73
  distinguished from theory of
    compliance 40–2
  distinguished from theory of law 32,
    34, 42–6, 56–8, 65–6, 73, 77
  Hart's theory 65–6
  sometimes descriptive/explanatory
    40–1
  sometimes normative 41
anarchist thinking 86–7, 97–8
Aquinas:
  on deriving human law from natural
    law 108–12
  on determination of common notions
    108–12, 224
  and the indexing of law 52
  and the institutional nature of human
    law 107–13
  on the moral force of law 61, 92
  and natural law theory 1, 7, 32, 80,
    166
arbitration, analogy with law 126–7,
    129, 132–3
arguments of principle and policy
    248–9
Aristotle 111, 224
Augustine:
  and the moral force of law 61
  and natural law theory 1, 7, 80, 85–6,
    166
Austin J.:
  and inclusive legal positivism 3, 84,
    177, 180, 182
  and institutional nature of law 106
  on laws not properly so-called
    101–2
  on legal positivism 1, 9, 32, 168 n.
  on positive morality 108
  and semantic theories of law 104 n.
  on the separation of law and morals
    41, 60, 61 n., 64
authority 136
  the argument from 123–40
  peremptory nature of 124–35, 173

background morality:
  in Dworkin 44–7
  see also political morality
background rights 47
Baier, A. 146
basic intuition, Raz's 77
Baum-Levenbrook, B. 201 n.
Bayles, M. 105
Bentham, J.:
  advocates inclusive legal positivism
    3, 84, 180, 182
  the causal/moral argument 86–98,
    103
  as legal positivist 9, 60, 168
  on limits of sovereignty 177
  on natural law 86
  on obligation to obey law 13, 64–5
Berkeley, G. 148
bias, the argument from 105–6, 140
Bork, R. 116–17
Brandt, R. 28 n., 152 n.
Brink, D. 40 n., 67 n., 69 n.
  on legislative intention 255 n.
  on plain meaning cases 238 n.
Brode, P. 69 n.
Bronaugh, R. vi, 57 n.
Buckley, L. J. 37
Burton, S. 187 n.

Canadian Charter of Rights and
    Freedoms 6, 66–7, 71, 115, 135,
    139–40, 142–65, 167, 170, 173, 176,
    185–6, 204, 208, 219, 224, 226–9, 256
Cardozo, B. 66, 214, 216
causal/moral arguments 86–98, 103,
    126
Charter societies 95–8, 102, 114–17, 122,
    134–5, 139–65, 223, 227–9, 262, 267
Clarke, S. 146 n.
cluster concepts 240 n.
coercion, legal theories as moral
    justifications of 13–16, 23–4, 27,
    29–30, 32, 59, 61–2, 132
Coleman, J. 82 n.
  on Dworkin's argument from function
    189 n.

Coleman, J. (*cont.*):
  on Dworkin's pedigree argument
    181 n.
  on inclusive legal positivism 81–2,
    230 n.
command theory of law 49
compliance, theory of 58–64
  not a theory of law 41–2
  connections with theory of law 64–5
conceptions of law, *see* Dworkin,
    interpretive conceptions of law
concepts vs. conceptions 68–9
constitutional adjudication, theories of
    66–72
constructive interpretation, *see*
    Dworkin, interpretive conceptions
    of law
Copernicus, N. 89
core and penumbra 8, 65–6, 122, 223,
    237–8, 242, 253, 269–72
  see also discretion; open texture;
    purpose in interpretation
Cross, Sir R. 36, 40–1, 105, 259 n.
  on binding rules of precedent 37

Danto, A.:
  on legal positivism 230 n.
Dehaven S. vi.
Denning, LJ 70, 216 n.
  on purposive interpretation 233, 256,
    264 n., 265–6
dependent reasons, *see* exclusionary
    reasons
descriptive/explanatory theories of law
    19, 30, 40–1, 91, 125
  not theories of adjudication 32, 42
  see also: law, theory of
determination of common notions
    108–12, 224
Dickson, Brian, CJ 67
  on purposive interpretation 144–6,
    256
Dilhorne, Viscount:
  on departure from precedent 261
discretion, judicial 65–6, 110 n., 148 n.,
    159, 192–229, 247–50
  desirability of 193–4, 250–4, 263,
    269–72
  having vs. exercising 207–19, 236 n.
  judicial testimony regarding 213–16
  necessity of 193–4, 207, 236–50
  strong vs. weak 35, 192–207
  and uncertainty 208–9, 248; *see also*

Dworkin; the discretion argument;
    open texture; plain-meaning cases
discretion argument, the 191–2
  a critique of 219–26
  and objectivity of morals 219–21
  and the pedigree argument 219
discrimination, in *Andrews* 149–54
Dubin, Charles, CJO 71 n.
Dworkin, R. vi, 4, 65
  arguments against inclusive
    positivism: the discretion argument
    191–2, a critique 219–26, and
    function, the argument from 221–3,
    and Hart 223–5, and Herculean
    reasoning 225–6, and objectivity of
    morality 219–21, and the pedigree
    argument 219; the pedigree
    argument 174–5, a critique
    175–82, not properly ascribed to all
    positivists 176–7, 180–2,
    applicable to Raz 182; function,
    the argument from 182–4, a
    critique 184–90; the validity
    argument 168–74
  on arguments of principle and policy
    248–9
  on concepts and conceptions 68–9
  on embedded mistakes 36, 54, 228
  on the force of law 12–13, 31, 33, 37;
    and theories of compliance 41–2,
    58–64
  on the grounds of law 9–13, 31, 33, 37
  Hart's internal point of view 27–30
  on institutional history 43
  internal scepticism 228
  on interpretation in arts and sciences
    24–6; parallel with legal
    interpretation 25–30
  on interpretation of laws 247–50, 255
  interpretive conceptions of law 5,
    13–15, 19–30, 91, 94; from
    participant's point of view 23–4,
    27–9; and immoral law 59–64,
    accommodated by flexible
    conception 60–4; inadequately
    distinguished from theories of
    adjudication 32, 34, 56–8, 77;
    inadequately distinguished from
    theories of compliance 58–64;
    morally justify coercion 13–15,
    23–4, 27, 29–30, 32, 59, 61–2, 132;
    normative in nature 15–19, 20–22,
    125, 128; not descriptive/

explanatory theories 40–1, 125; sometimes sceptical 23, 228; and value relevance 21–3
on judicial discretion 110n., 148n., 192–226, 247–50; compared with Herculean theorizing 218–19; fails to distinguish having and exercising 207–19; an inadequate phenomenological account 213–15; and the right answer thesis 206–7, 211; strong vs. weak 35, 192–5, 204–7; two interpretations of strong discretion 195–204; and uncertainty 208–9, 248
law as integrity 10–11; vs. inclusive positivism 126–7, 141, 166–8, 179–81, 231; vs. natural law theory 3, 7, 166, 178–9; vs. positivism 2, 8–11, 83, 247n.; and the functions of law 118–20
'law', two senses of 60–4
on legal principles 128, 169–74, 231; distinguished from valid rules 168–74
on legal rights 46–58; an alternative theory 73–8; a critique of Dworkin's theory 48–58; as distinct from background rights 47; as distinct from legislative rights 47–8; and indexing of law 51–4; and judges' powers to change law 49–58; as moral rights to legal decisions 46–7, 51, 73, 78–9, held against judges 48–9; as rights against Hercules 54–6, 78; species of institutional rights 47–8
political morality: implicit in law 43–4, 80, 235; distinct from background morality 44–6
on Raz on authority 136
on semantic theories of law 104–5n.
Dyzenhaus, D. 81n.

Einstein, A. 130–1
embedded mistakes 36, 54, 228
d'Entreves, A.:
on natural law theory 178n.
on positivism 229n.
evaluative vs. moral 19–22, 115–17, 120–1, 125–6
exclusionary reasons 124–40, 173n., 260
Perry's alternative 136–7

exclusive account of Charter challenges 156–63
the modified exclusive account 163–4
exclusive positivism:
arguments for, see: Raz
vs. inclusive positivism 3, 6, 79, 82–4, 87, 103–141, 155, 182, 226–9
explanatory power, argument from 113–17, 140
external observer perspective 5–6, 15, 23–4, 27–9
external point of view, see external observer perspective

family resemblance 240
federal paramountcy doctrine 171–3, 235–6
Feynman, R. 147
Finnis, J. 1
on the separation thesis 33
flexibility in law 121–2, 184, 245–6, 257–8
forces of law:
in Dworkin 12–13, 31, 33, 37
institutional 31–3, 42–3, 49–58, 66, 73–9; and precedent 34–40, 49–51
moral 32, 38–42, 58–64, 80, 92
foreign law and charter rights 157–9
Frankena, W.:
on natural law theory 178n.
Fuller, L. 2
on moral force of law 61, 80
on morality in jurisprudence 22
on positivism 10, 95–8, 177
on positivist methodology 16
on purposive interpretation 59n.
function, argument from 118–23, 140, 182–4, 221–3
a critique 184–90
and Hart 223–5
and Hercules 225–6

Galileo, G. 89
Gardiner, LJ
and the practice statement 259–60
German informer cases 98–101
Gilligan, C. 17n.
Goldsworthy, J. 2n.
Gray, C. vi, 204n.
Gray, J. C. 106
and rule scepticism 72–3
Green, L. vi, 100, 104n.
on value relevance 21–3
grounds of law 9–13, 31, 33, 37

Hampshire, S. 146
Hare, R. M. vi, 92, 93, 260n.
    on being overridden 173
Hart, H. L. A. vi, 2, 4, 9, 61n., 74, 77, 79,
    192, 229n., 230, 233–5
    advocates inclusive positivism 3,
        83–4, 140, 176–82
    arguments for legal positivism
        84–103; the causal/moral argument
        86–98, 103; intellectual clarity, the
        argument from 98–103
    core and penumbra 8, 223, 253,
        269–72
    descriptive/explanatory theory of law
        14, 20–1; distinct from, but
        connected to theory of adjudication
        32, 65–6, 73; distinct from moral
        theory of compliance 41–2
    on discretion: desirability of 193–4,
        250–4, 263, 269–72; on having vs.
        exercising 236n; necessity of
        193–4, 207, 236–50; in penumbral
        cases 223
    does not advocate semantic theory of
        law 104–5n.
    and Dworkin's argument from
        function 183–4
    and Dworkin's pedigree argument
        175
    on Dworkin's right answer thesis
        200n., 206n., 208
    on Dworkin's theory of legal rights
        59–60
    and Dworkin's validity argument
        168–9
    external observer perspective 5–6,
        23
    on flexibility in law, need for 121–2,
        184, 245–6, 257–8
    internal observer perspective 28
    on Kelsen's command theory 49
    on law and morals 22
    on natural law theory 84–6
    open texture 193–4, 237–50, 253,
        270–2
    on peremptory reasons 125n., 130
    on positivism and objectivity of
        morality 220
    on primary and secondary rules 75–6,
        234–5
    on purpose of rules in interpretation
        270–2
    rules of recognition 4, 43, 74–5, 234;

    a form of social rule 235; moral
        criteria possible in 175–82
Hartney, M. vi
Hercules 46, 54–6, 78, 225–6
    see also Dworkin
Hoadley, Bishop 72–3
Hobbes, T. 97, 100, 126, 220, 230
Hoffmaster, B. vi, 204n.
Hogg, P. 67n.
    on normative judgment and the
        Canadian Charter 154, 160
    on federal paramountcy doctrine
        172n.
Holmes, O. 208n., 214, 216
Hume, D. 148
    on causal/moral arguments 89, 94

inclusive positivism 1–4, 81–2
    advocated by Austin and Bentham 3,
        84, 177, 180, 182
    advocated by Hart 3, 83–4, 140,
        176–82
    arguments against: the discretion
        argument 191–226; function, the
        argument from 182–90; the
        pedigree argument 174–82; the
        validity argument 168–74
    vs. exclusive positivism 3, 6, 79, 82–4,
        87, 103–41, 155, 182, 226–9, 230n.
indeterminacy of laws, see open texture
indexing of law 52–4
institutional history:
    in Dworkin 43
institutional nature of law:
    the argument from 106–8, 112–13,
        140
institutional rights 47–8, 50
integrity theory 10–11, 42–58
    see also Dworkin, law as integrity
intention, legislative 255–6
internal point of view 27–30
    see also external observer perspective
internal scepticism 23, 228
interpretation 24–30, 247–50, 255,
        270–2
    rules of 35n., 76, 165n., 246–7, 254,
        261–2
    see also Dworkin, interpretive
        conceptions of law; purpose in
        interpretation

judicial discretion. See: discretion,
    judicial

Jervis, CJ:
  on plain meaning cases 246, 254
Johnson B. 71 n.

Kant, I. 100
Kelsen, H. 49, 77, 169
  as legal positivist 9, 168
  and pure science of law 18, 30, 105
King-Farlow, J. vi
Kohlberg, L. 16–17

La Forest, J. 145
law:
  co-ordinative function of 264 n.
  institutional nature of 47, 106–8,
    112–13, 140
  and morals 22, 33, 41, 59–64, 81
  obligation to obey 13–14, 33, 64–5
  settled vs. unsettled 113–15, 187–8
  as source based 175–6, 231 n.
  theory of: connections with theory of
    adjudication 65–73; connections
    with theory of compliance 64–5;
    connections with theory of
    constitutional adjudication 66–72;
    descriptive/explanatory 14, 19,
    20–1, 91; influences of value on
    15–30; need for flexibility in 61–4;
    not pure science 18, 30, 105; not a
    theory of adjudication 32, 34, 42 n.,
    56, 65–6, 73; not a theory of
    compliance 41–2; perplexing state
    of 1, 4–6; Raz's positivistic theory
    74–9; see also Raz; exclusive
    positivism
laws not properly so called 101–2
lawyer's perspective 32
legal officials 135–6
legal positivism, see positivism
legal rights:
  Dworkin's theory of, see Dworkin,
    legal rights
  Hart on Dworkin's theory 59–60
  primary and secondary 57–8
legal theory, see law, theory of
legal validity, nature of 170–82
Leibniz, W. 25
  on simplicity and the best possible
    world 19–20
the linguistic argument 104
Llewellyn, K. 233 n.
Lloyd, K. vi

Lyons, D. 67 n., 69 n., 82 n., 125 n.
  on the causal/moral argument 126
  on Dworkin's pedigree argument
    181 n.
  on Dworkin's right answer thesis
    200 n.
  on inclusive positivism 81

MacCallum, G.:
  on legislative intentions 255–6
MacCormick, D. N. vi, 52 n., 73 n., 232,
    234 n.
  on causal/moral arguments for
    positivism 86–98, 103
  on Hart's argument from intellectual
    clarity 101
  on legal positivism 1, 232
  on plain meaning cases 257 n.
Mackie, J. vi, 82 n.
  on Dworkin and settled law 187–8
  on Dworkin's right answer thesis
    200 n., 208
  on inclusive positivism 81–2
  on moral judgments 225
MacLachlin, J. A. 149 n.
Macmillan, M. J. 214, 216
meta-theoretical evaluative criteria
    20–30, 120–1
Mill, J. S. 3
modified exclusive account of charter
    challenges 163–4
Moles, R. 65 n.
Moore, G. E. 93
moral arguments in charter adjudication
    143–55, 176
moral-evaluative criteria, see
    meta-theoretical evaluative criteria
moral rights to legal decisions 46–9, 51,
    73, 78–9
  and judges' powers to change law
    49–58
  as rights against Hercules 54–6, 78
moral vs. evaluative, see evaluative vs.
    moral
morality:
  and judicial discretion, 226–9; see
    also discretion
  and jurisprudence 16, 22; see also
    value relevance; law, theory of;
    adjudication, theory of;
    compliance, theory of
  and law, see law

morality (*cont.*):
  objectivity of 219–21, 225
  positive 108
Morris, J.:
  on Denning 223n.
Munzer, S. 170n.
Murray, J. vi

Najm, S. 25n.
natural laws:
  basis for deriving human law 108–12,
    224
  and determination of common notions
    108–12, 224
natural law theory 1–2, 7, 32, 33n., 80,
    84–6, 166, 178–81, 229–30
  see also Aquinas; Augustine; Finnis;
    Fuller
Nixon, R. 136
Nowell-Smith, P. 4n.

open texture 65, 121, 192–4, 200,
    237–50, 253, 269–72
overlapping consensus 245, 268
overridden, distinguished from
    outweighed 173

Panagiotou, S. vi
paramountcy doctrine, *see* federal
    paramountcy doctrine
Parke, B.:
  on the golden rule of interpretation
    35n., 165n., 261–2
participant's point of view 15, 23–4,
    27–9
  see also external observer perspective
Pascal, B. 211n.
pedigree argument, the:
  a critique of 175–82
  applicable to Raz 182
  not properly ascribed to all positivists
    176–7, 180–2
  outlined 174–5, 219
penumbra of uncertainty, *see* core and
    penumbra
peremptory reasons 124–35, 175
Perry, S. 53
  and exclusive positivism 114
  on Raz and exclusionary reasons
    136–7

Philmore, LJ 37
plain meaning cases 238, 246–54,
    257–72
  see also: core and penumbra;
    discretion; open texture
political morality 43–6, 80, 235
positivism 1–2, 8–11, 16, 32, 60, 74–9,
    83, 95–8, 168, 177–82, 229–31,
    232n., 247n.
  arguments for: the argument from
    intellectual clarity 98–103; the
    authority argument 123–40; bias,
    the argument from 105–6, 140; the
    causal/moral argument 86–98,
    103; explanatory power, the
    argument from 113–17, 140;
    function, the argument from
    117–23, 140, 182, 184, 221–6; the
    institutional connection argument
    106–8, 112–13, 140; the linguistic
    argument 104; the pedigree
    argument 174–82
  and the separation of law and morals
    81
Postema, G. 52n., 125n.
  on co-ordinative functions of law
    264n.
  on participant and observer theories
    15
powers to change law 34–40
practice statement 259–61
precedent 36–7, 40–1, 105, 136–7, 236–7,
    259n., 261
  and institutional force 34–40
primary and secondary rules 75–6,
    234–5
principles 128, 169–74, 231
  distinguished from valid rules 168–74
pure science of law, *see* Kelsen
purpose in interpretation 59n., 144–6,
    233, 256, 264n., 265–6, 270–2
Putnam, H.:
  on cluster concepts 240n.

Radbruch, G.:
  on positivism and Nazi law 85–6
Radcliffe, LJ 70, 214, 216
Rawls, J. 91n.
  on overlapping consensus 245, 268
Raz, J. vi, 4, 60, 61n., 143, 170n., 185n.
  on analogy between law and
    arbitration 126–7, 129, 132–3

arguments for exclusive positivism:
the authority argument 123–40;
bias, the argument from 105–6,
140; explanatory power, the
argument from 113–17, 140;
function, the argument from
117–23, 140, 182, 184; the linguistic
argument 104

dependent and exclusionary reasons
124–40, 173 n., 260; Perry's
alternative to laws as exclusionary
136–7

descriptive/explanatory theory of law
19, 91; not a theory of adjudication
32, 42 n.

exclusive account of charter
challenges 156–63

on the external observer perspective
23

inclusive vs exclusive positivism 3, 6,
79, 82–4, 87, 103–31, 155, 182, 226–9

law as source based 175–6, 231 n.

on legal positivism 1, 74–9, 168 n.

on the limits of law 83

modified exclusive account of charter
challenges 163–4

on moral vs. evaluative elements in
legal theory 19, 21–2, 120–1, 125–6

on moral vs. legal evaluation of
judicial decisions 115–17

on morality and judicial discretion
226–9

on the obligation to obey law 64–5

on peremptory nature of authoritative
directives 124–35, 173 n.

on practical vs. theoretical authority
129–32

on rules of recognition 75

on settled vs. unsettled law 113–15

reactionary thinking 86–7, 96–7

Reagan, R. 116

reasons, *see* dependent reasons;
exclusionary reasons; peremptory
reasons

Rehnquist, W. 67

Reid, Lord 37

Rest, J. 17 n.

Richards, D. 69 n.

right answer thesis 200 n., 203 n., 206–8

rights, *see* background rights,
institutional rights, legal rights
legislative rights

Ross, D. 19

rule scepticism 72–3, 106

rules, *see* interpretation, rules of;
principles; primary and secondary
rules; rules of recognition; rules of
adjudication; secondary rules;
social rules

rules of adjudication 36, 49–50, 65–6,
75–9, 171

rules of recognition 4, 43, 65–6, 74–9,
112, 234–5
as duty imposing 75
moral criteria possible in 82, 175–82
and uncertainty 185–8

Russell, LJ:
on purposive interpretation 266

Sankey, Lord 41 n.

Sartorius, R.:
on Dworkin's right answer thesis
203 n.

Scarman, LJ
on Lord Denning 233 n.

secondary rules 74–9, 234–5

semantic theories of law 104–5

settled law 113–15, 187–8

Shiner, R. vi, 206 n.

Simonds, Viscount:
on plain meaning cases 254

simplicity criterion 19–21

Simpson, J. E. 146 n.

sceptical conceptions of law 14–15, 23,
72–3, 106, 228

Smith, A. 152 n.

social rules 235

Soper, P. 42 n., 82 n.
on causal/moral arguments for
positivism 88, 90
on Dworkin's argument from function
185 n.
on Dworkin's pedigree argument
181 n.
on Dworkin's right answer thesis
200 n.
on moral force of law 61–2

sources of law 175–6, 231 n.

statutes, authoritative nature of 138–9

strong social thesis 82–3

Summers, R.:
on Fuller 95, 97 n., 98
on natural law theory 33 n.

Sumner, LJ 37

Tapper, C. 170n.
Ten, C. 82n.
  on Dworkin's right answer thesis
    200n.
Tindal, J. 254
Tur, R. 170n., 185n.

Ullmann, W. 92n.
utilitarianism 91–3, 146, 260

validity argument, the 168–74
value relevance 21–3

Waismann, F.:
  and open-texture 237, 240–1
Waluchow, W. 82n.
Warren, J. 71n.
Wasserstrom, R. 41
  on Fuller and purposive
    interpretation 272n.
weight vs. overridden 172–3
Williams, B. 145–6
Wittgenstein, L. 239
Wollheim, R.:
  on natural law theory 179n., 180n.

P 24 Middle - this may be useful for discussing the APA f